TRAINING
AND
EXPLAINING

—

How to Be the Dog Trainer
You Want to Be

TRAINING
AND
EXPLAINING

—

How to Be the Dog Trainer
You Want to Be

Job Michael Evans

HOWELL BOOK HOUSE
New York

Macmillan General Reference
A Prentice Hall Macmillan Company
15 Columbus Circle
New York, NY 10023

Howell Book House
MACMILLAN is a registered trademark of Macmillan, Inc.

Library of Congress Cataloging-in-Publication Data

ISBN: 0-87605-781-4

Manufactured in the United States of America
10 9 8 7 6 5 4 3 2 1

JOB MICHAEL EVANS
is also the author of:

How to Be Your Dog's Best Friend (co-authored with the Monks of New Skete)(Little Brown)

The Evans Guide for Counseling Dog Owners (Howell/Macmillan)

The Evans Guide for Housetraining Your Dog (Howell/Macmillan)

The Evans Guide for Civilized City Canines (Howell/Macmillan)

People, Pooches and Problems (Howell/Macmillan)

To my Mother, Eileen, and to my Brother, John

———

Contents

Acknowledgments

This book is something of a sequel to one of my earlier works, *The Evans Guide for Counseling Dog Owners* (Howell, 1984). Why a sequel? Professional dog training and dog owner counseling have grown and changed dramatically in the past decade. There are new and diverse techniques—and trainers—on the scene. I felt a new effort was needed to coordinate the latest information, by sharing (of course) my own opinions and by interviewing other trainers.

After more than 20 years in the field, there are too many people to thank, but some must be mentioned by name because they helped specifically with the production and fine-tuning of the book you now hold.

I'm grateful to Carol Benjamin, who discussed many aspects of the book with me quite intensively and granted one of the interviews. I'm also grateful to my other interview subjects, Dr. Myrna Milani, Amy Ammen, and Dr. Ian Dunbar.

I am a proud past president of the Dog Writers' Association of America, and many members shared thoughts and insights that aided my writing.

At the risk of leaving other important names out due to forgetfulness, I will close by thanking my fine publisher, Sean Frawley, president of Howell Book House, and my longtime editor, Seymour Weiss.

I've enjoyed writing this book and especially conducting the interviews, even though I don't think I'm any threat to Barbara Walters.

Finally, I extend my thanks to all who have purchased my previous books, attended my seminars, or in any way helped me perfect my skills. You have made my life quite happy and full by helping me truly to enjoy challenging work. Again, thank you.

Job Michael Evans
Key West
January 1994

A Note to Readers

Before embarking upon any behavioral problem therapy for a problem dog, be sure that the dog has undergone a full physical evaluation by a veterinarian who is accustomed to looking for behavioral/physiological or clinical interrelationships. I cannot stress this point emphatically enough, as many behavioral and physical conditions overlap and influence each other.

Part One

—

ON TRAINING

Chapter 1

Training and Explaining

While many people *talk* endlessly about reaching their fullest potential, and every other television talk show focuses on fulfillment, in fact very few individuals do "reach for the stars"—not to mention achieve celebrity. Anyway, that's not the point.

Becoming a star shouldn't really be a major concern for any of us, although a healthy bit of ego helps personal initiative. When you consider the innate (although often clumsy) decency of dog folk, especially those who work with guide dogs, hearing dogs, and assistance dogs; humane shelter workers; and all who teach dogs to work with dignity and poise, you can't help but admire them. Their depth of commitment is inspiring, almost to the point of sanctity. We have truly made incredible progress in "service dogs," thanks largely to these profoundly motivated people.

PROGRESS AND PROBLEMS

Yet, there are problems. There are those who trivialize their own profession, not seeing it as a profession at all but as a Tuesday-night hobby, part of which involves yanking around other people's dumb dogs and providing a terrific chance to ditch the kids one night a week.

SOON IT WON'T BE SO SIMPLE

Part of the attitude seen in the burgeoning animal rights movement, especially within the fringe element that believes domestic animals should not be kept as pets, stems from the perceived arrogance of dog owners. Animal rightists act on their feelings against ownership and possession of what they feel cannot be owned.

There are new philosophical and political winds blowing involving efforts to ban certain types of dogs or all dogs in some localities, even in whole states. Releasing dogs from their crates at dog shows while an owner is otherwise occupied has happened. All sorts of threatening situations are developing at present.

TAKE A CLOSE LOOK

Look at animal rights groups. Many members are highly educated, articulate, philosophical, savvy, and very determined. They are also skilled in marketing and in high-powered lobbying even in the hallowed chambers of Washington itself. They really *believe* in their cause, and act accordingly.

NOW TAKE A SECOND LOOK

Now look at the dog fancy and specifically at the breeders and trainers in it. Too many breeders suffer from kennel blindness, contribute to genetic chaos, use faked x-rays, and claim falsified breedings as genuine. Too many breedings happen and, as a result, purebreds languish in shelters (although breed rescue groups do a good job of reclaiming unwanted pets and are, by and large, to be applauded). There is ample room for considerable improvement in today's fancier community.

Now, stroll around an obedience trial. There is swearing, backbiting, attempts at food training even within the ring itself, and an attitude toward the judges that can be condescending, suspicious, and lacking in respect.

Having attended many psychiatric conferences with my father, and having taught at countless veterinary conferences, I can tell you that with only a few exceptions our shows and trials look like jokes—bad jokes on ourselves.

SOME CLASS, NOT A LOT

With very few exceptions, dog shows tend not to draw large numbers of laypersons and passive spectators. Why should the uninitiated pay even minimal admission to spend all day in questionable weather or crowded conditions watching an event they do not understand? It is simply a bizarre spectacle for those who do not know what they are seeing.

Very few dog shows are narrated, fewer explained with panache and sophistication. Once again, just as the public immediately sizes up the mentality of "horse people" toward their chosen species and sport, spectators also come away with an impression of just who dog people are and how they tick. If they see a lot of self-involved, grooming-obsessed individuals who basically live for and with their dogs, it's easy for them to feel excluded. Wouldn't you?

WHEN THE TRAINERS GET IN THE ACT

Trainers don't help this image when they arrogantly present themselves as absolute authorities on all matters canine. Through their grand, sweeping pronouncements, the observer can easily tell that these individuals could have dropped out of fourth grade and are the type who think dogs have to study for their rabies test!

What I am saying is not critical, although those who feel uncomfortable with criticism will inevitably have objections. In fact, I am not criticizing, I am recognizing. This whole book is, in fact, a frank reassessment of our field.

WHAT WE NEED TO DO

We who train dogs professionally must learn to train well, explain training well, dress well, handle our students well, and handle ourselves with proper dignity. Too often, we make little or no effort to "sell" dog training to the general public. That is really a mistake.

We seemingly foster clannishness and elitism; sometimes we ourselves can't explain how and why we train. We must bring our profession up to par. We have to stop chiding ourselves as hobbyists. Millions of dogs still are euthanized each year, a great many for behavioral reasons. While many of us in the fancy do have to learn *balance* (not keeping too many personal dogs, not overloading classes), we also really have to get to work on our own problems. We need more, not fewer, people being taught to train and explain. With 45 percent of American households owning one or more dogs, I firmly believe there is a market for any good trainer.

THE PROMISE AND PROBLEMS OF SUPPORT GROUPS

In New York City, a group was begun in 1987 to combat anti–"pit bull" legislation, an obsession of then-Mayor Koch. Along with the AKC (American Kennel Club), what later became known as SNADT (Society of North American Dog Trainers) fought the bill and won. The group has had a stormy history, but it did manage to produce a Code of Ethics, certification tests, and seminars, and got trainers talking to one another.

On the West Coast, near San Francisco, there is a group called "Canine Discourse." The group has little formal organization as in SNADT or the well-known NADOI (National Association of Dog Obedience Instructors). A site and time for a meeting is simply selected, whoever shows up shows up, and a topic is decided on and discussion ensues round-table style for as long people want to talk.

This might be a better way to begin a dialogue than with highly formalized groups with intricate bylaws and election of officers. If you start a group in your area, it should be a real group, with set meeting times and topics announced in advance—but other than that, with minimal structure. I have seen how egos run amuck when a formal organization is established and the true vision of the group is all but lost. Simplicity might be the answer.

CLIQUES AFTER CLUB MEETINGS AND EXCLUSIVITY

In advocating the formation of such groups, I am not referring to cliques (usually friends who agree on all points of technique, so conflict and thus learning are conveniently sidestepped). Instead I mean discussion groups held on neutral sites, such as a church basement or a room in a restaurant, where *everyone* is invited and no one has to feel he or she is walking into "enemy territory," where a secret agenda is already set up.

DOG CLUB DIVORCES: OFTEN A TRAGEDY, OFTEN AVOIDABLE

It saddens me so much when I arrive in a given town for a seminar (and I have taught in over 300 towns in the United States and Canada) and the driver assigned to take me to my hotel launches into a long description of which club "broke off" from which other club, which in turn "broke off" from another club. Then there are the blow-by-blow accounts of meetings that I don't even care about and didn't attend.

What the organizers want by dumping all this unsolicited local gossip on me is my approval that what club "A" did was right and what club "B" did was wrong. I keep absolutely mum. It wasn't my fight, but listening in silence (I'm a captive audience anyway) *does* help me to identify the patterns of dog club divorces. Here's what is usually involved in such breakups:

- Differences over *training methodologies* these days usually mean the use of food in training, versus "coercive," "dated" training, terms used to describe trainers who do not use food. There are other methodological reasons for a divorce, but this is the main one today. This entire phenomenon has deep philosophical roots too complex to explore here.
- *Money* plays a part in many a split—often revolving around mismanagement by an inept treasurer. Instead of replacing the treasurer, the club splits apart.

WHAT DO I MEAN WHEN I SAY "TRAINER"?

I use "trainer" in this book all-inclusively, and I try not to genderize it. In fact, women dominate the training field. By "trainer" I mean class trainers, private instructors, research trainers working in academic settings, veterinarians involved in canine behavior studies, ethologists, zoologists, veterinary technicians, groomers, and many others. There is something here for all of you. Also, I am not and have never been upset by being referred to as a dog trainer. If you need to make up a new term, go ahead; I don't.

This is not a book that will teach you to train a dog, but rather a book that will help you to be the trainer you want to be, or dream of being someday. In a manner of speaking, it is a book of dreams.

For those of you contemplating getting into dog training as a complete change of career, you might want to check out the ever-popular career-switch book *What Color Is Your Parachute?* It is still widely available. You need a parachute to dive into dog training or exhibiting, so the book should be a good investment.

You will find essays in this book that may look eclectic at first, like the ones on dress and about fear. Yet any trainer who can't dress decently or deal with fear won't last long as a trainer. Since I in my early, seminal works explained the training exercises in meticulous detail, I will not repeat that information in this book.

When record producer Quincy Jones produced "We Are the World" to help feed Ethiopia's famine-stricken children, he met each performer at the door of the studio. Major stars like Diana Ross, Bette Midler, Michael Jackson, Ray Charles, and Bruce Springsteen stopped and listened to his succinct message, "Leave your ego at the door." They did, the results can be heard on the recording, and many hungry people got fed.

Wouldn't it be great if we in the dog fancy could also learn to leave our egos behind, mature, nurture our dogs and present them as the treasures they are to an adoring public? We're trying, I know, but we can do so much better.

Finally, this book is not the sequel to *The Evans Guide for Counseling Dog Owners* (Howell Book House, 1986). It is much broader in scope, and obviously much more opinionated! You may consider it a companion volume to that earlier book.

I wrote portions of that book while still at New Skete Monastery. They were short essays published under my own name in *Off Lead* magazine. Even though I had recently left the monks, I was pleased when those essays appeared in book form and I was able to dedicate that book to the brothers.

Just as years ago they had given me a skill, comfort, shelter, and rest for over a decade, I need to sincerely thank the brothers once again. I know I will find comfort, shelter, and rest at New Skete once again. For that I am eternally grateful to the Monks of New Skete.

Chapter 2

—

Serving an Apprenticeship

I firmly believe that anyone who wishes to become a class or private trainer should serve an apprenticeship under an experienced trainer. I did, and I'm now instructing two aspiring trainers. It's a responsibility I take seriously and, quite frankly, it is an honor. They tell me it is an honor to work with me as well, and everybody feels so honored we might as well be Boy Scouts!

All kidding aside, the idea of serving an apprenticeship *is* an age-old, honorable tradition stemming from the medieval guilds. In order to become a member of a guild you had to serve time under an experienced master. Let's say you wanted to become a blacksmith. You simply had to work, salary-free, for an experienced blacksmith until you learned the craft. You might even have to pay the blacksmith to work with him. This was an accepted procedure; if you couldn't say whom you had served and apprenticed under, nobody would hire you, and no one would patronize your shop if you went into business for yourself. You weren't allowed just to hang out your shingle and start blacksmithing. Indeed, if you tried, you would be black*listed.*

Things certainly have changed. These days, just about anyone can hang out a *dog trainer par excellence* sign. Serving an apprenticeship is sometimes viewed as the equivalent of serving time in prison. At a recent seminar, one aspiring trainer said to me, "I don't need no apprenticeship; the dogs will teach me what I need to know." Well, all I could think was, "I hope they teach you how to speak correct English because educated clients won't think much of you if you go around saying you 'didn't serve no apprenticeship'."

There is a valid point, though, in the idea that the dogs do teach the aspiring trainer quite a bit. Yet very often it takes an experienced trainer to tell the novice what the dog is trying to communicate. Yes, some training skills seem to be picked up by osmosis, but there is a didactic element in the learning process as well, and any aspiring trainer might as well face that early on. If you are not really willing to listen and learn, if you think you already know it all, you might as well forget about serving an apprenticeship. Your presumption will make any apprenticeship a complete sham.

I mention this because there is a certain humility to serving an apprenticeship, and what you learn about yourself at the hands of an experienced trainer can be enlightening, interesting, and often humbling. I certainly found that to be the case when I served my apprenticeship under Brother Thomas Dobush, the late monk of New Skete who took me under his wing over 17 years ago, I think (I'm still not sure) under orders from the abbot. Why he would voluntarily offer to educate *me* in dog training, at least the me I remember from those days, baffles me. I didn't know, like, or even care about dogs when I entered the monastery. And I certainly didn't want to *train* them. Indulge me while I recount some of my story, in order to help those thinking about serving an apprenticeship.

The monastery was New Skete, a collection of wood frame buildings that had been constructed by the monks themselves. In the center of the complex was a stunningly beautiful, eight-gold-domed Russian-style church. The place was surrounded by 500 acres of wilderness, silent, mountainous, and serene. The brothers were loving and gracious. The liturgical services were touching. The monastery observed the Byzantine rite—the beauty of the chant, the figures of the black-robed monks wreathed in incense, and the intensity of the icons swept me away. This would be home. But there was a rude shock: The monks of New Skete supported themselves primarily by breeding, raising, and training *dogs*. And they bred German Shepherd dogs.

AN ANIMAL LABORATORY

New Skete swarmed with dogs. When I entered the community in 1972, about 12 dogs were in the breeding program, and there was room for four or five dogs of other breeds that came for training. Only four years after inaugurating the breeding program, the monks had already made a small name for themselves, and luminaries in the dog fancy were visiting the monastery frequently, trying to impart as much of their knowledge as they could to the monks. One woman, Marie Leary, a pillar of the German Shepherd dog breed, remarked that the monastery was different because it was "an animal laboratory." She went on to add that she would rather work with the monks than many other novices in the dog fancy "because I know they're

New Skete was truly an animal laboratory and dogs were everywhere. German Shepherd Dogs in the house and usually a boarding/training kennel of naughty canines awaiting rehabilitation. Boy, did I start to learn fast! Here, the monks sit down for dinner surrounded by "the pack." (author's collection)

serious, they will be working with dogs for a long time, they will probably be famous."

The brothers were originally farmers. The farm years spanned 1966 through 1969 and at one time or another the monks had goats, chickens, pigs, Holstein cattle, Hereford cattle, sheep, and even pheasants. Without realizing it at the time, the monks were receiving a grassroots education in animal psychology and behavior. The monks had a mascot dog, Kyr, a German Shepherd who had "flunked out" at Seeing Eye school because of a problem with his pedigree papers. He was a beloved pet, but he either ran away or got lost, and the monks never saw him again.

The house was empty without a dog, and the other animals just did not fill the bill. Besides, the farm had to be phased out. It was not financially feasible and the monks were moving to a new location 12 miles away, high on Two Top Mountain. Brother Thomas Dobush, who died in a tragic automobile accident in 1973, had thought seriously about a breeding program, partly as an experiment (insofar as Brother Thomas "experimented" with anything) and partly as a means of livelihood—especially now that the farm was being phased out.

He contacted prominent breeders, procured some bitches, and, on a very small scale, began breeding litters. More and more serious breeders and professional trainers recognized his sincere interest,

11

which was spreading quickly to the other monks and visitors. They imparted their knowledge graciously and openly, which is invaluable in a field that is self-learned. I was overwhelmed by the electric current that seemed to flow between Brother Thomas and the resident dogs.

Brother Thomas began to train the dogs to live in the monastery as a group, and maintain quiet and order. "I didn't want them in kennels," he said, "a Shepherd's mind will rot in a kennel." But there could be no infighting within the monastery pack. Each dog was assigned to a brother who was primarily responsible for its care. The dogs came to dinner, and as the monks said grace, they fell into down-stays and waited out the meal. During the meal, the dogs would remain anchored, and if one got up, it was immediately ordered to lie down. The dogs placed themselves behind the horseshoe-style refectory table, flung out along the dining room walls as if by centrifugal force. Feeding the dogs from the table was absolutely taboo. Even though I was afraid of the dogs, and held on to some lingering resentment, I wanted to feed them. I believed that if I fed them the dogs would "like" me, and it was very important to be liked by the dogs if you wanted to stay at New Skete. It never occurred to me that most of the dogs were simply not *interested* in me. I was just another guest, and a kind of regal aloofness is, in fact, written into the temperament section of the breed Standard of the German Shepherd dog.

During my first meal with the monks, while I was still staying in the guest house and petitioning to be accepted into the community, the dogs eyed me with detached curiosity, calmly watching me as I took my place at the table, but they did not break their down-stays in order to greet me. One, Bekky, snoozed softly, and the others licked their paws, groomed themselves, looked at each other, but did not get up. Not one gazed at my plate or drooled. "Good God," I thought, "this is incredible." I had never seen dogs behave that way, with such mastery, such self-control, such quiet dignity and poise. I realized that many of my negative feelings toward dogs stemmed from the obnoxious conduct of *badly behaved* dogs that jumped up on me, or just didn't listen to anything I or their owners asked them to do. I began to think for the first time that maybe, just maybe, I could get to know and like dogs.

But as quickly as that thought entered my head, the old myths took over. Poised behind me were two large females, lying down a few short feet away, directly behind my chair. I couldn't turn around to see what they were doing without making a fool of myself in front of the other monks, but my nervousness mounted as I reflected on the myths and rules I had learned in childhood. These were German Shepherd dogs. I half believed that before the meal was over, one of them would lunge at the table, steal a platter full of food and scamper away. But worse than this, German Shepherd dogs *bite* people, sometimes even *eat* them. My mother had told me plainly: *Never* trespass on a German Shepherd dog's territory. *Never* pet one. *Never* turn your back on one. Here I was, sitting, eating a meal, in a strange place, with strange people, with two strange German Shepherd dogs lurking behind me. The end will be merciful and quick, I thought, I'll never know what hit me, and I forced another forkful of mashed potatoes down my dry throat.

Then the abbot checked to see if everyone was finished eating and rose to say the closing grace. The rest of the monks rose in unison, and we sang grace after meals, but the dogs remained in position. When the last note was sung, the monks turned to their respective dogs and said, "Okay!" and the dogs leaped up. Everyone was patting a dog, and a large self-assured bitch, Jesse, sauntered over to me and placed herself squarely in front of me. She did not jump, nudge, or nuzzle, but she looked as if she definitely wanted something and wasn't going to move an inch until she got it. "Well, pet her," Brother Thomas said, "like this." And he took my hand like a baby's and moved my palm back and forth over the dog's forehead. We both laughed at my behavior and Jesse too seemed to be smiling. My defenses crumbled and I knelt down in front of her and ruffled the rich coat around her neck.

"You can't stay here unless you like dogs—or can get to like them," Brother Thomas commented.

"Oh, that won't be any problem at all—no problem at all," I answered in the most blasé tone I could fake.

"Good," he responded. "Maybe tomorrow you can help me with the training. We have two dogs brought in recently. One is a Labrador that soils the house and the other is a Great Dane that bites."

My throat was dry again. A Great Dane that *bites*.

So there I was, a skinny college student entering a monastery that raises and trains dogs for a living, being asked by the then-head dog trainer-monk to serve an apprenticeship. I believe serving an apprenticeship is essential in preparing to be a private trainer. In this connection, the only life experience I have is my own and there is very little chance of acquiring any other, so you must tolerate still more of my personal story.

BROTHER THOMAS

Even now, years after his death, it is difficult to write about Brother Thomas. I simply did not have enough time to know him well, although I worked closely with him for a year. It is an irony of

A smiling and somber Brother Thomas was my first training mentor. Whatever he did—work, pray, laugh, teach, sing or speak—he did with class. (author's collection)

monastic life, where people live more or less on top of each other, that while the monks might get used to each other and even find themselves taking each other for granted within a short period of time, it takes months, even years to really come to *know* a brother monk.

In 1972, the breeding and training programs at the monastery were in high gear. There was a lot of branching out going on—into training, as owners asked that their dogs be taught to behave like the New Skete Shepherds did; into boarding, as owners asked the monks to care for their pets while they were away. Brother Thomas was trying to do everything almost single-handedly, and eventually he asked if I wanted to be his apprentice in training. I had strong reservations, for I still had not warmed up to dogs to a great degree.

But Brother Thomas actually saw this as an asset, not a problem. "Good," he said, "you won't become emotionally involved with your students." He made it quite clear to any dog that checked in for training that it was there to learn. The training could be enjoyable, but come, sit, down, stay, stand, and the rest of the command words and actions all had to be mastered. He also made it clear to me that I was there to learn. I was his *apprentice*. He used that word, for I remember looking it up to see if it applied to someone learning to like dog training. I thought of it as a cobbler's term.

Once the lines of communication were open, we embarked on a study program that involved a tight reading schedule, twice-weekly drill sessions, and oral tests. Since I had never excelled in sports, and weighed in at a slight 136 pounds when I entered the monastery, even the tiniest Pekingese could take me for a walk. Learning to work with dogs was an education for both mind and body. My sense of coordination was way off. I lacked an all-important skill that a dog trainer must have—timing. It is the ability to time your moves with what the dog is doing, to time your corrections so the dog understands what it is that was done wrong. Brother Thomas had to work extremely hard with me in order for me to gain the poise and confidence necessary to train effectively. The dogs knew how incompetent I was, and acted accordingly. But as soon as Brother Thomas took the leash, each dog calmed and did its work. Then, handing the leash back to me, the dog again became wild. It was frustrating, embarrassing.

I reached points when I wanted to throw down the leash and walk out, or wind it around Brother Thomas' neck and choke him. What saved me was the lavish praise he would heap on me when the dog and I were working together as a team. "Wonderful, good! He's all yours, you've got him! Do another quick down—oh—wonderful!"

He dictated push-ups to increase my arm power, for hauling around 100 pounds of dog sometimes takes superior arm strength—at least until the dog is at heel. He taught me to say "No" without whining it; to *tell* the dog, not ask the dog, to do something; to make eye contact; to "pin" a dog with my eyes; to praise verbally and physically. After six months, I felt the difference. The dogs responded to me warmly, but obediently. My body was in tune with the dogs'. I had "a dog in me," as Brother Thomas used to say. Having "a dog in you" meant that you no longer responded like a human, but like a dog.

He felt that a trainer developed a soft heart by training, for even though a trainer must be strict, dogs do teach compassion and patience. He felt that in training dogs one could learn spiritual discipline. He had very few persons with whom he could share such feelings and was flabbergasted when an occasional rigid layperson or clergyman would express the belief that there was nothing special or spiritual about working with dogs.

It is easy to see him in interchangeable roles: as guestmaster, as dog trainer, as writer, as editor, as liaison between the monastery and the outside world, as teacher, as mentor, even as cook. He was aware that he had many skills, and perhaps felt frustrated that he was using so few of them. Yet he was doing so much. He himself certainly scratched the surface of this paradox in his editorial for the first issue of *Gleanings*, a monastic/literary journal he began shortly before he died.

> It is not given to a man that he know the importance of his own life. But if he can be humble enough to allow the whole of his being to experience the whole of his world, he may begin to glean something of its meaning.

And later on in the editorial he brings in dogs:

> Learning the value of silence is learning to listen to, rather than screaming at, reality. Opening your mind enough to find what the end of someone else's sentence sounds like, or listening to a dog until you discover what is needed instead of imposing yourself in the name of training.

Brother Thomas died tragically in 1973. I co-authored with the Monks of New Skete *How to Be Your Dog's Best Friend*, which went on to be a very popular book among dog lovers. In 1983, finding the monastic life too confining, I made the difficult decision to leave. I did not know where I would settle, but I knew I had served a real apprenticeship and subsequently acted as head trainer and dog-owner counselor for 10 years, eventually training an apprentice monk myself.

FORMAL OR INFORMAL APPRENTICESHIP?

The point of this perhaps long-winded recounting of my own apprenticeship is not to give myself an ego-stroke (as you no doubt observed, it was anything but that), but to give aspiring private trainers a model—a criterion—on which to judge their own educational process.

If you are really lucky, you are going to find your Brother Thomas. And you will love him (or her) and alternately want to thank or throttle your mentor. That is the pain and glory of serving a formal apprenticeship. The lines of communication will be clear: Like Tarzan and Jane, it will be me Teacher, you Apprentice. Well, at least that eliminates any confusion as to roles, and in my opinion, speeds up the learning process. My advice to you is select the very best trainer you want to work with, if you can, and offer to serve an apprenticeship. I like everything up front. Then both parties know who is teacher and who is student. It's hard work for both parties, but at least it's a clear, neat set-up that facilitates learning.

However, there are some who will not be able, for many reasons, to serve a formal apprenticeship under an experienced trainer to gain training and counseling skills. Perhaps you are the type of person who simply cannot geographically get to your mentor. Or perhaps you are of a personality slant that would make serving an apprenticeship a living hell—indeed, perhaps you are a very experienced obedience class instructor who knows *darn* well how to teach exercises but simply needs to learn counseling and in-home presentation. All of this is fine. Guess what? You can still serve an apprenticeship and no one ever has to know it. Here's how.

Simply select the person that, if all those other considerations were not operable, you would *choose* to serve under. Then, don't miss a chance to observe that person working with a dog. Perhaps the individual shows in the conformation ring or participates in obedience trials. You should be at ringside, notebook in hand. What is it that makes this person's handling skills so special? Why do the dogs respond so nicely to him or her? Don't just stand there and marvel at the person's harmony and grace and timing. Standing there awestruck won't help you to learn anything nor decipher exactly what it is that produces such good results. Chances are it's not magic or witchcraft. But you'll never find out what it is if you don't look for the reasons behind the results.

If you force yourself to observe that person, you'll start to figure out the "secret" faster than you might think you would. Probably it's in the person's body language and vocal tonality, and most probably in the quality of eye contact he or she makes with a given dog. Masterly handlers know how to walk up to a strange dog and establish themselves as leader, as *Alpha*, very quickly. Often part of the secret is simply radiating an air of superiority to the dog by a serious (but not threatening) look in the dog's direction, and a body posture that is assured without being stiff. Look, try to see, then observe deeply and memorize what you think you've observed. You can have that "gift" too, but you have to know what you're asking for. Congratulations; you're serving an informal apprenticeship by forcing yourself to really study another person's handling skills. And they don't even have to know what you're up to! Finally, try not to be mesmerized by the dog—of course study the canine part of the team too—but keep your eye on your secret mentor, especially his or her eyes, hands (check out the fingers and what they do to the leash), and footwork. Get on your job, apprentice! You'll be surprised at how quickly you pick up the tricks of the trade.

Chapter 3

Beyond Fear: Understanding Your Emotions When Training Aggressive Dogs

I am thoroughly sick of hearing macho dog trainers—by no means all men—claim that they are not afraid of aggressive dogs. In researching the available literature, I've found tons of advice for fearful *owners* of canine grouches, but very little for those of us who must train them. Why has this remained such a closed topic?

First, it remains under-discussed precisely because the macho train-ers have "decreed," if only unintentionally, that anyone who is afraid of an aggressive dog just shouldn't be training one. As if fear of such dogs just didn't exist. As if anxiety and even despair on the part of trainers just isn't real. Psychologists call this syndrome "denial." I call it foolish.

This denial leads many trainers to believe that only a few possess the "hidden secret" to working with aggressive dogs fearlessly. Sup-posedly, this inside information gives these trainers, and *only* these trainers, the advantage with the aggressives. And so, a growing num-ber of trainers now openly advertise that they "just train puppies," or just "don't 'do' aggressive dogs." Conversely, there are trainers—many of whom seem to communicate that they have that "special some-thing" that turns canine sinners into saints—that service mainly the owners of aggressive dogs. Often these trainers carry client loads of belligerent beasts precisely because no other trainers in the area will train such dogs.

What is being overlooked by both the fearful and the fearless is that every trainer who deals successfully with aggressive dogs some-how *learned how* to train such dogs successfully. Working proficiently

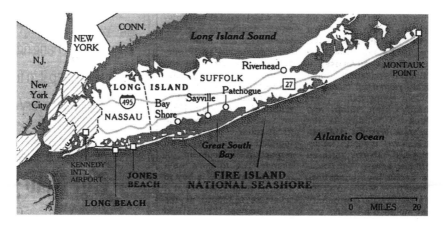

Fire Island and its fragility—and being stuck on the island during Hurricane Bob certainly was a study in fear. Naturally I was working on this very chapter at the time!

with aggressive dogs is not a divine gift bestowed from above only on certain trainers. It is a *learned* skill.

What isn't often explained—sometimes because the competent trainers just can't seem to verbalize the concept—is *how* each trainer confronted this fear of aggressive dogs and made an emotional journey beyond fear. With this in mind, I began interviewing many experienced trainers about the subject. What I discovered made for fascinating listening and helped me to articulate my own journey out of fear and into a position of being able to provide concrete help to aggressive dogs and their owners. It took some personal self-searching. In short, the first step in working with aggressive dogs is to work on your *own* fear of these animals. To work on fear, examine it.

ANXIETY OR FEAR?

Let's first distinguish between anxiety and fear. Anxiety usually involves consternation over a *future* event and what might happen when it occurs. But anxiety can also be based on past experiences and what occurred during those experiences. Fear, on the other hand, is a much more immediate phenomenon, and is often experienced *during* an unpleasant event.

For instance, I was once stranded on Fire Island during a serious hurricane. The police came door to door and informed everyone that the storm was just 300 miles away. It would very possibly make landfall on Fire Island—a barrier island that is 32 miles long, but only at most one mile wide at any point. It is, in fact, one long sand dune. It is not a smart place to be during a major storm, not to mention a hurricane. The storm had veered north so quickly and so erratically

20

Dogs pick up fear as quickly as we telegraph it. When the hurricane passed over, my Dalmatian flung himself into my and my partner John's laps and started to shake so severely I thought his spots would fall off. The humans are smiling fake smiles to reassure the dog. We were all terrified. (Kevin Bacon)

that tracking devices had failed to chart it. By this time, the police said, the bay side of the island was far too choppy to risk ferrying islanders back to the mainland. We were stuck. We could expect to be in the thick of the storm in about three hours. We would be in the storm about 12 hours, or, possibly much less if we were killed.

The police then wished us their very best, and moved on to give the same information to residents of another cottage. They then went back to their steel-reinforced station down the boardwalk. They did not issue any invitation to join them, but left us in our wood cottages, most of which are set on stilts, in sand. By the way, all this happened at three A.M. I began to experience considerable anxiety. Naturally, I was working on this book at the time.

By the time the hurricane bashed the barrier island, I had graduated from anxiety to fear. My Dalmatian was pacing around like a lunatic. The house was heaving heavenward. The windows, although taped, were squeaking; the rain was torrential and the roar of the ocean was deafening in the extreme. To complete the scene in true Hollywood fashion, the electricity on the entire island went out and all phone service died. By this time, my eyes had widened to the size of saucers and my breathing became hyperventilated. I was sitting in a wicker easy chair bracing myself. My dog flung himself onto my lap and started shivering so violently I thought his spots would fall off.

CHECK YOUR RESPONSES

From my studies of fear I've learned that all of our physical responses to immediate fear—widened, watchful eyes; bracing oneself; heightened breathing; extraordinary sensory perceptions—are all necessary protective human adaptations to being threatened and are *good* signs. These are indicators that the feelings of fear are being recognized and processed within the mind and body.

All of these protective ploys happen when you confront an aggressive dog. What the effective trainer has learned to do is not to hide or deny these manifestations of fear, but rather make them *work* for him or her.

For instance, opening up one's eyes out of fear can allow you to check out an aggressive dog with your peripheral vision. This is quite an advantage because a direct, prolonged stare at an aggressive dog can often trigger an attack—yet the dog must be observed so that it can be corrected. Bracing oneself is a necessary stance, and fortunately it is a natural human reaction to fear. Otherwise, I know some pretty tiny trainers who would have been toppled long ago by some pretty big dog brats!

Proficient trainers learn by trial and error to brace themselves without tightening the dog's leash, which will telegraph anxiety right down the leash and into the dog's cerebral message center. If you watch the upper torso of expert trainers of aggressive dogs, you will see that there is a real economy of movement. They are braced for action, even if their legs are moving. Please note that the natural ability to brace oneself against fear is a different reaction than simply freezing.

The brace is, instead, a mid-point stance adopted as one decides to freeze, flee, or fight. If a trainer of an aggressive dog decides "mid-brace" to freeze, it probably is a ploy to figure out what to do next. If a trainer "flees" it usually means the trainer will move about with the dog in order to distract the dog. Of course, flight is also an option and sometimes a necessity. But don't expect to get paid if you decide on this course of action! Finally, if the trainer uses the brace to decide to "fight," he will be in an excellent physical stance to correct the dog.

At this juncture the trainer's adrenaline will be up, the torso conveys dignity (which is never despised by dogs), and the correction has a "natural edge" to it: swift, clear, and proceeding out of a braced, yet poised-for-action person. The aggressive dog takes all this in.

The late, great trainer Jack Godsil, another mentor of mine. If you watch the torso, legs and even the buttocks of skilled trainers of difficult dogs, you will see authority expressed with minimal movement. Study Mr. Godsil's stance: the body language is perfection. (author's collection)

Remember, aggressive dogs are often the dogs *most skilled* at reading human body language.

RELIEF IN RESPONSE

It should be readily apparent at this point that the natural reactions to fear built into the human psyche are excellent defense mechanisms trainers can use to their advantage. It should also be apparent how foolish it is to deny that one experiences fear. That very denial will often slow or even shut down the body's excellent protection ploys. In my opinion, your fear will never disappear, and it *shouldn't*. Your fear *protects* you if you use it correctly, and enables you to help the dog by teaching and correcting.

So if you think the key to working successfully with aggressive dogs is to somehow magically "get over" your fear of them, you are deluded. If anyone who is proficient with aggressive dogs has sold you such hogwash, they are either lying about their own reactions, or just incapable of understanding what goes on inside of themselves. Freeing yourself of fear is an ongoing process in which natural reactions are respected, yet refined. In short, facing down fear tests your ability to do your best in a new and possibly threatening situation.

When Franklin D. Roosevelt cautioned us that we had nothing to fear but fear itself, he certainly wasn't denying that things in the United States were in awfully scary shape at that time. He wasn't denying fear at all—and we've since found out that he himself was damn afraid of the ongoing Depression and the impending war. He was telling the country to process the fear and deal with its problems. Dealing with dangerous dogs means facing, accepting, and using your fear of them. It means living through an economic depression, or a simple recession. It means facing a hurricane on a sand dune. You might flinch, shake, and shiver, but you *can* face down fear.

BUT HOW?

That said, if you wish to go beyond fear, a little self-righteousness can go a long, long way. Of the many trainers I interviewed, all of whom have had success rehabilitating combative canines, all mentioned that at some point in the training process (usually when the dog attempted to bite them or others), they felt a moment of *supreme indignation* toward the dog. Some mentioned that they also felt indignant toward a negligent or over-permissive owner. Before the 'non-judgmental' trainers begin judging, let me hasten to add that indignation is *not* anger. Instead, indignation is strong, yet controlled displeasure at something deemed unworthy, unjust, or base—such as the rude behavior of an aggressive dog. One trainer put it this way, using a verb in the first sentence that revealed her age—and intelligence:

> When an aggressive dog comes at me, I draw myself up arrogantly and feel insulted. I feel like a battered woman who has finally seen the light and just won't take it anymore. How *dare* this dog try to attack me, or anyone else for that matter? *How dare he???!*

If you are incapable of at least a little indignation, even when unjustly insulted, you will never be able to "draw yourself up," in short, to brace yourself in dignity, regardless of what techniques you use. If you have read enough pop psychology (and the doggie versions of it that are floating around), you've probably been taught that anger is "bad," and, as one dog writer (a Ph.D. in psychology) recently decreed, "Dogs should be educated in an atmosphere of non-judgmental and non-aggressive guidance." This is okay as deep as it goes, but it certainly won't help anyone to distinguish between anger, which is useless in dealing with aggressive dogs (or any dog), and indignation—which is *very* useful.

Another trainer, Jan McKeag of the Western Pennsylvania Humane Society in Pittsburgh, who works every day with problem animals, said, "If you're going to let fear just overtake you, you'll never accomplish anything. Instead, while of course I am afraid, I feel a strong obligation to help the dog out of its bind, and to do that the dog must respect me."

Perhaps it is a misunderstanding of fear, and the denial of it, that has led to an increase in trainers who no longer train aggressive dogs. Some even believe that they should be routinely euthanized. The truth is, we trainers sometimes have problems going beyond fear. I suppose it *is* easier simply to eliminate aggressive dogs by killing them, but it's just another form of denial.

Please note that there are many aggressive dogs who *need* to be euthanized. Even *after* training some will remain unpredictable and intractable, and will always present management problems. Remember also that many trainers are wise to make the decision not to handle aggressive dogs, especially if the trainer has a physical handicap or a real psychological phobia. But I would be less than honest with you if I didn't note that there are many extremely competent trainers who could literally save many, many dogs if they were able to figure out fear. Don't sell yourself short on your ability to face fear.

In my own evolution as a trainer, it was never possible for me to decide what kinds of dogs I wanted to train or not to train. "To train or not to train" was never an option for me since I lived under a vow of obedience. Whatever dogs were brought to the monastery's boarding kennel were the dogs I trained: young, old, stupid, smart, clean, dirty, grouchy, or sweet. Believe me, people would drop off the absolute dregs of canine society, lie through their teeth during the intake interview about the dog's aggression, and hope against hope that the saintly monks would turn a bastard into Benji. Often this happened, sometimes it didn't. The point is, I was forced to learn about aggressive dogs and to deal with my fear of them. Those of you who are religiously inclined might be interested to know that I prayed a lot about my fear. There is one psalm (number 22) that I loved:

"Be not far from me God, for trouble is near. No one else will help me. My strength is spent, dried up like burnt clay ... Dogs surround me; a pack of evil ones closes in on me...."

and later it goes on:

"Hurry my strength, hurry and help me. Save my neck from the sword, my precious life from the grip of these dogs."

Remember also that the phrase "Do not be afraid" pops up 366 times in the Bible. That means that if you read daily, you'll probably run across it every day, no matter where you open the book. You'll even have one phrase left over for leap year! If the Bible, or any book, helps you to go beyond fear, use it. Respect the naturalness of the feelings of fear. Remember to take your time with this inner work. Taking a fearless look at fear isn't easy, but it's often part of becoming a better person. For professional trainers, facing fear is an obligatory part of being the professionals we are called to be.

Chapter 4

First Night Freak-Out

It's the first night of class. The canine students have lined up with their handlers. You look down the line-up. There's someone who looks like Randy Travis, complete with cowboy hat and a wild Dober-man. Next to him is a Dolly Parton clone with a Toy Poodle in tow. She has on four-inch spiked heels; it's a wonder she hasn't impaled her Poodle. His nickname—no surprise to you—is "Dodger." But that's nothing compared to the person with the Siberian mix called "Tug." You wonder, what could be the tremendous mystery behind this dog's name? Could it be, by some incredible chance, that this dog has a problem pulling on the leash? Shock of shocks—he does! That's his precise problem! You're going nuts, as in NUTZOLA, because not only is Tug tugging, everyone else in the class is acting up like souls in torment. Chaos reigns supreme. You wonder if you will ever be able to complete the evening.

We haven't even discussed the equipment (a gracious term) with which the dogs are outfitted. There's a 12-foot chain that still has the screw-in spike attached to one end. (It's the one that holds the dog in the backyard, and has for the last six years.) There's the Venetian blind cord hastily snapped off the window shades when no other "leash" could be found, and the jump-rope stolen from the youngest girl in the family as the parents tore out the door for "doggie class."

The Charge of the Beserk Brigade follows as more members of the class explode into the training site. Somewhere in the air are registra-tion forms floating about, and somewhere quite distantly, one can hear the already parched voice of the instructor screeching some-thing that sounds like "Class ... claaaasssss ... Claaahhhhhssssssss." Welcome to first night at many an obedience class. Welcome to first night freak-out. Welcome, quite frankly, to hell.

Does it have to be so bad? I've had the good fortune, simply by the timing of my seminars, to witness many opening-night classes.

27

I'm teaching an old-style first-afternoon class at New Skete—before I learned how to employ more innovative techniques. Notice the dogs, some up, some down. Notice the participants, some slumped over, many checking out their dogs, not listening to the instructor. (author's collection)

Since I often arrive in town on a Friday afternoon, many an organizer or club president will ask me to attend and critique the Friday evening class. I usually do, and whether by accident or design, I've hit many first night freak-out Fridays. The old saying, "Thank God it's Friday" becomes "Freak-Out—it's Friday!" for many an instructor. On the sidelines, I've been able to compare what the Friday Freak-Out instructors do and contrast their procedures with my own approach to class.

Before you say, "Oh good God, here he goes again—pontificating on how his methods work and others don't," understand that I'm really not that talented in teaching classes. In fact, I have taught very few classes and observed far more. To class instructors who are having difficulty with teaching their classes, I'd suggest just that: *teach less and observe more.* So, I hope I can help with some advice, but I will try to keep in mind that no matter what structural ploys one devises to avoid first night freak-out, some tension is inevitable, built into the very structure of opening a training class.

As Diane Bauman (*Beyond Basic Obedience Training*, Howell Book House, 1988) so succinctly states concerning obedience training, "Learning is stressful ... any time you have been placed in a learning situation, you have felt the tension which comes from concentration and an inner need to succeed.... No matter how you try to sugar-coat obedience training, learning for a dog is stressful." I would add that the first night is the most stressful night of all. Let's see what we can do to remedy the situation in a positive fashion, rather than just bemoan the harsh realities.

DOGS OR NO DOGS?

The first decision any instructor must make is a highly controversial one: Should dogs be present the first night or not? I will admit my bias up front: I include dogs in the first session, but in a very structured way. Nevertheless, it's important that we examine both sides of the question. Let's start with the arguments for having a dogless first session. (By the way, as far as I can ascertain, dogless first nights are by far more common than first night sessions that include dogs.)

Many trainers feel that dogless first nights are more productive because the evening invariably is quieter, less hectic, and less stressful. It is easier for lay dog owners to watch a demo dog being put through its paces, and thus become acquainted with the exercises that will be taught. Some instructors feel that they simply cannot concentrate on their clients with 10 or 20 untrained dogs roughhousing and spinning out of control. Other trainers want to explain the underlying philosophy of the course and feel that barking, whining, and perhaps snarling dogs will make this impossible. In most instances, the first night of class is usually a dogless affair. If you are the type of instructor that sincerely cannot handle first nights any other way, I'd say stick to your current training regime. Go dogless that first night.

TRY SOMETHING NEW

If, on the other hand, you want to include dogs in the first session, here are some tips. First, some validations for your gut decision. I think your reasoning is right.

Running a dogless first night communicates to the humans present that dogs are somehow uncontrollable, wild, too "bad" and "naughty" to be present. Whether the instructor *means* to communicate this or not, this is what *does* get communicated: "They" can't be here with "us" because "they" are just too crazed and "we" have no way to control "them." The course then kicks off on a them versus us basis. Think it over: Is this really what you want to communicate concerning the human/canine bond, especially on the first night?

Another drawback is that it's impossible to fit absent dogs for proper collars (whatever equipment is used) and so this important preliminary is automatically delayed one week—and the problem dogs (those most in need of help) are left too long with oversized collars, non-functional collars, or worse, no collars at all.

Contrast the chaos of a standing class with the order produced almost immediately with the use of the "sit-on-it" technique. The dogs cannot move the handlers and rather than attempt to pull away, simply lie down. This frees the class to listen to the instructor. (Rob Nevin, class photographer, Dealing with Dogs, Campbellville, Ontario)

If, on the other hand, the dogs are present the first night, correct equipment can be issued to all the dogs present. The proper use of the equipment can be explained, and most importantly, owners can shuck the useless equipment they've been struggling with to date.

Remember also that if you conduct a dogless first night, you have already added one more session to the course. Since there are no dogs present to "work" or teach, there are no dogs present that need to be taught. You can't teach absent students. From a business standpoint, this just isn't using one's business noodle. You have automatically added one session to your course—and will have to pay for the hall or area in which the class is located, not to mention paying yourself for your time. For non-profit clubs sponsoring classes, this might not be a big concern, but it can be for the small entrepreneur.

My preference, obviously, is to have dogs present for the initial session. Instead of teaching the traditional heeling that first night and in order to avoid chaos, I believe in teaching a modified 30-minute down. I call this method the "Sit-On-It" method and I described it

originally in *The Evans Guide for Housetraining Your Dog* (Howell/Macmillan, 1987).

During dinner, TV, reading, or entertaining, keep the dog umbilical corded but don't hold the leash—sit on it. If you hold the leash during this time you will encourage the dog to fool around with the "give" in the leash, and you will not have both hands free to do whatever you want to do. Slip the leash under your bottom and try to trail it off to the side of the chair. Measure out only as much lead as your dog needs in order to lie down, no more. You can do this by simply pushing the dog down for a second (or giving him the down command, if he knows it) and then feeding out the appropriate amount of leash. If you give the dog too much, the dog will simply chew on it or dance around on the end of it. When your dog pulls against the dead weight of the leash, it will become quickly apparent that the object (your body) is immovable, and, like most of us do when straining to move a heavy object, the dog will give up trying. At this point, many dogs will attempt to explore other options. These might include stress whining, chewing on the lead, jumping up on you, or chewing the flooring. *Cancel all of these options through discipline.* The fact is, with this method of umbilical cording, *there are no options,* and the only acceptable response is for the dog to settle down and be quiet. If the dog stress whines, growl at the dog and make eye contact (do not whine back); if the leash is being masticated, whip it firmly up and out of the dog's mouth with a stern "No." If the dog jumps up on you, grasp the lead close to its neck area and yank down on it hard, with a "No."

If the dog chews the flooring, use the swat under the chin method or the shake. Do not give the dog a toy during this period. The message is no play, no toy, no pet, *nothing*.

It is a shock for many dogs to find out that no other options are available, but most quickly adapt and do the next most sensible thing—they go to sleep. It is even harder for many owners to enforce this method of umbilical cording, especially if they are used to making their dog the center of attention, catering to its every need and shoving something in its mouth every two seconds. The message, "I like you, I love you, but there are times when you must leave me alone and if you have to eliminate, just hold it," will, to some owners, be emotionally wrenching.

To adapt this method for obedience class, be sure that folding chairs arranged in a semicircle are provided for the participants. I would also suggest clipboards so that class members can easily fill out a behavior case history or make notes during the class.

Let me briefly outline exactly what goes on in the first session of one of my classes. Now that you understand the "Sit-On-It" technique, you will readily see how it enhances control of the first night learning experience.

As the class participants file into the training site—or are dragged in by their dogs—they are handed a clipboard with a blank behavior case history form. This form includes a checklist of problems. The handlers are asked to check any and all problems they experience with their dogs. Class size is held to 15 to 20 participants, and there is one instructor and one assistant. The assistant issues standardized training equipment, fitting each dog correctly on the spot. Decisions about varying training equipment for certain dogs can be made at a later time if necessary, but I like all dogs outfitted in a similar way so that the use of the equipment can be clearly demonstrated to all. The participants are directed to their chairs, which are arranged in a semicircle approximately five feet from each other.

Of course, each participant is greeted warmly, and the instructor personally introduces himself/herself to each individual, human and canine. I cannot stress sufficiently the importance of a good first impression. Even if participants try to bring up problem subjects right away, do not begin your relationship with a heavy discussion of "the problem." But do remember that 90 percent of the people who show up *are* experiencing behavior problems with their dogs. Indicate that you want to know about problems and help with them, but the first step is to become informed about them—and this is where the behavior form comes in. Shift back again to how very pleased you are that they have taken the first step in resolving problems by simply showing up tonight. Remember, everyone likes to feel welcome, and everyone responds favorably to a sincere greeting that comes from a warm heart.

During this time both the instructor and assistant should be on the lookout for any potentially dangerous dogs. Be ready to take the owner and dog aside. My usual procedure is to sideline aggressive dogs with their owners, counsel them after class that they must have at least one private, preferably in-home session, and then if possible reintegrate them into the regular class. Instructors who harbor aggressive dogs in class are, in my opinion, unintentionally cheating the other participants in the class. They are also cheating (and fooling) themselves because it is simply not possible to conduct a quality class if one is living in terror of being lunged at, snarled at, or otherwise accosted by an aggressive brat.

If any sidelining does have to be done, do it diplomatically and quietly. Simply separate one chair and let that person and the grouchy dog sit near the registration table with the assistant for company. Of course, the assistant will have duties later in the evening, but at least they can keep each other company for now.

Once everyone is settled in their chairs, or sidelined in their chairs—and by the way, this happens infrequently, since the questions you ask during the initial phone conversation usually will weed out aggressive dogs—it's now important that the main instructor be formally introduced. The assistant can do this, and a printed introduction is not out of order. Even though the instructor has already made personal contact with each class member, a short introduction accomplishes several objectives.

First, owners will usually make some attempt to finish their forms if they haven't already, and will make an attempt to quiet their dogs. This buys the instructor time to further "case the class" as to who is Alpha to their dogs, who has a shot at becoming so, and who a given dog thinks is a pushover. The introduction also presents the instructor as the helper, gives his/her qualifications, and indicates clearly that the assistant and the instructor work together and have an orchestrated class routine.

Too formal for you? Want just to "be folks" and greet participants informally at the door, or worse yet, remain cold and aloof and not be introduced at all? Well, choose your own poison is all I can say. I've found that this procedure works very well. You owe it to yourself.

After the intro, I choose the most unruly dog in the class and demonstrate how to make the "Sit-On-It" technique work. Students can place their clipboards and other items on the floor, and use the

33

other side of the chair to manipulate the leash encouraging the dog to leave them alone and lie down. It's easier for the instructor to take the most unruly dog, because that dog will need firmer, well-timed corrections. By observing the instructor, the humans in the class will probably cut the corrections in half, and be twice as slow in delivering them—which will be just about right for their dogs!

READ AND LEAD

I quite naturally use my own texts during my classes, and a copy of my book on city dogs, *The Evans Guide for Civilized City Canines* (Howell Book House 1988), is issued to each student (the class is run in town), along with leash, collar, and behavior form. By the way, the cost of everything is included in the course cost. I do not like to confront clients with added extra costs at the door, which makes them feel obligated to shell out more money than they expected to spend that night. I ask someone in the class to read aloud the sections on being Alpha and the section on eye contact to the group, who follow along in their own texts. Babyish? Not at all. Concepts like Alpha and eye contact explained in print in a book class members get to take home (where they know they can read it again) have more impact than an oral explanation.

In my case, it doesn't exactly hurt that the instructor wrote the book, but the reasoning behind the technique can work in any instructor's favor regardless of whether you use your own text. Remember, reading encourages reflection.

By this time (and this will amaze even the instructor and assistant, and certainly the class) many of the dogs will have "hit the dust." During the initial period, the assistant can help anyone who doesn't seem able to correct the dog quickly or firmly enough, but 20 minutes into the class, most of the dogs will have realized that every other option they may want to take has been blocked, and they will decide to "crash." The dogs will observe other dogs going down (one reason the chairs are arranged in a semicircle) and a certain chain of mimic behavior will kick off, the "smarter" (or lazier—it depends on how you look at it) dogs "informing" other dogs about what they are supposed to be doing. It's neat, civil, sane, and provides an atmosphere of near quiet. Using this method the owners have a nifty control technique they can use during real-life events like dinner or watching television. They also learn about leadership and eye contact, and how to ignore their dog when it pesters them.

Eye contact is demonstrated next by the instructor. It is then practiced one by one by the class members. Discipline techniques are also taught, and the class ends with short 10- to 15-minute sessions on various behavior problems, according to those indicated on the behavior forms (which the assistant has tabulated). These sessions can involve breaking up the class into separate groups and having the two teachers counsel each group, or, if everyone or almost everyone has indicated having the same problems, the class is simply kept in session as a whole. Occasionally, two separate "break-ups" of the class will have to happen, but this is not common since almost all beginners will have some of the same problems. Remember, a class that does not address the existence and elimination of behavior problems *the first night* isn't a quality class. Solving problems is why the majority of the students are there—*not* to learn ornamental ring-style exercises.

Homework for the first night should be done over the next week. Here it is:

1. One 30-minute down each day using the technique we learned tonight.
2. Two formal eye contact sessions using the technique we learned tonight.
3. Read the sections in the book outlined and those pertaining to the behavior problems your dog has, and discipline these problems if necessary—always deliver the softest correction possible.
4. Show up next week, immediately take your chair and "Sit-On-It," and get ready to read about, see demonstrated, and practice heeling. Your days of being pulled around like Ben-Hur during the chariot race will shortly be over. Initial class time? One and one-half hours, including registration and problem troubleshooting and solving. Subsequent sessions will glide in at just under one hour each.

I hope this guide to avoiding first night freak-outs has helped. It took me years to develop and is essentially an integration of some of the techniques I have used in one-on-one training sessions in my private client sessions.

Notice I do not force my class members to perform active exercises on the first night of class. They are scared, insecure, under-confident, perhaps even wary of the instructor. I feel that given a choice, they would rather sit than be yanked around by an unruly ruffian. The structured "down" they learn is something they can employ right away, at home, during real life—and how many times have you heard clients say on the phone, while inquiring about attending an obedience class, "Sometimes I wish he would just *lie down and leave me alone!*" Think it over.

Two final tips: Try to avoid scheduling classes against very popular prime-time television programs. Remember to dress well. Wear practical, but beautiful clothing—people must look at you for the whole evening, so make it a treat, not a torture. A little attention to personal presentation helps anyone's image.

Chapter 5

Subsequent Classes

If I sounded dictatorial and demanding regarding structure in "First Night Freak-Out," it's because I sincerely don't want you to have one—a freak-out, that is!

As for subsequent classes, even though some trainers would like just as prescribed an approach, I find it is better to chart your own course at this juncture and teach what exercise *you* want when *you* feel *you* need to teach it. Bear in mind that I am referring to the standard "be-good-at-home-and-don't-get-in-my-hair-anymore" classes (still commonly called "Novice Classes"—as if everyone is "ring-bound").

Some trainers find it easiest to teach *heel* now (I do) since basic control has been established via the Sit-On-It method over the last week.

Based in Manhattan as I am, good, tight, rock-steady heeling is essential for my clients—and my reputation! In a city where everyone (well, everyone with half a brain) "pretends" not to notice anybody else (the first advice New Yorkers give newcomers is "Don't make eye contact!"), the reality is everyone *is* noticing everything.

No New Yorker wants to be bothered by a lunging dog. It is the lack of heeling that will be noticed. So will you, and in a way you don't want. This is ultimate sin, since you came to New York *not* to be noticed and instead notice everything else. Got it? Well, maybe not, but the point is big-city dogs must learn to heel for functional as well as social reasons.

A DETAILED DESCRIPTION

For this reason I wrote in *The Evans Guide for Civilized City Canines* what is probably the longest, most detailed description of every

Not everyone can be a master teacher of the heel like the magnetic Jack Godsil. Notice the inclination of the dog's head and the tailset, but any instructor usually demonstrates heeling well, or at least more proficiently than the students. The trick is to make heeling seem practical. So I suggest "taking it to the streets." (author's collection)

aspect of heeling in print. I will not repeat it here, not the specific methodology at least, since you can find it in my other book. But in terms of how I train and explain the exercise, I ask the seated students (leashes tucked underneath their rears) to read aloud about heeling. Reading aloud together is very helpful. Remember, the read-aloud-from-a-standard-text has become one of the salient (and salable) features of the "Barney" dinosaur character. I personally find this repugnant and patronizing to any child over two and a half weeks; notwithstanding, the technique works.

OUT ONTO THE STREETS

After a few hectic, tripped-up, tangled, and bumbling attempts at heeling are made inside, just to get the hand position basics down and the collars correctly positioned, we hit the town.

While many trainers would never dream of leaving their sacred training sites for practice in a (horrors) real-life arena, I suggest it be tried. The results will amaze you. The dogs, used to being outside, feel great. The humans feel great because heeling is most often employed outdoors. The wildness factor goes way down. Plus, despite their innate love of the outdoors, dogs in training tend to be a little disoriented. You can use that fact to gain control.

In fact, the fullest explanation of teaching heeling will be found in your own experiences. The main emphasis is to make heeling a real, integral part of the dog's life, not some cornball exercise the dog performs by walking or running around in an indoor area where every other dog is doing the same thing. *Get outside*, even if it's just a heel around the parking lot, and practice there.

You will find distractions galore even here (the dog will lunge to get into his car—if he's smart enough to identify it), and he'll be totally shocked when you take the exercise right back indoors.

DISTRACTIONS ON HEEL?

When I suggest the foregoing inside/outside ploy, some trainers say, "The dogs won't be ready for that many *distractions* at that early point." I just laugh. I have had *first-time* heeling lessons circling the block of the Empire State Building. I think I know just a little about ignoring (and getting the dog to filter out) even the most horrendous urban distractions. Distractions? Get real. You can handle it. More importantly, dogs can handle it.

I think many trainers, especially beginning trainers or those who fixate on the dog alone and cannot take in a whole landscape, use this concept of "distraction" to justify an unproofed dog's shoddy performance. Ring people trot out the word constantly to explain why a dog is "ring-wise"—a word that should be expunged from the English language.

Sure, dogs get distracted; don't you? So train your dog and yourself to deal with distractions, usually by polishing the dog's and handler's concentration skills. There are methods the real pros use to achieve this and if you watch them at ringside, you will see what I mean.

It's best to refrain from complaining about distractions on the heel, or any other exercise. If you think about it, *all life is a distraction—*

"Take it to the street" is exactly what I did during classes in New York City. Let's make heeling appealing was my selling point—but it isn't easy with the distractions of such a wild, fast-paced town. Don't worry, wherever you are; you can handle it. (Charles Hornek)

there are some moments of quiet contemplation, but most of life is distraction. So what are you so shocked about? Train, don't complain.

Again, *how* you teach heeling (or any exercise, for that matter) is not the main concern of this book. The fact that you teach it well, explain it carefully, and put the exercise in a context that is usable is of utmost importance.

THIRD TIME OUT

On the third lesson I usually drill in the sit-stay using a variation of the Volhard "progressions" you find in *Training Your Dog, the Step by Step Manual* (Howell Book House, 1982). Again, these steps are introduced inside and then taken outdoors where an open car door (or other distraction) is used to get the dog to break the stay. Some trainers skimp on stays, but remember: For shy or aggressive dogs they must be rock-steady.

During the third lesson I also introduce the down position—simply maneuvering the dog into position using one of the time-honored, yet humane methods described in countless technical training books.

The Down

I also use my own "special spot" technique, in which the gentle area between the scapula and the upper thoracic vertebrae is pressed downward and "wobbled," easing some but not all dogs into the down position. For full details see *People, Pooches and Problems* (Howell Book House, 1991).

The challenge here is to explain *where* the spot is, train the client to accept manipulating it without undue nervousness, and train the dog to accept the manipulation.

The easiest way to be sure the client has the spot located is to simply stand with the dog at heel position, place your own thumb and position index finger in the proper place, and then ask your client to stand directly behind you, placing his thumb and finger over yours. Then slip your hand out and your client's thumb and forefinger will fall onto the right skeletal spot.

The Recall

The recall dominates lesson four. Again, there are myriad methods for teaching this exercise. But it's almost universally agreed that no repetitious recall practice can take place without first teaching a solid sit-stay, and unless the class has calmed itself to a degree that the recall doesn't resemble a circus. Spend the whole session on this, take the exercise outdoors if you can do so safely, and cap off the lesson with some down exercises. You might add a *short* stay to the down, just walking around the dog, correcting if necessary.

Remember, your clients still have the "Sit-On-It" technique to rely on, and next week we will introduce a freelance 30-minute down anyway.

Week Five

In *The Evans Guide For Civilized City Canines* (pp. 196–201) I detailed how to park a dog in a 30-minute down. Training and explaining this exercise takes some time and you may find enough "justifications" to get your clients to make their day by doing a 30-minute down each day.

Do It on the Spot

There is one way I handle the mystification some clients feel about the necessity of a daily long down (and some simply pretend to be

The long down in action. Do not stare at your dog, and use the corrections for breaks detailed in the text. Remember, the long down is important because it teaches dogs that they have to do what we say, when we say it, and for as long as we "say" it. It teaches dogs longevity in commands, improves memory and has many other benefits. (author's collection)

mystified because they have not done the required homework necessary to secure the long down).

What I do is have the whole class have their dogs placed on a long down during half of the sixth class—usually the second half hour after heeling. Sit-stays and recalls have been rehearsed, since the dogs are now tired and ready to relax.

The three-part corrective sequence during the long down is the same as it basically is in *The Evans Guide for Civilized City Canines*:

(a) The first time the dog breaks the down, give him a firm "NO" and replace him.

(b) The second time the dog breaks, say "NO!" and then go give the dog a firm tap under the chin. This is perfectly justified—you have dumped a lot of work into this dog by this point and you must be strict. Strictness and a no-nonsense, look-you're-doing-it-like-it-or-not attitude is essential.

I have seen classes where long downs were being practiced (attempted is the more appropriate verb). When the dogs break the down—and some of the craftier critters will break 30 or 40 times—the handlers simply return to the dog and without anger (even "method anger," as in "method acting") simply continue to reposition

42

the dog in the down. The dog soon learns that this is a grand game. It's also a supreme exercise in dominance for the dog (think it over) and an even more extreme expression of frustration for the owner.

If the dog breaks the third time, tie him up, or, no matter how humiliating it might be, go back to sitting on the leash. Then go home and practice more.

FINAL WEEK

During the final week, week six, I review all of the exercises. I do not conduct a "graduation" ceremony since we already have enough anthropomorphism pervading the dog world, and besides, during graduation ceremonies, someone inevitably gets unintentionally put down. Also, training is an *on-going, life-long process* that transpires between handler and dog forever, not just during a class. "Graduation" from an obedience course is really an oxymoron. Finally, awarding graduation certificates means that many owners will frame and enshrine them on some prominent wall forevermore.

If the dog slips in his training, or simply acts like a hooligan the night the "award" is being touted as the greatest accomplishment since Lassie saved Timmy from a fire, your training school or service looks like it grants pieces of paper but might not know how to train dogs. It's not exactly good advertising.

CLASS LENGTH

Why is my class so short—six weeks instead of the usual eight or even 12 weeks? First, 12 weeks is too long. I have to ask: What could an instructor be teaching in making novice students show up week after week for THREE MONTHS? I can only suspect that they are teaching frivolous exercises like "the finish" (useless for most lay owners) or just diddling around to seem impressive.

The reason I have condensed my class so much is that clients view a one-and-one-half month commitment to training a dog in a much more tolerable light than they do a 12-week ordeal.

Also, and this might sound inconsequential to some of you who are financially well off, in many families both husband and wife are working (often just to make ends meet) and a sitter has to be hired for the owner to attend class. Finally, psychologically, when attempting to obtain almost any goal, people want to see *a light at the end of the tunnel.* They want to feel they can accomplish the task in a reasonable amount of time, and the shorter time frame actually encourages students to do their homework between classes.

Why then are there still so many over-long courses? Part of the problem is that the sponsoring organization or obedience club simply has not discussed any kind of restructuring. Another part of the reason is: Clubs simply mimic what other clubs in the area do. Finally, and perhaps most sadly, there are instructors who think that they are so stunning as speakers, so entrancing as trainers, so scintillating in the knowledge of even arcane dog lore, so knowledgeable (translate: opinionated) that a captive audience might be enthralled with their every word. In short, ego fuels their effort.

I train in New York City where people love their dogs deeply (there are more dogs here than in Paris), but nevertheless lead very busy lives. I learned long ago to tailor my material carefully, so that dogs got trained and people got happy because they didn't have to spend forever accomplishing the task.

Chapter 6

Finally, a Code of Ethics

I belong to a fascinating group of pioneering trainers. The Society of New York Dog Trainers was founded in 1987 in order to promote and perfect our profession in the Big Apple and environs. Recently, the Society was renamed the Society of North American Dog Trainers (SNADT) and is now open to dog trainers throughout the United States, Canada, and Mexico. Charter members include Carol Lea Benjamin, Mordecai Siegal, Brian Kilcommons, Nancy Strouss, Arthur Haggerty, myself, and a host of other prominent and concerned New York area trainers.

From the list of popular individuals given above, one might think that a copy of the nasty best-seller *How to Swim with the Sharks (and Not Get Eaten)* would be stashed in the briefcases of everyone attending meetings, but instead a genuine spirit of cooperation, love of our chosen profession, and equality is truly present. Meetings are lively, well-run, and usually include an educational presentation by a member or a guest speaker. Recently we had a behaviorist explain what he felt were the differences between dog trainers and animal behaviorists, and other programs have centered on specific training techniques and the "pit bull" controversy.

As in any fledgling organization, incorporation, membership rules, and of course, a solid code of ethics* were early priorities. I co-authored the code and it was later reviewed by a panel and edited for final publication. To my knowledge, it is the first code of ethics published by such a group and it should be of interest to many who read this book. While it is not as complete as I might have wished, it is, as they say, a damn good start. If every locality had an organization such as ours, there would be fewer sleazeball trainers around, and the trainers who are trying to learn and do quality work would be greatly

---

*Reprinted with permission from the Society of North American Dog Trainers.

inspired. I certainly have been. We welcome your interest, and for more information, you can contact: Society of North American Dog Trainers, 441 East 92nd Street, c/o the ASPCA, New York, NY 10128, Attention: Jacque Schultz. Membership applications and other information will be sent promptly.

One more word about the code. If you are a trainer, read it slowly and carefully. Do you feel its standards? If you don't, shouldn't you? In the "olden days" of Catholicism (I know I'm dating myself), we used to have this terribly torturous but incredibly useful exercise called "An Examination of Conscience," during which you raked your soul over the coals and determined how you were failing in life in order to prepare for Confession. Later, not being content with this alone, I joined a monastery where they had something called "Chapter of Faults," in which the other brethren did this for you! Either way, self-examination can be elevating and revealing, and any good code of ethics aids that effort.

CODE OF ETHICS FOR THE SOCIETY OF NORTH AMERICAN DOG TRAINERS

The following Code of Ethics was written and approved by the members of the Society of North American Dog Trainers (formerly the Society of New York Dog Trainers). SNADT is a not-for-profit corporation founded in 1987 in New York City.

In dealing with the question of ethics, the Code sets down guidelines for the professional and personal conduct pertaining to animals, by which members of the Society can relate to each other, to their clients and their dogs, and to the public at large.

If members subscribe to and follow the Code of Ethics, our profession will gain added respect and confidence from the general public. Moreover, differences between members of the Society can be more easily resolved. It is vitally important, therefore, that the Code be comprehensive without constraining members of the profession. The Code of Ethics of the Society of North American Dog Trainers is modeled after the Principles of Veterinary Ethics embraced by the American Veterinary Medical Association (AVMA). However, it has been adapted to serve the needs and concerns of the dog training profession.

Attitude

The Code is deliberately structured in a broad and general manner, but the trainer who accepts the GOLDEN RULE (Do unto others as you would have them do unto you) as a guide for general conduct and who makes a reasonable effort to abide by the Code should have little difficulty with ethics.

SNADT believes that dog training is an essential service for a humane and rational society that cherishes dogs in the human environment. Dog training is an honorable profession worthy of public respect and esteem.

Membership in this organization must represent the highest standards of ethical behavior and humane attitudes towards animals. Aggressive or unprincipled behavior in pursuit of favorable business dealings will eventually conflict with the more specific guidelines of the Code. The Code is intended to light the path to elevated professional standards, to the humane treatment of animals, and to further the value of common decency. It is created for the purpose of stabilizing and improving conditions for the community of dog trainers, their clients, the public at large and, most important of all, for our student dogs who cannot speak for themselves.

Deportment

Members of the Society should always conduct themselves in a way that brings credit to themselves and to the profession as a whole. Members should be good citizens and of high ethical and moral character. No member should use a college degree to which he is not entitled.

Methods

This code makes no attempt to dictate to members which methods should or should not be used, as these vary from dog trainer to dog trainer. Instead our Society serves as a clearinghouse and a place of dialogue for members to share ideas and techniques.

Members agree that they will only use humane methods of dog training. The public may have misconceptions of how dogs are to be trained. Interpreting a training method and its effects is subjective and can be difficult for the novice to understand. Under no circumstances will brutality under the guise of a training method be tolerated.

Guaranteed 'Cures' and 'Secret' Methods

Trainers who use the unqualified term "guaranteed" in their advertising or other promotional efforts do a disservice to the profession, since there is no sure way to "guarantee" the cooperation and performance of three separate living beings: the trainer, the client, and the canine student. Similarly implied magical methods or cures are unethical and misleading to the public.

Testimonial and Endorsements

No member of the Society shall represent the organization with public or private endorsements or testimonials pertaining to products or services or equipment without the expressed consent of the officers of the Society. No member of the Society shall use the name of the Society in connection with a product or promotion without the consent of the officers of the Society. Mention of membership, however, without implication of endorsement in advertising and in the media, is acceptable.

Consultations, Retrains

When members of the Society consult with each other they do so for the good of their students and their clients. Consultations should be conducted in a spirit of professional cooperation between trainers. If a client consults with another trainer, the present trainer should avoid criticism of the previous trainer and focus on the situation at hand. Grievances are more constructively taken up on a person-to-person level, or in extreme cases, especially when violation of this Code is in question, through the Society itself. Clients should be freed of involvement in professional disagreements, as such involvement inevitably detracts from the services needed by them.

Advertising

Advertising means newspaper, magazine, and periodical announcements, professional cards, office and other signs, letterheads, Yellow Pages ads, newspaper ads and any other form of communication directed to the public at large or private clients.

A false or deceptive or misleading statement or claim includes, but is not limited to, a statement which:

1. contains an unqualified prediction of guaranteed results;
2. refers to "secret" methods of treatment or special services which is characteristic of false, misleading, and deceptive claims;
3. concerns any illegal transaction;

4. is not identified as a paid advertisement or solicitation unless it is apparent from the context that it is a paid advertisement or solicitation;
5. contains inaccurate statistical data of numerical claims based on past performance;
6. contains a material misrepresentation of fact;
7. derides the profession, other members of the profession, or their methods;
8. contains false titles or bogus implied endorsements;
9. infringes upon another trainer's signature mark, copyright, business name, or slogan.

When referring to SNADT membership in advertising, the following are the approved formats:

1. Professional members—Professional Member, SNADT (or Society of North American Dog Trainers).
2. Associate members—Associate Member, SNADT (or spelled out).
3. Professional members who passed certification—Professional Member, Certified Level (I, II, or III), SNADT.
4. Non-members who passed certification—Certified Level (I, II, or III), SNADT.

Records

Members of the Society involved in active training must keep records of their clients and canine students.

Communication with the Public

Members of the Society who write newspaper or magazine columns or make radio or television appearances should stress that their replies to questions are provisional and that active training cannot be done, in a full sense, in a broadcast, over the telephone, or in a published article. They should never hesitate to mention that certain problems may need the personal attention of a dog trainer.

Use of Books, Articles, and Reprints

Members of the Society who use the work of others in the form of books, articles, or reprints should clearly identify the author of the work. Books or articles used professionally must credit the author.

Drugs and Medication

Members of the Society shall refrain from dispensing prescription drugs unless they are veterinarians. Suggestions of prescription medication for behavior modification must always be done in cooperation with a licensed veterinarian.

Commissions, Rebates, and Kickbacks

It is unethical for a member of the Society to offer financial remuneration to a veterinarian in exchange for referrals. This practice falls outside of the AVMA Code of Ethics, which veterinarians are bound to follow. Rebates to groomers, pet stores, other trainers, or other professionals fall within the discretion of each individual member, but if the second party belongs to an organization which outlaws the practice, members of the Society should not ask the person to compromise their adherence to such a code.

Fees

If fees are quoted, they must be quoted accurately. If a "free" consultation is offered it must truly be free. Additional charges for leashes, collars, or other equipment or services should be quoted in advance.

Group Classes

It is unethical to overload a class for monetary profit only. Dramatic growth in a class once it has commenced should be avoided. "Ideal" class size varies from trainer to trainer, but certainly a ceiling is reached when the trainer/handler ratio exceeds 1:25. The ideal ratio is much smaller. Members should make every effort to stay below the prescribed level.

Legalities

It is every member's responsibility to be aware of all local, state, and federal laws pertaining to dogs and to inform their clients about them when pertinent. Members of the Society are encouraged to report any suspected act of cruelty or neglect to the appropriate law enforcement agency. Members are bound by local, state, and federal laws pertaining to animal cruelty.

Referrals for Purchasing/Adopting Dogs

Society members shall direct prospective dog owners to sources whose philosophies and practices are consistent with the philosophies and practices of the Society.

Efforts should be directed to the neutering of pet dogs to help address overpopulation of dogs as a social problem. This in no way implies that breeding and showing dogs in conformation or obedience is not endorsed by the Society.

Persons who are interested in breeding and/or selling dogs should:

1. have an extensive knowledge about their particular breed(s) and bloodline(s);
2. strive to eliminate or minimize genetic defects from their breeding stock;
3. offer their puppies sufficient handling and socialization;
4. limit breeding and/or selling to no more than five different breeds within a five-year period;
5. educate prospective dog owners about the necessary aspects of care needed to properly raise a dog (emphasizing the dog's physical, behavioral, and developmental needs);
6. inform prospective owners of the applicable regional consumer protection laws ("lemon laws");
7. follow the highest professional and ethical standards.

Breeding kennels and other facilities should be kept clean, provide adequate shelter, and subscribe to the standards set forth by the American Boarding Kennel Association.

Good Samaritan Referrals

In the event that a Society member receives a request for training services from a person with serious need and without the appropriate financial resources, that person, if not able to absorb the cost himself or herself, should refer the prospective client to a trainer or organization that is willing to help absorb the cost.

Chapter 7

—

False Training

"Sit her in front of you," advised Seymour Adelman, "look her in the eye and think of a number. Think of the number, don't say it aloud." I guided the five-year-old Sheltie into position in front of me and looked down at her. She looked back up at me. Our eyes locked, and I thought of the number five. The dog barked five times. I thought of the number eleven, and the little dog barked eleven times. Then I went blank and thought of zero. The Sheltie hesitated and then barked four times. "Isn't that fantastic!" the dog's owner shouted, and asked me to tell him the numbers I had been thinking of. I didn't have the heart to tell him about the zero.

Sable is the latest addition to the long line of dogs who like to count, read, multiply, and subtract. On a certain level, there is nothing noteworthy here. There have been reports of exceptionally learned dogs since the sixth century. But to think five and have a dog respond with five barks, to think eleven and then hear eleven yips, even to then think zero and get four barks (after all, the dog was working for a food reward—she probably felt she had to say something!) does entice the imagination.

My response, however, was not to become fascinated with the individual animal, but to drag out my materials on canine counting, ESP in dogs, and especially my account of Clever Hans, the prototype of genius animals. Getting interested in Sable for Sable's sake wasn't really a responsible attitude toward the phenomenon. And Sable herself didn't need my interest or adulation; she counted, broke down words into syllables, and performed other feats in order to gain a food reward, which usually consisted of bologna or other cold cuts, and because she was intentionally or unintentionally cued—even by myself.

The "Clever Hans" Syndrome

Clever Hans, too, worked for food. He achieved worldwide fame in 1904, at about the height of the Darwin controversy. Hans was owned by a mathematics teacher, Mr. Von Osten, and mathematics was indeed the horse's specialty. By tapping out the number with his hoof, he could add, multiply, and because of a special code Mr. Von Osten had devised, could also reply to more complicated conceptual questions. The horse became celebrated, especially in his native Germany but also throughout Europe and the United States. Intellectuals and academics came from far and wide to see Hans. In her brilliant book, *Look Who's Talking*, Emily Hahn notes:

> Hans captured the public fancy in Germany. He was the subject of popular songs, and you could buy picture postcards of him and bring home little toy Hanses for your children ... Nobody said that Hans was a music hall entertainer: he was considered to be another thing entirely. People who might be supposed to understand horsey matters—such as cavalry officers, the director of the Hanover zoo and well-known zoologists—announced publicly they believed in Hans, that he was 'sincere.'

In the same way, many members of the dog fancy want desperately to believe in a counting dog, and by extension, in the possibility of fantastic mental abilities in their own pets. It is a deep-seated need, correlated with belief in one's own intelligence and savvy. In 11 years of training dogs, the most frequent question I've been asked after working with a given canine is, "Well, tell me the truth now. Is he smart?"

A Press Party

And so, when a dog like Sable appears in a suburb of Chicago, the newspapers and television stations immediately descend. Television shows that specialize in the exotic do a feature. Dog magazines feel a responsibility to alert the fancy to the existence of such an animal, and to try to explain the phenomenon. Lost in the crush is careful scientific evaluation and research to determine the facts of individual cases. The fact is, many scientists do not know how to evaluate such phenomena and others just don't care. Journalists are also in a bind, for unless they simply report the story on a comic or superficial level, they must carefully tread the thin line between debunking the whole concept and irresponsibly buying the story. A related problem is the reaction of the animal's owner if the animal's intelligence is questioned. Clever Hans' owner died in 1908, after extensive testing showed that Hans was being cued, unintentionally, by slight body movements and by reading slight changes in the eyes of his handlers. Even though Mr. Von Osten's innocence was never called into question, Emily Hahn notes that "He was so downcast up until the time he died in 1908 that it is not too much exaggeration to say he was broken-hearted."

IMPARTIAL STUDY NEEDED

For careful scientific evaluation of a dog like Chicago's Sable, extensive double-blind testing would have to be done, as it was in the case of Clever Hans. To catch subtle body movements and changes in the handler's eyes, video equipment would be of use, as well as a camera trained on both handler and dog as given interactions took place. Unfortunately, as one eminent professor of animal science admitted,

> I'm absolutely confident that something in the owner's personality lets the dog know exactly how much to respond, perhaps a blink of the eye or something else, and the owner may be completely unaware of that. I'm interested in all things pertaining to dogs but I'm not willing to go to an awful lot of trouble in this particular instance ...

And when I described Sable's feats to Dr. Erich Klinghammer, professor of psychology and ethology at Purdue University, his immediate reaction was, "Are you sure this isn't the Clever Hans syndrome?" These gentlemen don't mean to be unkind, but this kind of story is, for them, so old it should have been set to music years ago.

Still, even exacting scientific evaluation cannot explain away all the incredible actions of animals. We simply do not know enough about the functioning of the brain and the senses, and until we do, we can leave the door open to the possibility of extrasensory abilities on the part of our pets.

The real question, perhaps, for those of us outside the scientific community—and so prone to anthropomorphic extrapolation when it comes to smart dogs—is not "Can a dog count?" but "Should a dog count?" I am not recommending furthering the Cartesian split between animal and man, not suggesting we "keep dogs in their place." My suspicious and cautious feelings, rather, have more to do with what I fear is often the endgame for human handlers of wise pets. Is the dog who counts simply an ego boost to its owner? If not, why is it that such animals invariably attract the attention of the local, regional, and then national press long before any careful scientific evaluation is done? Admittedly, there is great public sympathy for such pets. The resultant publicity and attention can provide a real high for both dog and owner, at least until the situation becomes unmanageable, as it often does.

FAMILY TENSION

Sometimes talented dogs can become the cause of extreme tension within the family. Mrs. Adelman explained that she has refused to join in the publicity hoopla surrounding Sable and bemoaned the fact "the dog gets more attention than I do. She sits at the table with us. She gets on the bed. I just can't see it—let her be a dog, for God's sake."

It was this last comment that I think says more than if Sable had started to recite the Gettysburg Address. For, despite the apparent frustration with the dog and criticism of her, the bottom line is a concern that her animal identity is being exploited. It was interesting to me as a trainer that Sable did not listen to even the most basic obedience commands. Throughout our interview, she repeatedly tried to scale her owner and myself, had to be pushed into a sit continually, demonstrated a pronounced heart rate and at times barked randomly even if no question was posed. On one level she was an animal with perhaps extraordinary abilities, but on another level—perhaps more important to her happiness as a dog and a member of a "pack"—she was lacking in social control, introverted, indulged. In the same way Clever Hans was, as Emily Hahn explains, "high strung, nervous and moody, possessing strong likes and dislikes." For all the voluminous literature on Hans, I have yet to discover if he liked to run free in a field, nibble grass off the ground instead of sugar cubes out of a hand, jump fences or hurdles, and do the usual horsey things horses like to do. Is it possible that gifted pets become our personal clones? What, ultimately, is in it for *them*?

All of the above speculation in no way denies the mystery of animal ability. As Dr. Michael Fox remarks, "Animals are not dumb creatures living in a twilight world of partial awareness. Indeed, they may open the door for us to a different reality, a world of which—because of our state of mind and lifestyle—we are no longer a part." Is it our own alienation from the natural world that makes up attempts to drag the gifted pet into our own artificial realm? Is it a better dog if it can count? Can a dog count, and should it?

55

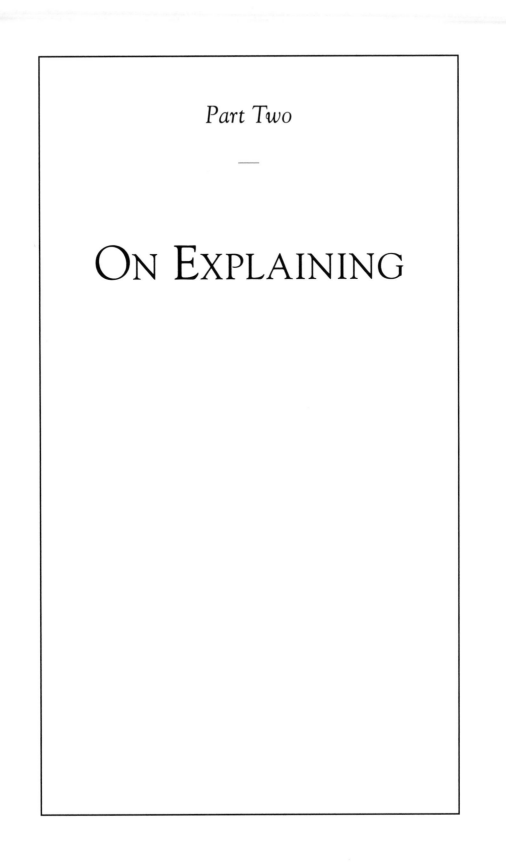

Part Two

—

ON EXPLAINING

Chapter 8

The 10 Unbreakable, Unshakable Rules for Dog Trainers

This chapter flows out of a talk I did in Toronto for a highly sophisticated audience of trainers. I was the keynote speaker, following five days of extremely intensive talks and workshops given by another trainer. I fully expected to find an exhausted, comatose crowd. Instead, I found the talk had created excitement before I had even arrived, since the seminar participants had been given the 10 (actually 11) rules in photocopy form—but with no remarks.

Why such interest—especially when some of the listeners thought that perhaps I would give super-tips on methodology, hints that would perfect their training techniques? Of course, I intended to offer nothing along those lines, not during this talk, not to this audience. Instead, the excitement being generated before the speech was because the audience sensed that I would be talking about the psychological, emotional, and financial lives of trainers—and that's what they *really* wanted to hear about, and that's what most other speakers don't (or can't) talk about.

SUGGESTIONS, NOT REALLY RULES

When I started to teach veterinary seminars on a regular basis (and, by the way, as a non-veterinarian it was hard to break into this speaking circuit, and incredibly heartening to be so nicely received), I learned that the practitioners present were interested in surgical and clinical techniques only insofar as they simply had to attend a certain number of such talks in order to fulfill the requirements of a given conference. Meanwhile, the roster was liberally dotted with talks that had a psychological or financial focus. Trainers should take the cue here. I once had a budding trainer say to me, "I think if I explore my *inner child* I will be a better dog trainer. As for money, it doesn't really matter to me." I answered immediately that perhaps it would be more valuable to explore her *inner adult* and show just a little concern for the value of a well-earned buck. For instance, with money one can buy food to feed oneself and those one loves. For that matter, one can pay the therapist who is helping one explore the inner child. With serious examination of one's inner adult one can easily become more compassionate, better at listening to others, less self-absorbed, and more. Conversely, a person busy dissecting his or her inner child might become quickly discouraged, less able to listen to others or take a careful case history, and, the worst result of all, become an extremely boring person. So this is *not* twelve-stepping, folks.

That's why, with one exception, I've kept the "rules" centered on practicalities. Have you ever really found anyone who is truly interested in anyone else's inner child? I mean other than the inner child directly involved. Troubled trainers bore clients. But spirited, sustained, sociable persons who train well and teach well are a joy for clients to be around. Keep all this in mind as you peruse these "rules." Again, I don't need to pontificate, and I am not criticizing fellow trainers—recognizing, perhaps, but not criticizing. Let's run down the rules, and then go over each one individually:

---

10 Unbreakable, Unshakable Rules For Dog Trainers

1. Get educated
2. Train how you are comfortable training
3. But train the dog
4. And train the owner
5. Keep careful records
6. Have your work evaluated periodically
7. Be honest, be ethical
8. If possible, keep a journal
9. Keep up—increase your knowledge
10. Pay yourself first
    And ...
11. Take time to love

---

1. Get Educated

Getting educated in dog training can be a subject of much debate. Mostly the debate centers on how one should gain knowledge. Examining someone else's specific background rarely helps if one intends simply to copy it and, presto, become the perfect trainer one imagines that person to be. Duplication is not education. For instance, very few individuals can (or should) join a monastery that specializes in breeding and training dogs in order to become like a trainer who stayed in such a station for 11 years, eventually to leave and set up a dog training business in New York. I trust you get the point.

The answer is, of course, get educated the way you can get educated. Let's start at the most limiting level—with the aspiring trainer who is trapped by geography, family duties, or a disability. Obviously you can read. Probably you do. But you should pace your reading of dog books carefully, concentrating on the ones that really strike a responsive chord in you, and mixing your dog book reading with reading on other species, psychology, communication skills, so-called "assertiveness training" texts, and general books about nature. Avoid pop psychology books.

Read the Original Materials

Never ignore the "masters" in the field, no matter how dated you are told they are or feel yourself they have become. Within the "old-timers" in the field is an oral tradition that somehow got itself into print. *Remember, back then, trainers trained, rarely wrote. Now, trainers who have rarely trained write quite a bit.* Got it? So beware of what and who you read. But *do* read.

That said, let me say that some junior trainers become absolutely obsessed with reading to the point that they become late-night readers who are no longer absorbing anything they read, just passing print in and out of their eyeballs. Training literature should be *studied*, not simply read. If the writing is entertaining, that's sweet, but in my experience, don't expect it to be scintillating. But if you skim or skimp on a given book, especially a poorly written one, chances are you will miss its (muddled) message and feel frustrated that the effort you put into reading even low-quality writing is a total loss. It's sort of like listening to a boring person—sometimes, words later, after you wake up, you can discover that you've learned something.

Non-Readers, Get With It!

I should also mention, especially for the younger set, those weaned on MTV and television in general, that there must be a *commitment* to reading if any knowledge is to be gained. *You* have to do the reading. *You* have to do the work. If you don't like to read, an admission very few trainers will make, don't expect to be anything more than possibly technically brilliant in the field. If you do not like to read, chances are you will not be acquainted with what your clients have read, and in your ignorance, you will look foolish. Your technical brilliance will remain impressive, but you will be viewed with a certain suspicion by anyone who has done more homework than you.

Reading also influences one's vocabulary, which in turn influences one's ability to take a concise behavioral case history, or listen to one that is being delivered orally, which often happens in on-the-spot class interactions. Clients will often use vocabulary terms or slang that an effective trainer needs to know. Also, like it or not, we are becoming an increasingly multilingual country. Canadian trainers who live near French-speaking population centers have long ago learned to give commands or instructions in French or English, whatever the language of choice may be for the client and dog. Many American trainers will soon experience this challenge, usually to attain some fluency in Spanish, or they will find blank spaces amongst their class participants and private clients.

Beginning trainers often get hung up on what, exactly, they "should" read. They want a concise list. This makes them feel advanced and "in control." Seasoned trainers continue to read until the day they no longer train, but they are often not as obsessed with *who* they are reading, but rather, with *what* is being said. See the Annotated Bibliography following the text for some tips.

My own practice, which I developed during my monastery years when we were obligated to certain periods of *lectio divina* (mandatory holy reading), was to juggle three or four books at a given time, books ranging from light to serious reading. You might try this. A lighter text tends to make it easier to read the more complex books, and for many readers, variety is simply the real spice of a rich reading life.

2. Train How You Are Comfortable Training

Even 10 years ago, a "prominent" trainer would choke on giving out this advice. Many of you are acquainted with the "do-it-my-way-or-else" syndrome or the more common, gentler-sounding, "but-we-have-always-done-it-this-way" mantra that gets repeated by instructors in clubs that run classes. Often the instructor who obviously is under criticism or is being implicitly asked to at least try another technique will adopt an icy stare that would freeze over Greenland twice when confronted with anyone who might suggest change.

While the prima donna instructor might feel superior, yet threatened, the questioners simply want a way to train that is more comfortable for them. Obviously, they feel resistance to the imposed methodology. This is an important juncture, because whether dogs get trained or not often hangs in the balance.

THE COMFORT ZONE

The idea of being "comfortable" with what one is doing is extremely important. The problem, of course, is that in this New Age, everyone wants *immediate* comfort. Few things hold more potential for comfort than food, so it is not surprising that trainers who overuse food often claim (with incredible conviction) that this methodology makes them feel more comfortable.

The case that food training often "works" is mentioned, but it's not always clear whether it works for the owner, the dog, or on a general level of pure happy feelings. There can be a frivolity in feeling totally "comfortable," and I would only ask you to consider that pandering to your own comfort may not always be professional, often involves avoidance of any risk, and can wind up as a form of what I've called "Dog Training Lite."

I am waiting for some trainer to use this term as an advertising ploy, use it with a straight face, use it as a marketing gimmick, just as Pepsi and countless other companies have attached the adjective to their products. Dog training, my friends, cannot be done in a "lite" fashion. No matter what methods are used, invariably *some* degree of force will need to be exercised that might make the client or trainer uncomfortable. If you cannot handle discomfort, get out of dog training.

So, what's the point of rule #2? Well, what I mean here is not simply "dog training lite," but rather a *self-groundedness* that flows directly out of "obeying" rule #1: Get educated.

COMFORT IN EDUCATION

You see, if you are comfortable in your educational expertise, in your presentation of your materials and methods, in your ability to take a case history, you will inevitably present yourself as a supremely comfortable, confident person. Now, unless you are a lucky soul, all you have to add are the vibrations that emanate from a warm heart, and your client will feel your comfort—and greatly profit by it.

On the other hand, if you are *conflicted* about how to train, unsure about which methods you teach well, halting in speech and in overall presentation, you will not come off as comfortable to clients or dogs. Often the dogs notice the conflict first, through your subtle body language and paralanguage cues. Transference then occurs as the dog figures out that you don't know what the hell you're doing. If the dog is aggressive, or prone to be so, this is a golden moment of opportunity for him. Tentative trainers searching for how to become comfortable in training often get bitten. Once bitten, often twice shy, as the saying goes, and meanwhile, while you center on which approach to base your work and with which you are "comfortable," you are not much use to clients or dogs. Please think it over: *Comfort often involves being at ease in discomfort.*

There is still another aspect of the comfort/discomfort debate. How does your client feel about your training techniques? Is he or she comfortable? We already know if you're not, they won't be, but beyond that, have you stopped to really look, listen, and learn whether clients feel comfortable about your training thrust? Often during a lesson itself there will be time to review the "comfort index" as the client works the dog and you watch and listen. This is the moment to remember and think about after the session—and you should be merciless with yourself. Was the client getting it? Could she execute the training techniques? Were they harsh, too soft, not appropriate, or simply not duplicable? Get comfortable with yourself. With clients. Worry about it a bit.

3. But Train the Dog

This might seem like an amazing "rule," but the fact of the matter is, some trainers are into diagnosis and not into dogs, at least not into the training of the species. With the advent of canine research of a more sophisticated kind, studies have aided trainers immeasurably, but there has also come a tendency, especially among academic trainers, to simply describe the cause of canine misdeeds and not provide solutions.

Trainers who are in contact with real, live clients and real, live problem dogs often don't give a damn about the *cause* of the bad behavior—they just want it stopped. This turns out to be a source of frustration for trainers and specialists for whom snooping out the cause of the bad behavior is of central importance. Understanding just how shallow clients consider "cause" is often the difference between actually training the dog out of bad behavior, or toying with "cause."

In my opinion, the trainer is hired to train a dog and its owner. Even after the first session, you are supposed to have *done something educationally* with the dog in question. You were not called in to chitchat about a problem or to simply diagnose it. Do your job! Train! Isn't there something, anything you can teach the dog during that first session? Of course there is, if only the "sit." Well, do it, because any amount of training leaves an impression on even the most dominant dog. Train! I've never seen a dog that is impressed with diagnosis or owner counseling unless the dog is also trained and taught.

4. AND TRAIN THE OWNER

Believe it or not, even in these relatively enlightened dog-training days, there are trainers who lack vital communication skills. Many do not know how to take a behavior case history, even on an informal level. Others couldn't care less about the owner environment and just want to teach the dog to get into certain body postures that will be useful for practical, day-to-day life. And they will still call this dog training!

In a way, I guess it is training, because nothing is being manipulated or motivated except the dog's body and mind. But modern dog training methods obviously also entail engaging the owner's mind and body in the process. The first step is to become people-sensitive, not just dog-sensitive. This proves no small task, frankly, for no small amount of trainers.

This might sound stupid, but it is necessary to say: Find out who the *owner* of the dog *really* is. There are classes, enlightened ones, where as a rule whole families are invited (or even required) to attend the opening night. Good thinking. Here, the instructor can ferret out just who is *really* in charge of a given student who doesn't give a hoot. While it might be assumed that the woman in a household is the dog's main caregiver (and thus its trainer), it's becoming a less safe assumption lately, and should be researched at least somewhat. Who is the owner? It's an appropriate question if you intend to train dog and owner.

By the way, never, ever fall for the line that the dog belongs to or is owned by a child or adolescent. This is patent nonsense. Sometimes clients will present you with the (untrue) information that the dog really belongs to Jennifer or Tiffany. Jennifer is seven. Tiffany is 13 and more busy planning her fantasy dating life than thinking about dog care or training. These two cherubs are not the "owners" of their dogs. Target who is. I'm saying don't train Jennifer or Tiffany, but target the main owner.

5. KEEP CAREFUL RECORDS

In *The Evans Guide for Counseling Dog Owners*, I talked about the necessity of keeping careful records. I provided two sample behavior case histories that I had been using myself and borrowed (with permission!) from other specialists. Amazingly, something took! Most trainers, especially those who work privately, now use some kind of form when interviewing clients. This was a real step forward.

If any problem in this area exists it is with private trainers who overuse the case history process, or the class trainers who underuse it. Your form should not be longer than one side of an $8^1/_2 \times 11$-inch sheet of paper, with perhaps a chance for a client to add something on the back. Class trainers really should consider a form that includes a chance for participants to spell out the real reasons they have come to class—precisely, a chance for them to list the myriad behavior problems they are experiencing with their dogs. If you provide less than a full chance for clients to reveal, in my opinion you are cheating those clients.

Needless to say, any trainer in this day and age who thinks that clients are really coming to class to teach their dogs the "exercises" and only such routines is severely deluded. Clients come to class or hire private trainers because from their perspective the dog cheats, lies, steals, is dirty, destroys things, or is just plain retarded. In short, insanity rules from the client's point of view. Ironically, our record-keeping is often the first step in restoring order to a seemingly lost relationship. The very presence of a form, whether filled out by a client or a trainer, adds a measure of stability to the training process.

RECORDS, BENEFITS

There are benefits galore to keeping good, clean records and not just for our clients, frankly, mostly for ourselves. First, good record-keeping forces the trainer to ask the correct questions. On a tired day, on an "off" day, it is altogether possible to lag in detection skills, or even to shut down on such skills and just "believe" whatever a client says about a dog. The client chart (whatever form one chooses) keeps the trainer on track. Any detective is nodding in agreement.

Secondly, good records help you to refer back to what you have taught or intend to teach. Especially for trainers who enjoy (the verb is correct in this economy) a good case load, it's easy to forget who learned what from lesson to lesson. If you goof in front of a client and unwittingly begin to teach an exercise already taught or push a point already pushed, you will be deeply embarrassed and wish you had kept careful records.

Finally, record-keeping helps any trainer to feel good about him- or herself. Inherent in the process is a sense of control over one's work, an ability to leave work behind since the essential facts are on record, and thus an ability to enjoy other aspects of life more fully. This freedom, in turn, relates to one's ability to spend time with others and not be obsessed with work to the detriment of others or one's own dogs. It all hooks in, if you think of it, and "putting it together" is what counts, to use a line from Steven Sondheim. Keeping careful records helps you to do just that. Believe me; otherwise things fall apart quickly.

Don't forget the possibility of litigation—something I've never had to suffer through, probably because I always kept careful records. Litigation in a litigious society is always a possibility. Ask some veterinarians. There are sue-crazy people out there and your record-keeping might be evidence you need at a strategic moment.

One last point, especially for academics or for trainers who wish to contribute to studies of canine behavior problems: The need for careful records is crystal clear, for if there is no clarity in standardized documents, there can be no correlation of data, no reference points for comparison, and no way to validate a study. Many aspects of canine behavior will remain forever "anecdotal" in nature. But surprising amounts of information can be cross-checked, validated, put under peer review, and eventually creatively used, through the simple task of keeping good, solid records.

6. Have Your Work Evaluated Periodically

Everyone claims to be open to criticism, but truth to tell, it's an exceptional human being who truly is. Even if one fulfills all the "dicta" previously suggested in this Mosaic chapter, fulfilling the 10 rules, kowtowing to every detail, it can still be difficult. One exercise that's difficult is to get oneself evaluated every so often. As a trainer said after I suggested this as a rule at the Toronto convention, "You must mean get yourself *humiliated* periodically."

But evaluation doesn't have to be humiliation. It's a point well-made, if protectively-made. Even the idea of having one's work sent up for review is threatening. I'll offer one of my own experiences that may help others to bite the bullet and get re-evaluated, whatever the risk of humiliation possible.

CERTIFICATION OR CRISIS

I was once ushered into the certification committee of the Society of New York Dog Trainers, which later became the Society of North American Dog Trainers. The certification committee was already rolling along nicely with prominent trainers, who had published and lectured widely, at the helm. I felt honored to be asked onto the committee. But I was still "grandfathered" in.

At our first meeting, between evaluating prospective certification seekers, the certification committee decided to review *each other* in our handling techniques with the shelter dogs that are provided as candidates for testing those who want certification. In short, I was not allowed simply to sit as a judge, but asked to train in front of a panel of sophisticated judges who were judging trainers who had just applied for certification.

Strangely, I was scared. Yet, I enjoyed the experience. I was getting re-evaluated, and, blessedly, by top trainers. Even as I resumed my job as a judge of others, I had a smile on my face. I had done what I would ask others to do. I had tested my skills, displayed them to the public, and the dog had responded nicely. Even at a basic level the dog had showed it was beginning to be trained, and thus liberated. I felt free, competent, and validated by my peers. Academics call it "peer review."

AN ALTERNATIVE: AVOIDANCE

Some trainers, however, will do anything to avoid such an experience. They may feel, for instance, that such re-evaluation happens every week in class itself. But look at who the "jury" consists of—lay dog owners who are troubled and come to class precisely because they lack competence. Is this a competent evaluative group for a professional attempting to perfect his or her skills by "periodic review" by peers? I think not.

How can you arrange truthful re-evaluations? Well, a very private way is simply to videotape yourself. This might involve a helpmate, since using a decent camcorder with a tripod will provide the best results, and someone will have to move that camera as you yourself move about. Another method is to videotape yourself and then stop-action (pause) the results. This exercise is very fruitful as you are free to really study yourself. All this can be done in privacy or with close trainer friends, although if you are serving an apprenticeship, it's really the priority for your teacher to see you taped and keep that tape close at hand, to compare with future tapes later on. The results can be incredibly revealing.

7. BE HONEST, BE ETHICAL
I think the "Code of Ethics" reprinted in this book maps out my feelings—simply read it over as many times as you feel necessary.

8. IF POSSIBLE, KEEP A JOURNAL
Such an exercise is an invaluable aid in perfecting one's observational acuity, vocabulary, and simple record-keeping skills. In a dog trainer journal, you simply record what you went through in a given day: your mood, the mood of the student, the mood of the client. Then record performance, because controlling moods in clients or in oneself is often the key to success or failure.

Performance itself, whether it be your own, the client's, or the dog's, can really be recorded more successfully on the carry-around records you need to tote anyway. The journal records your inner thoughts, desires, suspicions, observations, and hopes. It explains the trainer you hope to be. You will see that some journal excerpts open and close this very book—this is not an accidental or a literary ploy. Instead, my journal entries have animated my work, and helped me to see just how far I have come, and how far I needed to go. Keep a journal, and if you have no idea how to do this, consult *The Intensive Journal*, by Ira Progroff. Remember, I'm asking you to keep a journal, not write a diary. Think seriously for a moment about the difference between keeping a journal and writing a diary.

ADDED BENEFITS

Out of my journals flow articles and even books. While it may seem that currently everyone and their grandmother is penning a dog book, quality books usually result from months or even years of reflection. While publishing is not as important in our field as it is in ethology, anthropology, and other sciences, the "publish or perish" dictum has not been levied on our field as a sacrosanct necessity. Nevertheless, do try to drum up a decent article and get it out there in front of the public. Besides the headiness that comes from seeing yourself in print (and self-confidence is important in this field), there is a good chance that the article might win a prize (both the Dog Writers' Association of America and *Off Lead* magazine sponsor writing competitions), and at any rate, the information might lead to correspondence with other trainers, which is so important in a potentially very lonely field.

Finally, writing—journal-type, or for publication—always helps focus your mind. This can only help you to perfect your observational skills as a trainer, since writers are observers. Don't ignore this discipline—it is essential, satisfying, and in the end, supremely rewarding.

FIRST BOOK, FIRST TRIAL: WRITING HOW TO BE YOUR DOG'S BEST FRIEND

Early in 1976, we brothers trained a German Shepherd dog for an editor at Little, Brown and Company, a Boston-based publishing firm. When the client returned to New Skete to retrieve his now highly-trained dog, we gave him a complete demonstration of what the dog had learned. The editor liked the demonstration and the advisory talk that went with it, and suggested that we write a book on dog behavior and training. Eventually we did.

Of course, I am making a long story short. The genesis of our modest book on dogs was much more complicated, involving community discussions of the book's content and concept, the usual contract negotiations, and finally the long, arduous process of writing and photographing. It is this process that I should like to share with you since it is the underside of book publishing, the side few see. Especially in a book concerning animals, featuring text and photographs of living beings, the glossy jacket and promotional blurbs hide the real action behind the book. Perhaps our experiences will give an added dimension to the book for those of you who care to read it, and help others who write about animals.

Everyone and his mother, it seems, is currently writing a book on dogs. The market is filled with books on animals. Our particular slant was its concentration on the dog/owner relationship as the basis for healthy rapport between canine and human, and our "living lab" full of dogs. In the wrong hands, our story could easily have become an "elves and fairies" type of tale, instead of a practical book on training. We avoided romantic details, cute stories, trivial anecdotes of life with dogs. We used a direct, advisory approach, imparting knowledge in a readable fashion so that people could really begin to deepen their relationships with their dogs, not just think about it or envy others who already had good rapport. "How do you do it?" is a good question we are often asked concerning our dogs; we wanted to answer that question and at the same time say, "Look, you can do it too!" This is what any "how-to" book does, whether it is a book on dog training or on intimate areas of human development: It presents the reader with a vision of order and efficiency in whatever task it addresses itself to, and it encourages the reader.

HUMOR OR NOT?

Humor encourages like nothing else, and so we dotted the book with educational stories featuring good punch lines and occasional slapstick scenes. There was the story about the Newfoundland-Saint Bernard mix that knocked over the refrigerator, tore up floor tiles, ripped down the drapes, and then growled at the owner when she returned home! One reader wrote, "If it happened to me I wouldn't have thought it was funny at all, but since my dog's chewing is confined to my slippers, I began to count my blessings!" Cute or trivial stories about specific dogs that other readers will never meet or even care to meet are a waste of paper and do not communicate our own outlook. (Several people offered us snapshots and chapters on their dogs and their talents.) Educational stories, especially related in a funny way, can be a boon to training. At the same time, a secondary purpose is sometimes served: The owner learns that his dog can get itself into humorous situations, and yes, even become the butt of a joke. Dog owners are notorious in their reluctance to face their dog's deficiencies and failings. They have to be carefully eased into it. Yet, laughing at or with our dogs in a healthy, constructive way can be a key to understanding them, appreciating them, or, as the case may be, tolerating them. Unsurprisingly, one of the chief failings of most dog training books is their complete lack of humor. William Koehler's books are one exception. Whether or not one agrees with every method in his books, they are well written and occasionally very funny. But try reading 10 pages without a pause of some of the other top training books. If your head starts nodding, don't be surprised.

PHOTOGRAPHY

Canine photography can be an exasperating, demanding chore. When working with models the photographer cannot say, "hold that pose," or "turn to the left just a bit," or "make that smile a little broader." The photographer must adopt two roles. As a professional, trained to snap the shutter at the right moment, the dog photographer must also be a skilled observer of animal behavior, for only then can he or she capture the correct nuance of response. It takes a lot of film and patience to capture such elusive concepts as eye contact between human and canine, or canine loneliness. Shooting obedience exercises, praise, and discipline procedures can also be difficult. Technical precision is important if the reader is to know what to do, and when.

Canine models have to be chosen carefully. An Old English Sheepdog cannot be used to portray what eye contact means. A Dachshund cannot effectively display the technique of jumping a hurdle. In choosing models of one breed, one must be careful not to alienate owners of other breeds. An ugly specimen of a specific breed, when used as a model, can infuriate the ardent fancier who is concerned with having the beauty of the breed appreciated. Sensitivities abound and need to be appreciated.

In animal photography, as elsewhere, for every 10 good shots there are bound to be 100 throwaways—good but not quite on the mark. The photographer for *People*, used to photographing Jackie Onassis and others who smile on cue, was baffled by grinless German Shepherds and impatient, publicity-shy monks anxious to get back to work. After taking over 1000 shots, the magazine used three.

71

Finally, there are accidents of equipment, like the time Brother Marc and I laboriously concoted and posed seven models from our boarding kennel population—only to discover later in the darkroom that the camera shutter had malfunctioned. Meanwhile, the models had gone home.

HOW TO AND HOW NOT TO

A how-to book will suffer if it does not correlate photographs and illustrations with the text. At Little, Brown we were spared this difficulty. Our editor, Richard McDonough, had produced how-to books ranging from stained glass window making to woodwork, leathercraft, and skin care. He is an expert at the whole process, since all how-to books have certain common features. This experience held an added bonus since the editor reflected the feelings of the layman for whom the book was written. He posed questions about the final manuscript that would have occurred to the lay reader. Someone more knowledgeable in dogs might have brought the text up to such a level that the general reader would feel "out of his league" and so turn elsewhere. I learned that a good editor is not a mirror image of his or her author. Indeed, the editor can very well be the opposite to greater benefit.

Publishing companies are becoming more discriminating in what they accept from how-to authors of any persuasion, dog writers included. A famous name in dog training will no longer be the ticket to a literary contract. Dog training and behavior books, like any other books, will undoubtedly be judged in the future on their ability to communicate effectively and factually and on the ability of the text to move on the basis of language alone, and not by the number of dogs the trainer has trained, or his or her ability to lecture training classes. In the increasingly sophisticated how-to book field, a mediocre book just will not make it.

Despite the current spate of both poor and brilliant animal books (one need only look to the works of James Herriot, Michael Fox, Jane Goodall, and Emily Hahn to find examples of the latter), I think we need more books on dog training and behavior. Through these books, a new dialogue, a new consciousness, may develop concerning our canine friends. As our various sources of knowledge and experience are intelligently documented and pooled, they may lead us to new discoveries about dogs and their ability to learn and communicate that we may have never imagined possible.

A look at the literature concerning apes and chimpanzees reveals a similar growth situation, culminating in the breakthrough works of

Jane Goodall and Francine Patterson. Researchers like Dr. Michael Fox (who wrote the foreword to our book) and Emily Hahn (author of *Look Who's Talking Now*) already hint at the communicative abilities and possible symbolizing capacities of dogs. Their own insights are no doubt aided by the knowledge they gleaned from trainers and behaviorists. Assuming their years of actual experience with their subjects, these experts have perhaps more to offer to research in animal behavior than even laboratory scientists. Those of us concerned with dogs are gifted to have at our disposal a wide array of valuable laboratory experiments dating back to the beginning of this century. Subsequent breeding programs, rearing methods, and training techniques often hark back to the results of these laboratory observations. But a laboratory environment, manipulated by man, structured and organized by man, can tell us only so much.

There has been a split in animal studies concerning researchers like B.F. Skinner, who perhaps personifies the "laboratory approach," and Konrad Lorenz, who is more naturalistic in his approach. At this juncture, we need more accounts of canine behavior and training, in my opinion. Sentimentality and anthropomorphism must be avoided if accounts of training and behavior by laymen are to be accepted by the scientific community. The tendency in our culture is to humanize dogs and ascribe to them fantastic abilities that are in reality human projections. This must give way, at least among canine specialists, to a new approach that, while not ensconcing itself in the rigidity of the laboratory, does not also fall prey to humanization.

Helps and Hindrances

It is only through exchange and research that any real breakthroughs will occur in canine studies. We have tried to emphasize the importance of becoming a trained observer, with lived experience and the ability to communicate that experience factually, carefully, and clearly. With this kind of research in the dog world, we may truly be on the way to discovering the actual potential of our best friends, a potential that we may only have scratched to date—not because of our dogs' limitations, but because of our own inability to empathize, communicate, and understand.

Our attempts to understand animals can be severely limited by our Christian heritage, which seems to tell us, implicitly or explicitly, that man is separate from and superior to other animals. But this is not the emphasis in the Christian East, or in monasticism. The monk's job was to see the unity of all creation, to see it transfigured in Christ. Monks have always sought out nature, wilderness, and the animal kingdom with deliberate singlemindedness. Konrad Lorenz used to tell his students, "You must love the animal you are studying." Similar injunctions have come from monastic fathers like Francis, Segius, and Seraphim. So in a sense, every animal worker has to adopt a monastic stance, a scaling down of ego, for it is ego that frightens animals.

The name of our book is *How To Be Your Dog's Best Friend*, but this may be misleading, since some dog owners will attempt to *make* the dog their friend. A better approach is to contact the dog on its level, not yours, and say, "Let's be friends together."

As you can see, book publishing ain't easy—but do keep that journal!

9. KEEP UP, INCREASE YOUR KNOWLEDGE

I once attended a dog training seminar where a participant disagreed violently with what the speaker had to say. She began her comments by saying, "I've been in dogs *30 years* and I think…" She exploded into a diatribe about her methodologies, techniques, and for that matter, her personal needs and desires, adding again (and I think even *again*) that she had been "in dogs" for 30 years. The audience sat stunned until finally a woman of equal age rose and said, *"And you've been repeating the same mistakes for 30 years! It doesn't matter how long you've been in dogs and we don't care. Sit down and shut up."* At this point the audience applauded. It was an embarrassing, yet revealing moment.

The seminar speaker tried to save the moment by inquiring which seminars the 30-year veteran had recently attended. Finding out that the number was zero, he decided to move on with his material rather than make a bad situation worse. The sad fact was this participant really thought her education was complete. She felt she knew it all!

Yet in every other professional field, continuing education (CE) is either demanded or highly encouraged. In some states, veterinary CE credits can take considerable effort to earn each year, and there is a no-nonsense policy about the matter: If you fall behind in CE credits, your license to practice will be taken away. The same rules apply in the legal profession, among medical doctors, and in many crafts. The fact that dog trainers and specialists are not required by any special regulation to attend any particular lecture doesn't spare us from the obligation of special education—education that is continuing, structured, and serious.

BUT WHO AND WHERE?

Finding out about ongoing seminars specializing in dogs and their behavior isn't that difficult. A great resource is the American Kennel

Club Library (phone 212/696-8245) and the "Seminars" section in the AKC Events supplement. Another source is the seminar listing and the ads in *Off Lead* magazine (phone 315/339-2033). Still another approach is to scour the exhibit tables at dog shows. Here you will often find leaflets advertising the upcoming appearance of a given speaker, plus an outline of the material that will be covered.

Word of mouth isn't a bad way of gaining information on who will be appearing where, either. Even if fellow trainers are reluctant to share techniques, they are paradoxically very open about who is going where to listen to whom. With the exception of the "30-year" veteran mentioned earlier (and there is usually one at every seminar, so brace yourself and take a catnap during this interlude), most learning-oriented trainers get very excited when a big name is coming to town and will share information on site, registration, date, and time. Keep open, and you'll hear of such talks.

There are two aspects of giving and getting a seminar, and it might be useful to talk about them here—both from the point of view of your optimum enjoyment as a listener, and the comfort index for the speaker himself or herself. Successful seminars are not accidents. They are carefully concocted events.

GIVING AND GETTING SEMINARS

Because dog training is a learned profession, a field where most skills are learned on the job, those of us interested in accelerating the learning process must search out new ways of gaining greater knowledge. After all, we can only learn so much from the dogs themselves (even though, in the final analysis, they are our best teachers), and so we turn to those who handle dogs competently and are willing to share their skills. In short, we attend seminars and clinics.

I've been on both the giving and receiving ends of dog training seminars. During my years at New Skete Monastery I had to organize, prepare, and conduct seminars, and clean up and wrap up affairs after the day was over. I speak from a deep reservoir of respect both for those who give seminars and those who "get" them.

Let me share with you some ideas that will help you give or get seminars that are profitable for all. Let's examine the situation first from the point of view of the organizers—those brave souls who stick up their hands at club meetings and volunteer to organize such events. At the same time they stick out their necks, and in almost every club there will be sideliners ready to chop them off. So the first thing to realize as a seminar organizer is you can't please all of the people all of the time, and not even three-fourths of the time.

Something is bound to go wrong and you, the organizer, are bound to bear the brunt of the blame. Organizing a seminar can be a thankless task that deserves profound thanks. Get ready for that.

Begin by talking to others who have organized seminars. Read everything you can find on seminar organization. One of the best seminar-preparation guides I know of is *How to Talk with Practically Anybody about Practically Anything*, by Barbara Walters (paperback edition available). The final section of the book covers how to greet the speaker, how to get him or her settled, how to introduce the speaker, and much more. Ms. Walters says,

> Prepare the speaker for all known eventualities. Caution him about the elderly ladies in the front row who usually nod off to sleep just as the talk is getting underway. Tell him it's nothing personal—they always do that because they're elderly and the hall is usually warm. Don't be demure about the time you want him to speak, effusing that the audience is just *dying* to listen as long as he wants to go on. He's a professional and can trim his goods to fit the situation. He'll be much less offended to hear that he has exactly four hours and 40 minutes, because people must return to work, than to watch the room emptying long before he's reached his next material.

These and similar tips abound—it's a good "bible" for any seminar organizer.

Remember not to make the seminar organization committee too large. Often two, three, or four people can work together more effectively than a huge mob. Marie Ehrenberg and June Goodrich of Rochester, Minnesota, have organized many successful seminars. Marie says, "We work together so well as a team. We can cross-check everything between ourselves, accommodations, scheduling, pick-ups, delays, you name it. We've done it so many times you get used to what's involved." June Patrick and Anne Green of Pennsylvania's Back Mountain Kennel Club, also veteran organizers, offer this observation, "Two people are a good organizing committee. We make a good team. Of course on the final day we need extra hands, but if too many people are assigned to help, someone usually forgets something along the line. With two main organizers the heat may be on, but things get done."

What's the hardest part of organizing a dog-related seminar? Usually, said Marie Ehrenberg, "turnout—assuring that there will be an adequate turnout and scheduling the seminar so that it doesn't conflict with shows or other events in the area. After that, rental of a suitable hall, and once in a while, a speaker who is difficult to deal with or over-demanding, but that's rare among dog people."

Other than the preliminary talks for scheduling, arranging accommodations, and so on, the organizer's main burden falls on the day before, the day of the seminar, and the day after. On these days the organizers really appreciate a call from club members asking, "Is there anything I can do to help?" Even if it's the day *after* and you haven't lifted a hand to help, call and offer your assistance. Because not infrequently, when the speaker arrives in town, the organizers tend to panic. Have we forgotten anything? Will the registrants actually show up? Will the ceiling of the hall cave in? Will the dog defecate or urinate? These and other such nightmares run through organizers' heads, and if the speaker himself or herself is "wired" before the seminar (more on that later), the organizers are as well—they won't sleep the night before any better than the speaker, even though they themselves will not be "on stage" for any time longer than an introduction. Be attentive to the organizers and help out. After the seminar, thank them, preferably in writing—it will be much appreciated. Offer also to help clean the hall, and do all you can to lighten the organizers' work load.

Seminar organizers should consult with the speaker on how he or she prefers to be introduced. Some have a scripted introduction which is not at all vain; it is, in fact, a *courtesy* to the organizer and club. Others, by comparison, couldn't care less what you say by way of introduction as long as you don't say something negative or compromising. If the speaker doesn't offer advice, you should script an introduction together and not just rise and say, "Here's Mary Smith!"

The seminar organizers, not the speaker, should set the ground rules for the seminar *before* the speaker is introduced. For instance, if smoking is not allowed or will be confined to certain areas at certain times, this needs to be stated in advance of the seminar. At dog-related seminars, even the best behaved dogs act up and whine, growl, snort, giggle, complain, and otherwise manage to make themselves noticed. Don't ever bank on the good behavior of the dogs! State at the beginning that while we all know that the dogs present are trained (a nice way of putting it since training means different things to different people), we'd appreciate it if you'd remove your dog from the hall if he or she gets too vocal or too active. Don't leave this to the speaker; he or she will hardly want to deliver an admonition to a noisy dog or an insensitive owner.

It is also the responsibility of the organizers to advise the speaker of any prospective attendees who are likely to make the seminar unpleasant or prolonged for the participants. We have, for instance, within the dog fancy, the well-known "know-it-all" syndrome. Here, someone who "knows everything" about dogs decides to pontificate at a given seminar and monopolizes the floor, grilling the speaker on minute points. This, of course, delays the seminar and draws the participants in the process, although such audience experts think they are "proving" themselves to the crowd. This scenario is so much a part of dog seminars it should have been set to music long ago, but then nobody would come to see the musical! Such souls not only slow down the seminar's pace, but wind up making fools of themselves and possibly the rest of the seminar participants.

I once had an especially memorable experience with this syndrome. The participant was a member of the veterinary profession and whispered throughout the course of the day to another seminar participant. Whether he was agreeing or disagreeing with me, I didn't much care, as my main concern was not with criticism (I am quite open to it), but the fact that the seminar day itself was disrupted by this person's constant barrage of private comments and public complaints. I felt terribly embarrassed for him, and later, another veterinarian attending the seminar came up to me and apologized for his colleague's behavior. He had unknowingly made a fool of himself in front of the very people he sought to impress, and demeaned the veterinary profession in the process. Seminar organizers must be on alert for such cranks—and silence them. Their motives are often suspect, personal, and at any rate are not in the best interests of the other participants. Constructive criticism is one thing, and welcomed by any mature seminar-giver. Whispering, covert discussions, and badgering questions are another, yet I know from many seminar givers that such encounters are all too common.

Finally, the seminar organizers should not forget the speaker once he or she has finished speaking. For example, don't assume that the speaker wants to go home immediately—he or she may want to get some feedback and generally "wind down" after a hard day. Ask and offer alternatives. Does the speaker want to go back to the motel, or would he or she enjoy meeting the club president or prominent dog people present? I have met during seminars absolutely fascinating people that I would later have enjoyed a dialogue with, only to have been whisked back to my hotel to watch Grade B movies. Ask seminar speakers how they would like to "come down" and if they indeed *do* want to go back to the motel. Even if you (and others) are dying to socialize and "pick speakers' brains," respect their right to privacy. They've already given one seminar!

Next I have some words to the "givers," those of us who attempt to mount seminars and what we can do for those who attend them.

Let's talk about how to give a seminar, and my remarks are necessarily at my fellow speakers and seminar-givers, although organizers and "seminar receivers" might also gain from these comments.

I once spent an hour with a well-known seminar-giver. Over coffee we discussed the art of giving seminars to dog training groups and veterinary organizations. This person had just taught four successive seminars each weekend for the last month. He had just begun to rust out, and burnout wasn't far behind. He stared into his coffee, and in a lifeless tone, dramatically unlike his animated manner before an audience, explained that seminars had become for him "a form of mental rape." He detailed facets of seminars well known to most speakers: constant questions during breaks, lunch, and the seminar itself; the loneliness of motel rooms; being asked for instant evaluations of individual dogs and complex behavior problems; the tension of making plane and bus connections; the "let-down" period after the event is over; ad nauseum. He had had it. I listened sympathetically, yet sensed that something central was amiss in his attitude toward giving seminars. While I'm sure none of the exasperation showed during his seminars (he is fully professional), I wondered how long he could take the pressure without caving in (probably the day after teaching a seminar, never during one).

Concerned, I consulted a good friend who is an actress, a graduate of the Skidmore and Bennington College acting schools, a seasoned professional. She explained that the problem lies in attitude. "As soon as you start to put up a wall between yourself and your audience, you're sunk. There are mechanical tricks that speakers and actors use to psych themselves up to act or teach better, but with a person who holds a poor attitude toward the work, stage tricks simply produce a more mechanized performance, one that people see through immediately."

She went on to explain that the only thing seminar-givers have to offer, even granting the fact that they may harbor within their minds a goldmine of knowledge, is an inner quality of peace and happiness concerning their work—an ardent love for dogs, for teaching, and for instructing that shines through and inspires others. Seminar teachers are not superior—they are simply more learned, and able to communicate what they know attractively. In essence, the seminar-giver often gives more of *himself* or *herself* than concrete information.

If attitude is important, so is preparation. Barbara Walters comments in *How to Talk with Practically Anybody About Practically Anything,*

> The rule is preparation. Test pilots bullet into space with scarcely a heart flutter because they know their business; good public speakers, cheerily and effortlessly rambling on without a glance at their notes, have also done their homework. They've gone over and over the

points they want to make, the structure of the speech, even the flourishes of humor.

She adds that the best preparation a speaker can make is to learn the speech thoroughly—and then throw it away! The use of cards might help some speakers, or they invariably fall out of your hands, get mixed up, or suddenly blur before your shocked eyes as you begin the speech. Typed pages are a disaster, I know—I once relied on them. They are an invitation to snoozeville for your audience.

Preparation is very important for a person giving dog-based seminars because often the speaker must handle a dog while speaking; anyone who has done it knows that this complicates the matter of speaking style considerably. Some otherwise seasoned speakers tense up here, and of course this tension is telegraphed down the leash, and the dog responds accordingly. Sometimes hilarious results come from this tension, as the seminar speaker explains what will be done with the dog, tries to do it, and of course the dog does the exact opposite. My advice is to *go with the humor,* laugh at the dog and yourself and try again. It's somewhat perverse, but it seems that the more famous you are, the more renowned you are for your training methods and handling skills, the more the audience secretly (or even openly) wants to see you make some mistakes. It shows that you're really human, and usually something about the caliber of your humanity. If you stamp your feet, protest, get mad at the dog, or try to calm audience laughter, you cast yourself in a poor light. If you laugh, move on, and try the technique again, you've shared your humanity, your "inner quality" with your audience. Dogs are not machines to be programmed; they make mistakes, they have a sense of humor, a sense of playfulness which is one of the things you want your audience to appreciate about dogs (I hope)!

The problem of "mental rape"—the way my friend described seminars—usually centers on the plethora of questions, questions, questions that almost any seminar-giver receives from dog-people audiences. First, this is to be *expected* and appreciated. When you think of it, there is no reason why the seminar participants should *not* ask questions. On the other hand, questions can be asked at a totally inappropriate time or about a totally inappropriate subject, and this has to be tactfully indicated. Providing seminar participants with an outline of the day or evening often helps ward off questions during breaks that will be dealt with in the course of the seminar itself. An outline is also a good idea because the participants like to know what is going to happen to them, when they will eat, can take their dogs or themselves for a walk, or ask questions.

I never mind signing books and exchanging pleasantries during seminar breaks. But when a participant monopolizes me as seminar speaker, it's easy to get frustrated. On the other hand, it's all part of the job... (Judy Emmert)

Some people, however, even if provided with an outline, and even if you have *already* addressed a certain question in your prepared text, will approach during a break and ask for a "personalized" response. For instance, you present a unit on destructive chewing, outlining your basic approach to such problems. A seminar participant hurries up during a five-minute break and asks you what should be done about Tippy—who chews. You've just spent a half-hour talking about destructive chewing. Essentially what this participant wants is for you to repeat the half-hour speech about destructive chewing (in five minutes) using her dog's name as the sole noun in an identical speech. She will then be happy. The exposition in the seminar itself wasn't enough—she wants to hear it for Tippy. You now have three minutes in which to answer (two minutes of the five-minute break were taken up by the question itself,) the seminar participant is looking at you expectantly, her feet planted firmly as she stands directly in front of you. Tippy sits at her side munching a bit of trash he just picked up off the floor. All the other seminar participants are filing back to their seats, waiting for you to resume. You have several choices: explain the situation and ask her to come back, recap your talk in the two minutes, or remind her that you just covered her particular problem and risk incurring her ill will. It's a genuine no-win situation.

Sometimes a version of this happens within the seminar proper, with a person who dominates the floor with repeat questions or comments. There is the seminar participant who wishes to use your seminar as a platform for his or her own views, often by soliciting agreement from you concerning their favorite or not-so-favorite training methods. Be tactful and listen. Sometimes you just have to decline to answer the question, as I once did when an irate breeder rose to her full height and proclaimed to the assembly that all veterinarians were quacks and didn't I agree? Nothing is gained by such questions/comments and your reputation can be lost in an instant. Tact is of essence for the seminar-giver, because the "getters" don't always have it in large quantities.

The main point is never let *anyone* slow down the pace of your seminar with personal or peripheral concerns. The teacher must always guide and conduct the experience, remaining in full control, while at the same time being open, honest, and gracious with anyone who has a question.

And don't forget the immense value and in some situations the sheer relief of being humble enough to say "I don't know." You are not expected to know everything about dogs, and you are not the only resource available to those seeking information. It is also a good idea to give credit to all your sources, especially if an idea is new or unique. Rather than try to pass it off as your own, be gracious and give credit. It demonstrates that you, too, are still learning and appreciate the insights of others.

Find out what kind of audience you are addressing in advance from the seminar organizers and find out *again*, for yourself, the day of your seminar or speech. I usually begin by polling my audience right away, inquiring about professional interests and occupations. Don't automatically assume that everyone there is a professional dog trainer interested in your material exactly as you plan to present it. A good speaker can quickly tailor material to the group at hand.

Most of all, have fun. Present yourself as you are, just as you are, and enjoy your group. Find a friendly face and make eye contact with that person, scan the room frequently, and don't forget the value of loving touches for both dogs and people. Enjoy yourself despite your fright, the tension, the demands. And if you are riddled with doubts, worried over your material, scared stiff, just remember a famous line and keep repeating it, over and over. The line? "They can't kill me, they can't kill me, they can't kill me..." Fact is, they'll probably love you!

Personally, I find the greatest aid in perfecting my own seminars lies in attending those given by others, during which I can place myself at the disposal of the instructor, assume a learning stance, and watch how the seminar progresses in terms of dynamics. I also learn a great deal from every seminar I conduct, and I have conducted some during which I had so much fun that I wished I could have stayed on for weeks. There is a wonderful point in which a seminar takes on a life of its own. The participants all are comfortable with the speaker, as is the speaker with the participants; laughter flows, learning accelerates, and everyone is having a highly educational and humorous experience.

I think there is room in the dog fancy for many more seminars, and I wish that the "old-timers" in dogs would be more open with their hard-won knowledge by organizing it and presenting it in seminars instead of hoarding it. After all, like money, you can't take such knowledge with you, and it might as well be shared. My experience tells me that clubs, especially in the Midwest and West, are actively searching for new and different seminar speakers. There is nationwide a growing appreciation for seminars as essential learning tools. I would like to see the development of many more seminars, especially seminars focusing on breeding, genetics, canine nutrition, bonding, the psychology of the dog, behavior problems (especially aggression), and puppy management. The dog world is already overflowing with seminars focused on competition obedience. Clubs are looking for new topics and are continually expanding their horizons to better serve their constituents. Innovative seminar-givers will address these needs.

I know that I have gained a great deal of satisfaction from giving and attending seminars. To me, it is a way of sharing the knowledge I gained during my years at New Skete Monastery and in my private training consultations since. I feel I owe a debt to dog lovers who did not have the benefit of such an intense and full background in dogs, and feel a corresponding obligation to learn more and more about our shared passion—dogs.

10. PAY YOURSELF FIRST

Here's how it works: At the end of the week, you take out of the bank what you feel you should have earned that week. You hold the money or transaction slip in your hand and then you put it aside. Now, you calculate gas (home and car), electricity, and mortgage or rent, and you subtract that from what you thought you were going to pay yourself. Now look at what's left. That's what you pay yourself. *Put it in the bank.* Now, not later, now. Save it now or you probably won't have it later.

Almost everyone knows that credit card delusionary thinking permeates the American economy, but it starts on an individual level.

My advice is cut up those cards! Save maybe one, the one with the lowest interest, and use it only for major purchases. It is, for example, completely absurd to use any credit card to buy a meal—you will be paying for a meal you ate four months ago with interest added!

Simply put, too many trainers forget that they are employees under contract to themselves. Just as waste, corruption, mismanagement, and plain stupid financial practices take place in all huge corporations, it also takes place and even takes over the lives of many of the self-employed. It's an old, sad story and it need not happen.

FINANCIAL FITNESS

I recommend you attend a seminar that concentrates in this area. There are plenty available, but be sure you don't hook into one that is really aimed at executives from large companies. Sometimes promotional literature makes this clear; often it does not. Check carefully. The response when you announce that you run a dog training business will often be a giggle—a giggle you'll grow used to. Behind that giggle, though, is often an interest that may contain *entree*, possibly to a seminar that is a source of extremely high-level information. Use that giggle and that interest—because, you see, dogs are helping you at this juncture.

Pay yourself! No, money isn't the key to happiness, but as Joan Rivers says, at least if you have some, you can afford to *buy* a key. A terrific source book is *How to Succeed As an Independent Consultant*, by Herman Holtz (John Wiley & Sons Inc.). While it says nothing about our particular profession, it is full of useful advice and precious tips.

11. TAKE TIME TO LOVE
This moment needs some care. First, an apology. I know I said there would be 10 unbreakable, unshakable rules. Now, here appears an eleventh rule. But it appears as a literary ploy precisely to point up its importance.

There is an accusation that has been thrown at dog people, and continues to be thrown at us, that states that we are in love with dogs because we are incapable of loving humans. The pronouncement is usually ignored, laughed at, or even perversely agreed to, usually out of a desire to silence the offending accuser. It is, after all, a serious charge.

But, like most mythology, there may be a kernel of truth worth looking at. Since I spend considerable time around dog people, at seminars and shows, and since I come from a monastic background where I was taught that talk is cheap and silence is often golden, I've somewhat subscribed to the theory. Yes, quite possibly, many "dog people" substitute love of dogs for love of people.

One has only to look at the high number of overweight, even obese, members of the dog fancy who have no outlet for human affection and seem to care less about anything in the world except their precious pooches. Is this balance? Is this fair to the people who would like to receive even an iota of the love such souls prefer to bestow on their dogs? Can't one have a loving and fulfilling relationship with a soul-mate and friends *and* one's dogs? Why do I find, upon even casual investigatory questioning, that many dog owners are troubled at home, and add dogs to the problems they feel incapable of solving?

QUESTIONS AND ACCUSATIONS

I ask these questions not to accuse anyone or denounce dogs, a species I love dearly. Rather, I think human unhappiness is inevitably absorbed by dogs. Using them as a ploy to alleviate human misery inevitably backfires. Usually, the dog pays the price. If the human took time to love other humans, the results of that caring and love would spill over to the dogs in the household. But for the lonely, upset, paranoid owner who lavishes love on dogs and hopes that it will somehow bring him or her into closer contact with the love available within their own species, the results are usually mixed, skewed, and vague. The dog lover often returns to loving dogs exclusively—after all, it's safer, surer, and dogs don't dialogue. Their love can be imagined to be unconditional—something no human can promise—and they are not interested in past abuses, present desires (except their own), or future plans.

For the lay dog owner who wants this kind of life, this might be okay. It may be unexciting and boring to others, but okay for them. For the professional who offers training to others to help them live harmoniously with their pets, this myopic view of love and of its complexities can be disastrous.

The dog-obsessed trainer can mistakenly overrate the importance of the dog in the household, transferring his or her own love-of-dogs paradigm (not to mention imposing it) on the household. The neurotic owner elevates the dog in importance and enshrines it as a love object that is being under-appreciated, under-worshipped. No effective training can possibly take place under the cloud of such thinking. Meanwhile, the root of all the difficulty really might be within the *trainer*. Even though the clients may demonstrate the same neurotic syndromes, it's possible that the trainer doesn't have love in his/her own life.

This is what the West Africans call "deep talk" and if you don't get it, well, I suppose you just don't get it. But if you even suspect that the dog-love versus human-love "problem" is affecting your personal or private life, I think it is something you should explore. We can't accuse clients of that which we ourselves may be guilty.

GIVE YOURSELF TIME

Exploring it, however, takes time. Since dog-work tends to be all-consuming, it becomes easy to think about dogs and dogs alone, and ignore oneself. Self-reflection flies out the window, especially if such an exercise is expected to bring up bad results anyway. The ultimate result, if the syndrome is allowed to go too far, is that nobody human "gets in" and the dog person becomes truly a *dog* person. The surprising thing about all this is that there are many dog people who do not view this as troublesome—and a small number who view it as *preferable*. Some of these "doggified" people are out there working with a normal, well-functioning teacher. Their mind might be on your dog, but they are not that concerned with *you*.

What's the answer? For the trainer, it can be found in the word *balance*. Balance your love of dogs with a healthy, loving sense of respect. Seek out relationships with other people. Balance your feelings of comfort and control that quite naturally flow out of training dogs with the risk-taking and possible loss of control that might happen in human relationships. Stop running. Stop running away at the expense of your dogs, your clients, and, most importantly, yourself. Balance is the key. Take time to love. Perhaps even more accurately I should say, find out how to love yourself and then take time to love others. Everything you do with dogs, including falling in love with some of them, will flow out of that developed love. That takes time, doesn't it? Believe me, though, it's worth the effort!

9

Business Is Business

Dog training might be thought of as a hobby, but for many of us, it's how we put food on the table. We can never let ourselves forget this, especially if we have families to support.

Let's mention some special problems of private trainers first. What about taxes? Call the IRS 800 number and request its booklet on self-employment. Be especially careful in planning and calculating the amount of space you plan to deduct as office space. The rules have changed drastically lately, as they have for luncheon and dinner deductions—even if dogs are *discussed*, actual business must have transpired.

Get yourself a good accountant; a Certified Financial Planner is best. And get a good calendar. The calendar I have used for years, and that many trainers use because it seems custom-built for us, is manufactured by QUO VADIS Publications, Hamburg, New York 14075. It is called AgendaScope. It's the best I've found.

KEEPING RECORDS ON CLIENTS

Simple index cards might do for some, especially when accompanied by the use of colored markers. They are compact and simple to file.

Because I am much more "formal" in my interview approach I prefer the form William Campbell developed and you will find it in *Behavior Problems in Dogs* (check any dog supply catalog to order) or in its generously granted duplication in *The Evans Guide for Counseling Dog Owners* (Howell).

Some of us with a Sherlock Holmes mentality and a mild perception that dog owners are not telling us the truth, the whole truth, and nothing but the truth find these forms of great value. They keep us on track as trainers who track down and decode information.

Know and Observe Publication Legalities

One word of warning: You cannot simply duplicate another's card, nor use their training name if it has a copyright notice (©) or trademark symbol (™) after it. Nor are trainers allowed to excerpt sections from published books and distribute them freely to clients. I know we all love dogs, but authors must also make a living. Ask for permission from the author, who will then ask the publisher, who very well might refuse. Instead you have to bulk-order the book. Most companies have excellent, even incredible discounts for clubs (plus 800 telephone numbers to save you money placing orders) and accept credit card transactions. This is only fair, but dog trainers often have great difficulty understanding the concept. I have granted rights to many of my pieces and chapters, especially for use as handouts at shelters, but clubs have also duplicated practically whole books of mine without any permission and distributed them as freebies. "But we thought you loved dogs…" is often the sincere yet simplistic reply upon confrontation, and yes, I do love dogs. I also like to earn a modest income. So do you. Think it over, copycats.

As the information age explodes, books that one would have previously taken a trip to the library or bookstore to procure can be drawn up on computer. This electronic refinement is coming and will allow authors and publishers to clamp down, since what these clubs and private trainers are doing undercuts their authors, their profits, their ability to hire new talent, and in many cases, it's *illegal*. You need the express written consent of both author and publisher if you want to use material not your own. This is no lecture—just a word to the wise. Things are going to tighten up in this area. Be careful and avoid making trouble for yourself.

Advertising

Spreading your message involves more than just business cards. Flyers, trinkets, gift bones, you name it, it all gets used. Business cards themselves have changed from the standard "K-9 Training Academy" (another indication to the public that trainers can't spell—and you snickered earlier when I said some people view us as fourth-grade dropouts—still snickering?). Business cards now can be flip, joyful, even chiding and snappy. Some examples are presented for your information. You can press your own creative buttons and take it from here.

JODY ROSENGARTEN
DOG TRAINER · PET THERAPIST
230 SHARP HILL ROAD
WILTON, CT. 06897

The Buck Stops Here

STEPHEN J. JOUBERT
DOG TRAINER

LOVING AND HUMANE

Patience of Job:
training for dogs
and people

JOB MICHAEL EVANS

Dealing
with Dogs, Ltd.
Meet us on TV ONTARIO

Judy with Dudley the Doberman and
Joanne with her Golden Retriever, Chelsea

"
Outside of a
dog, books
are man's
best friend.
Inside of a
dog, it's too
dark to read.
"

—Groucho Marx

Amiable Dog Training
the friendly experts

AMY AMMEN

Here are several examples of what I consider top-notch, solid, and truthful examples of advertising. While business is business, ethics can't be tossed out the door, either. Phone numbers have been deleted in fairness to other trainers. The important aspect is to look at the presentation of what each trainer/school offers.

Chapter 10

The Question of Dress: Putting on the Dog

My advice here for women would be, *don't* keep it short and don't keep it sweet. For men the situation is much easier—if you are a certain type of man who has never given much thought about how you appear to others, you need to think about dress. With the exception of corporate businessmen or gay males, that includes the rest of the species, practically!

Let's take an overview of the "fashions." Some, not all, dog trainers opt for skin-tight jeans, so tight the date of a dime can clearly be read through the worn fabric. I have added immeasurably to my valuable coin collection simply by deciphering the date of the dime and then bumming change for the soda machine. My biggest bugaboo (perhaps an appropriate choice of words) is tank tops worn with the above jeans.

Here's an outfit I once saw in the South. The woman had on "those" jeans, "that" tank top, and had somehow fashioned an *umbrella* into a hat to protect her from the sun. She had broken off the stick part and somehow inserted a stretch band to hold the contraption in place. "Now I'm ready to teach my class rain or shine," she proudly announced. That might have been fine from her perspective, but many class participants were snickering and the dogs were backing away from her as if she was some sort of extraterrestrial.

Now I fully realize that everyone does not show up at class wearing umbrellas on their heads—but the extreme example cited herein perhaps points out just how far some trainers need to go in another direction.

I always tried to dress to scale when teaching on Manhattan's Upper East Side, and you should do likewise whenever you work in similar areas. After all, if the doorman is going to be wearing white gloves even while petting the Bulldog, the least we can do is to appear as well-turned-out as our surroundings. (Charles Hornek)

SO WHAT?

And why is the issue of any importance anyway? Well, if you have to ask, check out your head in a mirror—there may be an umbrella growing out of it! The issue *is* important because our field is regarded, frankly (not by all, but by many), as a low-end profession which attracts people who have flunked out of vocational schools—the type you have to pay for yourself and offer "guarantee of immediate employment upon successful completion of the course." You've seen the ads on TV, so I think you know what I mean. Dog trainers are acknowledged and perceived not to have any college education. Can dress help? It sure can.

But How Can Dress Help?

How you dress reveals who you are, what you think about who you are and what you do. Conformation exhibitors learned this truth years ago—and judges beat them to the punch long before that. Judges came to know that their authority and control was increased if they dressed one notch above whatever they felt their exhibitors would show up wearing. The famous Westminster show in New York City is a perfect example of this. During variety group judging the men are usually in black tie (although I did see one younger judge wearing black Armani, which looks as good as standard black tie) and the women judges are almost invariably in slit-to-the-thigh evening gowns. Sometimes the ladies will sport sequins below the waist, although no judge wants to be accused of freaking out even the temperamentally super-sound dogs that make it to Westminster because the poor dog was blinded by a sea of sequins! In fact, since the show is nationally televised, sometimes going into "repeats" throughout the year, viewers often have more than one chance to check out what's fashion-do and what is a disastrous fashion-don't.

We will skip the topic of hairdos and hair-don'ts. Mostly though, it all works glamorously and tastefully. An image gets purveyed, but more importantly *people feel good about themselves and about being at the show*. Because of the unrelentingly fierce competition in the obedience ring, and because of the masochistic mayhem that has infiltrated into some conformation shows, there are ambiguous attitudes about the question of dress. I firmly believe that the dogs notice the difference in attitude that dressing up produces, and adopt a positive "look-out-world-here-I-come" attitude. Many owners, exhibitors, and handlers fully agree.

Attitude Is Everything

In our profession, whether one is an instructor, a private trainer, or a competitor/exhibitor, attitude is everything. When you come into class smartly dressed, you *take over* that class, honey. You'll make them listen to you. Think about your clothes, that special brooch or other piece of power jewelry that draws attention to your upper torso—never to your breasts, no matter how pretty you may feel they are. Instead, draw their attention to your eyes, to your shoulder carriage, your stance, and the erectness of your backbone. All of this body language can be emphasized without a hint of implied arrogance. Be careful how you carry yourself and dress yourself.

Students study how we carry ourselves—and since they themselves often arrive at class with air of total resignation, we must present a correspondingly clear vision of competence and success. Of course, dangling pendants and clanging charm bracelets are out. Black, grey, and combinations of both convey authority and knowledge.

STANDARD ISSUE

As for wearing standardized club-issued jackets while training, I suppose that's okay—as long as they are not accompanied by the aforementioned jeans. One nifty side-effect: Class participants can readily recognize who is running the class or assisting if they need help. Just be careful. Make it look good. Most clubs can find a graphic artist even within the club who can choose a design and lettering style that looks a step up from the usual Upper Font lettering that fairly screams out the club's name, with the usual high-jump, surrounded by dumbbells. This might be a logo that conveys to some competition folks what obedience is all about but it's a source of secret amusement to regular dog owners who come to class because their dog pulls down the street or runs away; or lies, cheats, and steals things when he is home. Believe me, these people (80 percent of most classes) have no intention of coming within 85 feet of any high-jump, or picking up a dumbbell. Again, what you wear conveys a lot about what you believe and want to accomplish. By the way, don't wear such identifying clothing during private training.

MEN: LOST IN JOEY BUTTAFUOCO LAND

Joey Buttafuoco might dress for court appearances, but did you ever see him hanging around his house or at his auto body shop? It's the old tank top and jeans routine. Maybe Amy Fisher got a thrill out of it, but he looks a lot better dressed as he does in court. The point here is that men, too, should dress one level up from the way they think their class participants will. That's always a safe rule, period. For men or women, good sensible shoes should have *traction*. It is perfectly possible even in the smallest shoe stores in the smallest towns to get beautiful shoes with great traction. Just ask trainers in any area with heavy rainfall. Incidentally, mink oil protects fine shoes remarkably well, but please, avoid tennis shoes.

CLOTHING FOR THE PRIVATE TRAINER

This is a special subsection. I've worked for Calvin Klein, Mary Tyler Moore, William F. Buckley, Jr., and Kevin Bacon. The special question with these celebrities, and with any private client, is: What does one wear? Well, I can tell you right now, if you work for Calvin Klein, *wear Calvin Klein*. Similarly with any designer.

If you are working for anybody well-known, and in my opinion you should work not with the dog's subordinate caretakers but with the *owner* only, try to be sensitive to how they will feel with you on the street. This usually means that you should arrive in a jacket, which you can shed as you sum up the situation. Nor do I feel that women need to wear skirts, even in the most sophisticated neighborhoods. It is not necessary, it impedes movement, and it can be potentially embarrassing. Balance your outfit with what you think your client will wear.

DESIGNER FLACK

Once I wrote an article for *Dog World* after viewing a special display at Gimbel's about how to decorate around a dog. In this case the dog on display was a Dalmatian—known as a breed as a year-round shedder. The piece included super tips, down to fabrics and where to get them, and a quote from the store designer saying something about not living like a tramp just because you have a dog. I thought that was a sensible comment (unless you enjoy living like a tramp.) The same applies to one's style of dress. I suppose my arrogance is showing once again.

Boy, did I get mail on that article! "You arrogant New Yorker, we'll decorate any way we damn please!" Another wrote and said she had seen me at a seminar and the suit I was wearing was tacky and I should just go back to wearing the monastic habit (and also return to the monastery "where I belonged") and leave everyone else alone.

To be sure, making suggestions about decorating or dress is risky business. But if we want to bring our profession up to the image level the sheer work involved dictates it *should* have, shouldn't we make the mirror our first stop? Image might not be all, but to use Americanese, it ain't nothing. One final point: Be sure the color coordination between handler and dog is *perfect*. Who will ever forget the handler at Westminster who chose to show her Dalmatian in a white and black polka dot dress? The Rottweiler owner who competed in obedience in total black was another unforgettable. The dog wore more accessories than his handler did.

Chapter 11

—

What Is Style?

Even The *New York Times* now has a separate Sunday section on the subject of style. Trainers need style too. They need proper dress, class, preferably leather leashes, and good-quality collars.

A trainer with style also needs a sense of humor. A ribald, risqué sense of humor has become, in some ways, my style. To use the lyrics from the Sondheim musical "Gypsy," "You gotta have a gimmick."

However, I must distinguish between trainers who are running around using clickers, clackers, ultrasound devices, or other contraptions. The "gimmick," that is, what makes people listen and learn from you, should come from your own inward talent.

For Barbara Woodhouse it was her sheer size, her pageboy haircut, and her propensity to wear plaid. For Jack Godsil, although unfortunately he never made a video or wrote a book, it was his incredible timing and taste as he worked a dog—he could surely have easily become an important figure in Dressage (a precision equestrian sport) as well as in dog training.

Most of all, style should be genuine. Purveying style in a contrived manner can certainly be attempted, but it usually comes off as shallow and forced.

FAKE STYLE IS EVERYWHERE

One zap of late-night TV stations will reveal hundreds of options on developing your own self/style.

They almost always offer psychic tools and techniques (many derived from Christian Science founder Mary Baker Eddy or Scientology guru L. Ron Hubbard), but these ploys can't be easily superimposed on others who are:

What is style? The designer who conceived of this pose thinks it's having a Dalmatian to match the sheets, or vice versa. There is a Dal in the photo, if you can find it. Ultimately style might mean gimmickry, but it comes down to who you are. (Kevin Bacon)

1. Working with two humans and another species. (Dogs are never mentioned on these programs or tapes.)
2. Most promotions offer "teases" as lead-ins to get you to buy a complete package, a video, or an audiotape.
3. Finally, although such tapes and videos of this genre are somewhat helpful, they subtly appeal to those lacking self-confidence, those who feel innately insecure, or unsurprisingly, those who have been recently laid off or unemployed. Even if they try not to show it, these people are *damn angry* about losing their jobs, pensions, and security, and having to watch tapes instead of work.

NEGATIVES COMPOUND NEGATIVES

None of the above—the inherent complexity of the work, buying tapes to bolster self-confidence, marital difficulties stemming from money troubles, and the accompanying anger—will help one train effectively. It's always possible that a trainer comes to class or receives a client in a less-than-peaceful state of mind. But this needs to be distinguished from the trainer who is in ongoing crisis, when some of the troubles can only be resolved with the passage of time. This trainer needs a rest, or if it is necessary to get out of the house periodically just to escape an intolerable situation, a role-switch to assistant can be made. No explanation need be made. And in general, dog people are too chatty and too trusting about details of their own personal lives. Style is not self-revelation.

SILENCE IS PLATINUM

In fact, developing your own style consists precisely of avoiding this trait. Self-confession can make one look weak, nervous, afraid.

I once had a trainer come up to me after a training class and launch into a half-hour discourse about her alcoholic husband and her 14-year-old son who had just passed through juvenile court. Meanwhile, she had seven Shelties and no one to talk to, except me.

Her style in class was sloppy, she was poorly dressed, and her manner was tense, even brusque. She rushed her classes because if she was late, drunken "Harold" would be ready to fly off the handle.

Obviously, she needed therapy if her personal or professional lives were ever to improve, not to mention synchronize. When I mentioned this to her, she said they had tried one session together and it had disintegrated into a fight over the dogs.

I said try another therapist. She replied, "Harold won't go anymore." I said, "Go alone and tell him you are going alone. Tell him you have troubles and problems and if he doesn't want to go for himself, would he go for her problems? If the answer is still no, I'd say go anyway and, although I'm just the son of a psychologist and not a degreed one, my lay person's advice would be *dump this bozo.*"

THE SECRET OF STYLE

It's obvious from the above examples that the key to developing happiness is to have your own life together to the point when a smile is your usual expression. As Barbara Walters says, "Everyone responds from happiness that springs from a secure heart" (*How to Talk to Practically Everyone About Practically Everything*).

In short, finding your own style really means finding the warmth and kindness you feel towards dogs, people, and, perhaps most importantly, the bond you appreciate between the two—and then expressing this love.

In the end, it's not just humor, clothes, charm, a great hairdo, or even a personal life free of problems. Instead your own style will flow from within and needn't be practiced. It's simply *you*—your love for dogs and the innately beautiful person you are. Tap into this and you've found the secret of style.

Chapter 12

Phone Alone

Wondering about that title? I thought of it after seeing the popular movie *Home Alone*, in which an innocent youngster is left behind to defend the household against intruders. For some bizarre reason, which would be understandable only to fellow private trainers, I suddenly thought of an analogy between the kid in the movie and trainers held hostage in their own homes—not by burglars or even dogs—but by people calling on the phone!

Indeed, to a trainer, being home alone with the phone is to be truly held hostage—unless you know how to handle intruders. In twenty years of private training, I've learned a thing or two about how the phone "operates" (forgive the pun) in the dog world. Other than an electronic shock collar, it is potentially the worst piece of equipment we can use and abuse. I know one trainer, and she is not atypical, who clocks in 65 hours a month in training-related phone calls. If she had a 900 number, I would say, "Bravo!" but the 65 hours are work time for which she receives nothing in compensation.

This trainer has tried every "time-saving" gimmick the phone companies offer. You name it, she's got it: call waiting, call forwarding, a car phone, three-way calling. Despite all the time-saving frills, her phone time seems to have increased. Her husband, who used to receive some personal time when he arrived home from the office, now stares at the television while his wife soothes stressed-out clients over the phone. Recently, he's taken to singing a send-up of the "We're all connected" TV jingle. His translation? "It's all concocted …"

Again, this situation is not unusual. There is something in the nature of our work that seems almost to dictate endless chatter. Perhaps it is the fact that, inevitably, we wind up discussing two different species and perhaps even more different individuals during any one conversation. Perhaps it is also the fact that clients can more easily justify their dog's behavior over the phone, since the given behavior was not seen by the trainer. Clients often tend to "talk around" the problem, describing aggressive dogs as shy, daily housetraining accidents as rare occurrences, chronic jumpers as superfriendly. Since the behavior cannot be observed, it is up to the client to "sell" us on the fact that the behavior really isn't *that* obnoxious, even as they plead for help to eliminate that given behavior! This is stuff for psychologists—and I hasten to add that most of them don't do phone consultations.

Because it seems that the phone remains a big bugaboo for many trainers (I receive numerous inquiries about how to handle the problem) and because I believe that mastery over one's phone habits is an *absolutely essential* aspect of running a successful business, not to mention preserving one's sanity, here is a "hit list" of what to do and not do concerning the phone. The list is highly idiosyncratic. The tips aren't in any concise order, so read through them all—and feel free to use any that you think can work for you.

MESSAGE MACHINE MAYHEM?

Let's begin at the beginning. Get an answering machine. Buy a top-of-the-line model that will give you years of service. Consult *Consumer Reports* or ask around. Mine is Code-A-Phone model 5530, and it's going on four years—and if my phone machine doesn't get a daily work-out, I don't know whose does. Get one with a tap-in feature so that you can collect messages from other touch-tone phones. And get one that has a three-digit tap-in code, so that you don't have to worry about someone accessing your machine—it does happen.

Your phone announcement is very important. My original one said "Hello, this is Job Michael Evans at Patience of Job: Training for Dogs and People. Your call is important to me. Clearly, you're interested in the finest quality training for your dog. At the sound of the tone, etc. …" By the way, there's nothing wrong with a little "ad" inserted in your message, but keep it short and sweet, not over five seconds. Also, announce within the message that the tone is coming—it gives clients a chance to think about what they want to say. A nice touch I've heard on some messages is to ask the client to leave their name and the dog's name as well.

Remember to record your announcement and then call on another phone to hear for yourself what it sounds like. Remember, any announcement that uses (or abuses, as is most often the case) background music usually comes off garbled and unintelligible over long distance regardless of carrier.

Some trainers install call waiting in order to not miss out on potential business. They think it will be a financially beneficial feature. It may well be, but in my opinion it can be personally and professionally damaging. When clients call a trainer, they want that trainer's ear. They are usually very concerned about their particular problem and are insulted when the trainer says, "Oh! Just a second, I have another call coming in ..." Who *cares?* What you have signaled the client, regardless of your good intentions, is that someone or something else might be more important to you than whatever it is the client has to say. The caller you just intercepted also gets the same message if you put them off and return to caller #1. That's insult on insult, and pretty soon, with the fabulous call waiting feature you will have succeeded in insulting half your clientele and alienating tons of friends. You'll soon be home alone to phone alone if you keep this feature on your line long enough. Call waiting might work in the world of finance or stocks, but considering the intimate nature of the relationship between trainer and client, it's a killer.

A quick anecdote: I know a trainer who was called by a client about a beloved pet that had been hit by a car just after a recall lesson. The client didn't reveal immediately the fate of the dog, but was in the process of describing how he had dutifully practiced that morning, drilling the dog in the recall. The trainer nodded in approval over the phone, murmuring "Good...good..." The client went on to describe how he had trusted the dog a little too much ("He was doing so well on those recalls") and so decided to give the dog full off-leash freedom ... "OH, JUST A MINUTE I HAVE ANOTHER CALL COMING IN," announced the harried trainer, oblivious to what the outcome of the off-leash experiment might have been—in this case a sad one. When the trainer returned to the caller, the line was dead. Needless to say, I hate call waiting.

The complaint, of course, is that if one doesn't get call waiting, people will just get an "annoying busy signal," as the phone company puts it, and immediately call another trainer. This just isn't true. If you come highly recommended and have sterling references, prospective clients will keep trying until they reach you. They might then say, "Gosh, you're tough to get hold of!" Don't waste a minute apologizing for the busy signal. I usually just say, "Well, I guess that's the price of popularity, but I'm glad you got through now. What can I do for you?"

Remember also that there is nothing wrong with using your answering machine to screen calls. Sometimes this is necessary, especially when you know a given call will take up a lot of time and can be just as easily listened to at a more convenient time. One word of caution, however: Never let more than a day go by without returning

101

your calls! If you are on vacation, word your announcement message in such a way that clients know not to expect a return call until a certain date. DO NOT say that you are not at home or away—even in small, "safe" towns this is an invitation to robbery.

The Initial Contact

Let's continue on with our discussion of the "evil" telephone and its incomparable potential for torturing the trainer. Let's discuss handling that first important inquiry from a prospective client. Here, trainers can take a tip from Dr. Ruth Westheimer. During her radio or TV call-in shows, Dr. Ruth always seems supremely pleased as she says "Hello! You are on the air!" The greeting is sincere, without being too sweet. However, as the caller reveals the difficulty he or she is experiencing, Dr. Ruth begins to interject notes of caution as to just how much she can be of assistance over the phone. For instance, she'll cut in with, "You know the only thing I can tell you about that problem is that it isn't an easy one. I would have to sit down with you in person and be able to ask you many, many questions in order to be of help." Even if the client continues to rattle on about a given problem, a boundary has been drawn. I'd advise trainers to do the same. Let clients state the problem, presenting it with all the intensity they will usually muster while exposing it, and just listen. At a strategic point (you will get better and better at telling the exact moment), interject that you can only do so much on the phone, other than listen sympathetically, and that the best course of action would be to set up an appointment between the two of you.

After all, if you are trying to make a living at this business, not to mention do quality work, seeing the client face to face is the only way to really be of help. Get ready, though; often clients will continue on describing and diagnosing their dog's difficulties even after you clearly indicate that you need to see them in person. Listen a bit more, say nothing, and then repeat that it is necessary to set up an appointment. I should be able to end this article here, but it is amazing how many otherwise savvy, even brilliant, trainers cannot steer their clients through to making an appointment and instead stay on the line, attempting to "do therapy" over the phone. And so, for those with aching wrists worn out from holding too many phone receivers too many evenings, here are some further tips on keeping that receiver on its hook and out of your hands.

If you try to answer too many questions on the phone, especially during an initial call, you may find, ironically, that you never hear from that client again. You might have confused them. Please be aware that many clients are simply using the Yellow Pages to check out whatever trainers are listed. They are most probably simply comparing prices, and, perhaps, methods. While *you* might think that these callers have all the time in the world to hear about how superior your methods are to others, the fact is that caller has 12 more calls to make in order to "cover" the available listings and present the financial manager of the household with a price breakdown. Unfortunately, many callers couldn't care less about methodologies and only want to know what the training will cost. The trick is to reveal to the client your cost, but instill a respect for the methods you use. Not an "easy sell," as they say in the business, especially when the client has a load on his or her mind to be dumped pronto.

Indicate clearly from the beginning that you work with dogs *and* people. Don't assume the client understands this. They may think that you will simply come and train the dog, and that by magic, without any participation on their part, the dog will become saintly overnight.

Remember: *Everyone* wants a quick fix—and if they think they can get one out of you over the phone (for free) it's worth a shot. Lay owners often have no idea that the problem behavior their dog exhibits is perhaps only the tip of an iceberg of potential problems. Remember this as you direct them to set up an appointment, especially if you are a trainer who is lucky enough to have a waiting list and the appointment has to be delayed. Without necessarily offering any "quick fix" solutions, you could offer a phone tip that might make life with the dog at least bearable until you can arrive with more complete advice. For instance, if the dog is anointing the house with urine, you could suggest, on the phone, that they limit water to three times a day, confine the dog to one room, and not allow the dog to sleep on the bed. But be sure to emphasize that much more is going on here than just those three tips will cure. At least you will have given the client something to do while waiting for you to come.

Even follow-up phone calls, once you have begun actively working with a client, have to have some structure. Establish some ground rules. Ground rule #1 in my opinion is that current and past clients *should always have phone access* to their private trainer. To me, unless the "past client" is someone I worked with over a year ago, this is part of the service a private trainer offers—quality time for current clients. Even so, there must be some restraints. One veterinary counselor I know sets the hours of 5:30 PM to 8:30 PM as a good time for clients to call her. She finds this time suits her schedule and works for her.

Another trainer prefers to "clear the decks" (meaning his desk of phone messages) by 10:00 AM, and he starts returning and taking calls at 8:00 AM I hope, for his sake, that all his clients are morning people.

Still another trainer likes to use her cellular car phone and asks clients, both in her verbal instructions to them and on her home phone's message tape, to leave *two* times the *client* will be available to receive her return calls. In this way, she can make very effective use of car travel time between clients. Smart gal!

Whatever method you decide on, get the phone *on the hook and off your mind* as much as possible. Otherwise, I can practically promise you a first-class case of trainer burnout within three years. And as I mentioned earlier, don't think that running out and getting every gadget and service available to "enhance" your phone capabilities will help you better negotiate the phone problem that is built in for private trainers. No phone gadget will enable you to hang up the receiver more quickly. Indeed, the vast majority of these gimmicks are designed to keep you on the line as much as possible.

TRAINING OVER THE PHONE—POSSIBLE?

What about phone consultations? You know what I mean: Trainers or behaviorists who sell their services over the phone, sometimes using 900 numbers. I'm sure there is some nice money involved, and plenty of gullible fools out there who will call. I'm equally sure such services will become more and more visible in short order. This is, after all, the age of the 800 and 900 number, but I think the whole idea is bad. Compared to personal training, I fail to see how a phone consultation can substitute for taking a full behavior case history, or physically demonstrating techniques. I suppose it's workable if the trainer clearly indicates that the phone consultation is a poor substitute for personal interaction. Remember: You read it here, as the "information explosion" continues on into the 21st century, phone training and even fax training will come into vogue—and probably go out of vogue just as quickly. I don't buy it. As long as a real, living, breathing, thinking dog is not present, how can we call it dog training? And I'm assuming (perhaps a stupid assumption on my part) that a real, living, breathing, thinking client is present also, along with an enlightened trainer. This is supposed to happen courtesy of whatever phone company is in use? I don't get it.

Finally, don't rip that phone out of the wall! While the phone isn't the trainer's dearest friend, it is of service. It enables us to retrieve messages that we would otherwise miss, and it helps us to encourage current clients and reach out to new ones. Occasionally, and sadly, it serves to bring us the news of the death of a student—and to comfort the owner. It is an invaluable tool, one, like our collars, leashes, and trusted books and notes, we couldn't do without. Perhaps more than anything else, the phone keeps us in touch with fellow trainers with whom we can discuss cases, puzzle over the problems of problem dogs, talk about the latest "hot" training book, encourage each other to go on in a field that sometimes seems very lonely, and, yes, even complain to each other how much time we have to spend on the phone! If you're a trainer, and you ever even suspect that perhaps your own mother doesn't love you—take heart, Ma Bell does!

Chapter 13

—

Westminster: Training and Explaining in Action

There are dog shows and there is the Westminster Kennel Club show, held the second Monday and Tuesday of February at Madison Square Garden in New York City. Who would come to a dog show on two weekdays? Try about 7,000 to 10,000 spectators, nearly 3,000 exhibitors, and press from all over the world.

The Westminster Kennel Club held its first show in 1877 and has continued to hold an annual show ever since. It's the oldest annual dog show in the United States and the second-oldest sporting event, bowing to the Kentucky Derby by only two years. Entries are limited to 2,500, and although it's not the largest dog show in America, it's certainly the most prestigious. It's the only show limited to champions only.

You might think that the Westminster Kennel Club must have a huge membership in order to stage such a show, but membership in the all-male club is limited to 70 and is by invitation only. Many members are wealthy or famous, but they all work on the show, and it's the most smoothly run show in America. "Westminster is the annual gathering of the dog world," said the late William Rockefeller, a Westminster member, "and we feel a sense of responsibility to set an example for dog shows across the country."

One of the reasons Westminster is such a great learning experience is that it is a *benched* show. This means that unless a dog is being shown, groomed, or exercised, it must be stationed on its assigned bench—a small cubicle in a large hall off to the side of the show

There is no place like the Westminster dog show, to see training and explaining in action. The supreme moment of glory, when even the press "loses it," is Best in Show which the unforgettable German Shepherd Dog, Ch. Covy-Tucker Hill's Manhattan, won in 1987. He is shown here winning the Herding Group at Westminster in 1986. What you can't get from a win picture is the crowd going into pandemonium mode.

rings. This provides an unusual opportunity for spectators to get a close-up look at their favorite breeds.

Not too long ago, more than half of all dog shows in America were benched. Today, fewer than a dozen benched shows remain. "It is only at a bench show that breeders, exhibitors, handlers, and spectators have the time and opportunity to enter into serious discussions about their breeding programs," said William H. Chisholm, a former Westminster president. A special feature occasionally added to the extravaganza is the Parade of Former Westminster Winners—a nostalgic line-up of great champions that strut their stuff to unrestrained cheers. These extraordinary dogs are also benched both days so that spectators can visit them and talk to their owners or handlers.

GOOD WALKING SHOES

Many spectators come on Monday morning, stay all day and into the night, and then return Tuesday to repeat the process. When I asked Thelma Boalbey, head of public relations for the show for many years, what advice she would give first-time spectators to Westminster, she replied with just four words: "Bring good walking shoes." If you decide to attend the Westminster show, the following tips will make your trip more enjoyable.

Get a general pass for both days. This allows you to stroll about and also leave the Garden if you need to go back to your hotel or want to do some sightseeing. Judging stops from about 5:00 PM to 7:00 PM on both days, which gives you a chance to get dinner or visit the benching area when it is less crowded.

Although the general pass is fine for most of the show, try to get a reserved seat for the Best in Show judging on Tuesday night. A slightly elevated seat is best unless you are lucky enough to secure a box seat. You'll want to be close to ringside to view the judging of the seven best dogs in the show.

EXCELLENT EXPLAINING

Few dog shows today are narrated, fewer still are presented with the style and wit of Roger Caras, a well-known author and animal authority. You'll delight in his commentary on the personalities of the various breeds as each Best of Breed winner takes center stage during Group (semi-final) judging.

You'll be reminded by Mr. Caras that show dogs (and their handlers) love applause. Spectators can get *loud* at Westminster, and as the Best in Show judging nears on Tuesday evening, the noise level can reach football-crowd highs. Watch the press and see what dogs they applaud for. They generally refrain from the hoopla until an irresistible dog comes along, and then they let loose.

Clap all you want, but keep in mind that flash photographs are very disturbing to both dogs and handlers. Save the picture-taking until you have the permission of those concerned.

If you're looking for grooming tips, you can see many of the country's top groomers at work as you wander through the grooming area adjacent to the benches.

During the day, avoid the main aisle between the rings set up for breed judging. It gets clogged very easily, and your best bet is to consult your program for the breed and ring you're interested in and make your way to it via the side ramps.

Beware the ticket sharks hawking cut-rate tickets at the door of Madison Square Garden. They prey on out-of-towners, and their tickets are often fakes or have been used already and are invalid.

If you like to dress up, Westminster is the show for you. Judges wear black tie or elegant gowns, and exhibitors dress to the nines, as do many spectators.

On Tuesday evening, one dog out of the thousands competing will win the judges' hearts and the oohs and aahs of the entire crowd. For dog show excitement, you can't beat the glitter and glamour of New York's Westminster Kennel Club show. The dogs are well trained and the show is well explained. You can't ask for more than that. It's a living, breathing example of the best that's possible in the collaboration of dog and man.

Chapter 14

—

The Vexation of Veterinarians

Veterinarians are rarely vexed over surgical or clinical matters, but when hit by an onslaught of clients asking complex behavioral questions, their attitude can change from sweet to sour in seconds.

First, canine behavior is either not taught or barely taught in veterinary schools. Secondly, veterinarians are great absorbers of canine folklore; since they might not be up on the latest behavioral knowledge, they literally have to fall back on what they heard at home. Thus, often folklore remedies like hitting a dog with a rolled-up newspaper or rubbing the poor dog's nose in feces might still get dispensed by some practitioners.

However, the days when veterinarians can claim ignorance on behavioral matters are flying by quickly. Most veterinary conferences now include sessions on canine and feline behavior, delivered by top experts. In states where there are stringent continuing education requirements (and you'd be amazed at the list of which states do and do not demand continuing education), access to behavior talks is easier.

Some vets make a personal, ongoing effort to keep up on the latest trends in behavior. Others develop a solid referral system with quality trainers—probably the wisest solution.

I think most lay persons haven't the slightest idea of how hard and taxing (literally!) it is to operate a veterinary practice. The veterinarian simply doesn't have the time to discuss complex behavioral problems. It is not a matter of not wanting to take the time but literally a matter of really not having the time to give.

This is why I usually suggest that a veterinarian search out and request a presentation from one or two or three trainers or specialists.

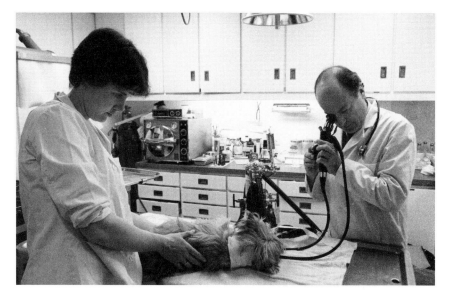

The main vexation for veterinarians is how in the world to balance the warmth and compassion needed to deal with clients with the ever-advancing clinical and surgical techniques they are bound to learn. But there is a way, and many practitioners are finding their own answers. (Courtesy Lewis Berman, DVM)

Working with more than one trainer is useful in case a trainer develops a waiting list, or one trainer specializes in a certain area.

Veterinary conference overload. This is more precisely emotional overload. At three veterinary conferences in which I was employed to teach on behavior of canines and their humans, I was amazed at the number of "bedside manner" courses being offered concurrently.

To be sure, there were the usual clinical and surgical offerings, but also offered were courses on "How to Have a Warmer Practice," "Telephone Etiquette," or "60 Hot Tips That Will Make You More Money." Apparently, this is what the attendees need and want to get that special "edge" for their practice—otherwise program planners wouldn't schedule talks on these subjects.

Strictly speaking, there is nothing wrong with such talks. The presentation may indeed "soften" the veterinarian as to the needs of the client and patient. But why is such "softening" necessary?

Certainly telephone etiquette should be part of every receptionist's repertoire, but this is not always the case. Here's an example from a cross-file comparison published in one proceedings book from a meeting of the American Veterinary Medical Association:

Telephone Etiquette: Good and Bad

BAD RESPONSE	GOOD RESPONSE

Greeting the Caller:

"Hello," or, "What do you want?" or, "Who's this?"

"Hello, Dr. Gray's office, Mrs. Woods speaking."

Verifying the Message:

"What name did you say? I can't hear you." or, "What did you say? Talk a little louder."

"Would you repeat your name for me, please?" or, "Would you spell that for me, please?" or, "Would you mind repeating the information?"

Acknowledging:

"Okay, I'll see if I can get her."

"Thank you, I'll call her to the phone."

Leaving the Line:

"Just a minute, I'll try it," or, "Hold on, I will see what I can do."

"Would you mind waiting while I check, please?" or, "I have to leave the line for a moment and check your file, Mr. Jones; can you hold for about three minutes?"

Screening Calls:

"He wants to know who's calling," or, "If you tell me who is calling, I'll see if I can locate him," or, "Well, who is this?"

"May I say who's calling, please?" or, "May I give him your name?" or, "He is with a client at the moment. May I take a message?" or, "Will you please wait while I see if he is available."

©1986 by American Veterinary Publications, Inc.

Ignorance isn't bliss. Half the time, the poor veterinarian doesn't ever hear such good or bad conversations. One can only imagine what happens when the receptionist (who, remember, often doubles as a technician) talks about training on the phone to a troubled client.

Unless instructed to refer to trainers, many try to dish out advice solely on their track record of trotting animals to and from the waiting room.

This is why it is essential, when presenting a portfolio, for the savvy trainer also to include the receptionist or technician in his/her presentation. A great deal can be gained.

As for practice tips, such as the ever-popular ones offered by Marty Becker (who works the veterinary conferences), they are useful presentations, but mostly result in audience validation or affirmation. But attending is well worth the effort.

What's missing in many presentations is the owner/animal bond triangle, which the trainer or veterinarian essentially only inserts himself into briefly (if intimately at times). This triangular configuration is the true key to dealing successfully with owners and their pets. While we can try practically everything imaginable to perfect that bond clinically, surgically, or behaviorally, we remain essentially outside its orbit.

Unintelligent, unprepared trainers who become over-involved and try to enter the orbit usually wind up spinning around as crazily as those already in orbit. At all times, we must be compassionate yet remember the role of distance, loving and yet remember that love has limitations.

Part Three

—

INTERVIEWS ON TRAINING AND EXPLAINING

Chapter 15

The Interviews: Dog Talk

A distinctive feature of this book, from conception to the time the publishers accepted the idea, was to hold interviews with some of the top trainers around. Frankly, I surprised myself in suggesting such a feature for this book. Trainers can be notoriously secretive with even mundane information they consider "their own." Perhaps it's because professional dog training remains a lonely field, which in turn naturally attracts loners, so secrecy and shunning sharing are the rule. We have no trade associations, no unions, no lobbying groups that have any real clout, and some, but not all, of the professional groups formed to share information have disintegrated into monthly shouting matches (also know as "meetings") where nothing is shared and everyone and everybody's ideas are torn apart.

A DINNER TO REMEMBER

It makes me wonder if the situation is any better than when I originally came to New York to open my training business. A prominent, established trainer planned a small intimate dinner party for me. I was too innocent and too fresh out of the monastery to suspect anything but the best of intentions; here were my colleagues, welcoming me to the city. Instead, as soon as we were seated, a pall settled over the table. Glasses clinked, but the toast was hollow. With clenched teeth, one trainer asked another, "So, how is business?" which received an icy, "Just fine, fine" as a reply. And so it went.

Mercifully the host called an end to the whole affair early on, making up some excuse about an emergency with a biting Rottweiler (at eleven PM?). I have yet to figure out that dinner, but it remains in my mind as a vivid vignette of how trainers pretend to share while not wanting to do so. There is always the hope that someone will talk

117

about themselves and their life "in dogs" realistically and openly, but everyone else waits for someone else to do just that. Now I think what was expected of me on that dinner date was to reveal the "hidden secrets" of the monastery's training program, and also to explain why I had the audacity to come to New York City with a somewhat established reputation and threaten the training business of others—as if there are not enough unruly dogs to go around for many trainers.

A Dinner I've Chosen to Forget, and Another Way

I said earlier I wondered if the sharing situation was any better these days than it was at that disastrous dinner. Among some trainers, probably not; among a few others, it certainly is. Some of the latter I count as close friends, for I cannot be friends with trainers who simply won't share or who prefer just to take. That's probably why so many of my friends are in religion, the arts, or academic circles where the word dog is barely pronounced except using its backward spelling, or if one is needed for a walk-on in a play, or being studied as a fossil in class. For me, this has been the perfect balance for my necessary contacts with "dog people," who sometimes tend to have one-track minds. I am not saying anything new here—this has been recognized in the dog world as the myopia it is for years. Nor am I saying anything critical. When I say that dog people often can *only* talk about dogs, I'm not criticizing, I'm recognizing. But is this a *good* productive trait?

Because I think this seemingly inbred inability to broaden one's base of thought is so limiting it eventually affects even one's dog work, I had to be careful whom I selected for the following interviews. Ultimately I needed to talk with people who knew something about *life*, not just dogs; about *love*, not just bonding; about *symbol* and *substance*; about communication and motivation. I hope you enjoy the interviews as much as I did while conducting them. They will draw you in by the depth of their thinking, their love of their profession, and their uncompromising love of dogs.

I can guarantee that you won't feel like an invited, yet unwanted, dinner guest. Instead, at these interviews you have a special seat at the table as an honored witness—so listen in. I would suggest you read the interviews in succession, although they can be read independently.

Finally, while I tried to keep myself out of the interviews as much as possible and truly listen to my subject, inevitably they themselves would draw me into the process flow. The give-and-take gave each interview a life of its own.

Chapter 16

Carol Lea Benjamin

Most people know by now that Ms. Benjamin and I are friends. She wrote the introduction and did the illustrations for my first book after I left New Skete Monastery, *The Evans Guide for Counseling Dog Owners*. The *American Kennel Gazette* reviewer at the time remarked that, while the text itself was innovative, the cartoons kept the book from becoming a "preachy textbook." I think "textbook" was code for "prayerbook," actually.

Reading any of Carol's books softens the heart and at the same time strengthens one's determination. There is understanding with compassion, a compassion that includes humane discipline. Even now, all these years later, I continue to re-read her texts.

Carol and I met at the monastery in 1981. She and her husband, Steve, had come to discuss the possibility of procuring a New Skete Shepherd, which they later did. Scarlet made many friends for people and dogs during her lifetime. I had learned earlier on, in my monastic role as guestmaster and kennelkeeper, to keep myself sheltered from "worldly" contacts, not to reveal feelings, to hold "oneself" with dignity and essentially to keep everyone at arms' length. I was quite good at it at the time. In fact, that's probably why I got the guestmaster job, because as the guest's initial contact, friendly yet appropriately distant, I instilled in any guest's mind the boundaries as they existed.

What I had not counted on, and what most visitors didn't even try with monks, was humor. But as soon as I met Carol, we discovered a mutual talent for making each other laugh. I knew right away that I had found a kindred soul. Our relationship blossomed so that she and her husband made many visits to New Skete, and once Carol came alone, for a meditative break.

And she did meditate and use the time to reflect and write. I was busy with my own complex monastic schedule, but usually after

Carol Lea Benjamin and her dog, "Dexter." (Stephen J. Lennard)

Vespers, we would have time for a leisurely walk down the two-mile dirt road that dead-ended at and isolated the monastery. One of my fondest memories of those years is walking down that road with Carol and talking about the antics of naughty dogs we'd trained. In the end, we were laughing so hard, we could hardly stand up. Over the years, we've talked about many serious subjects, but we've never lost that wonderful ability to make each other laugh.

Carol Lea Benjamin is a professional dog trainer with over 20 years' experience with dogs of all ages and with all kinds of problems. She is the author of seven books on dog behavior, *Mother Knows Best: The Natural Way to Train Your Dog; Dog Problems; Dog Training For Kids; Dog Tricks* (with Captain Arthur Haggerty); two books widely given away by shelters to adopters, *Second-Hand Dog: How to Turn Yours Into a First-Rate Pet* and *The Chosen Puppy: How to Select and Raise a Great Puppy From an Animal Shelter*; and her latest, *Surviving Your Dog's Adolescence: A Positive Training Program*. Ms. Benjamin has also written two novels and four nonfiction books for children.

In addition, Ms. Benjamin has written and illustrated numerous articles on dog behavior for magazines such as *Time, The American Kennel Gazette, Apartment Life, Dogs U*S*A*, The German Shepherd Dog Review*, and many others. She has taught dog behavior seminars all over the United States and in Canada and has participated in many radio call-in shows and television shows, including Daywatch (CNN) and CBS This Morning, sharing her expertise about dogs.

Ms. Benjamin has won many awards for her dog writing, including the Gaines "Fido" (Dogdom's Writer of the Year, 1985), the first Kal Kan Pedigree Outstanding Pet Care Journalist Award, 1988, a New York State Humane Association ABCDE (A Book Can Develop Empathy) Award (for *The Chosen Puppy*), 1991, and the Dog Writers' Association of America's highest honor, the Distinguished Service Award for Extraordinary Achievement and Communications Excellence, 1990. Her award-winning column, "Dog Trainer's Diary," has been published in *Pure-Bred Dogs—American Kennel Gazette* since 1979, making it the longest-running column by an individual in the over 100-year history of the American Kennel Club's official magazine.

THE INTERVIEW

Job Michael Evans: *I don't really want to ask any stupid questions. No interviewer would, but I need to ask the standard one that might sound stupid: How did you start in dogs? Can you tell me a little bit about what your experience was when you were a little girl and how you hook that up with what you do now? I'm very interested in that type of past history in the people that I'm interviewing. I think it helps other trainers to get balance in their own dog work if they know what other dog trainers have in their background. For instance, some dog trainers are not necessarily born of deeply dog-involved families.*

Carol Lea Benjamin: Do you remember the experiment Konrad Lorenz did with geese when he let them follow him instead of their mother when they were in the imprinting period? From then on, the geese would only follow him. Well, when I was a little girl, my family had a dog named Snowflake. The family story was that Snowflake taught me how to walk. My understanding is that I got imprinted on Snowflake. And dogs have held my attention ever since.

When I was in high school, I wanted to be a dog trainer, but the only kinds of dog training I knew of at that point were training for the army, which did not appeal to me, and training for The Seeing Eye. When I was 15, I met a boy who said he had a job working for The Seeing Eye in the summer and subsequent summers, and then he would eventually become a trainer. I got so excited at the thought that you could do that that I nearly passed out. I was very, very shy. It took me a week to work up my courage and finally I called The Seeing Eye. I said I'd like to work there in the summer, muck out kennels, do anything, and then I was going to go to college, because my father would have killed me if I didn't go to college. There was never a choice in my family. It was, "You're going to

121

college." So I asked advice on what courses I should take to help prepare me to be a trainer so that after I graduated I could come back and be a trainer of Seeing Eye dogs. By the way, I am using Seeing Eye properly. This was The Seeing Eye, in Morristown, New Jersey. The person on the phone listened very politely. I think I must have done it all in one breath because I was so scared. And when I finally finished, the voice on the phone said, "I'm sorry. We don't hire women. We did during the war, but not now." And he hung up. As far as I knew, that was the end of my dog training career.

More than 15 years later, I was given a Golden Retriever as a Valentine present—of course, I picked him out myself. I had always had smaller dogs and I found his energy level too high and I didn't know how to manage a dog that big. I had always had terrier-type random-bred dogs when I was a kid and had taught them all kinds of tricks with no trouble at all, but I was beside myself with a Golden, which is pretty funny when you think about it. Anyway, I saw an ad in the paper for a dog school, 10 lessons for 25 dollars—well, *that* certainly dates me, doesn't it? I figured, what could I lose? You got to sign up the night of the graduation of the class before. I walked in, it was a big beautiful room, the mats were out, and I got to see the several classes that were graduating, people and dogs working together with such tremendous rapport, such mutual pride. In moments, I had this overwhelming feeling that I found what I was born to do.

I took my dog, Oliver, through the 10 weeks and at the end of the 10 weeks, I went up to the trainer and asked if I could be his apprentice. In the strangest negotiation that ever happened, he looked at me as if he were asked that very question 50 times a day and said, "Sure, kid." So that's what I did for the next year and a quarter.

JME: *So you were kind of an assistant, but not really?*

CLB: Yeah, really. I swept the floors. I ran errands. I taught my own class. I handled dogs in his classes that the people couldn't handle. He was a firm believer that you take a dog when the person is having trouble. I know a lot of people now feel that that's a no-no, that you never take a person's dog. He took their dogs for demo work, even though he had his own trained dog there, and we took dogs to show people how to do it, so they'd be inspired, so they'd succeed.

JME: *So you were doing a lot of different things.*

CLB: I was very active. I did everything.

JME: *I mention it because my experience with even small classes where they have one or two assistants these days is it's all very stratified as to* who does what. It's not the kind of deal where you do a little of everything. They seemed focused on the idea that they're an assistant for a while and then they'll get to be the head honcho rather than doing all of the nitty-gritty stuff that really teaches you everything, every aspect.

CLB: Different people are comfortable with different ways of working. This was a great opportunity for me. I learned a lot and the experience of handling so many dogs gave me the confidence to finally go out on my own. And I loved every minute of the work because I was learning to do the thing I wanted to do more than anything in the world.

By the way, if I were starting now, I'd have a shot at The Seeing Eye. They do have women trainers now and they are very good at the work. But by now I know how great it is to work for yourself.

JME: *So when you finally went out on your own, you called your school "Oliver and Me."*

CLB: Oliver and Me. I gave the dog first billing.

JME: *What do you feel about the dog training field today? Many people feel the current vista is not at all promising in terms of getting dogs trained. Others seem to feel that all sorts of exciting innovations are a positive trend. If one doesn't believe that New Age training, for want of a better term, is liberating the field and comforting owners (it's interesting that there are not many claims for its effectiveness in training dogs), one is considered dated and is essentially discarded. I think you are familiar with this syndrome. What are your thoughts?*

CLB: My policy on the new fads in dog training is "Don't ask. Don't tell."

But I can speak for myself. I believe in things that nurture a relationship between a person and a dog and a dog and a person. I rely on the growth of the relationship rather than relying on gimmicks and equipment and treats and all kinds of junk you're supposed to have to throw at the dog or alert the dog. I think a normal, sound dog feels that the entire world is very attractive but the most attractive thing in the world has to be the owner. That doesn't mean that the dog will gape at the owner all the time, but if the owner needs the dog's attention, even when the dog is out in the park playing with other dogs, he or she can get it. To me, having a trained dog means you can get the dog's attention and the dog will come to you because you are the best thing in his life.

I believe in addressing a dog's mind. I believe that the dog is a thinking being, capable of figuring things out, adding things up, capable of learning from both experience and observation, capable of learning the rules of a game and augmenting the fun with new versions. To me, the easiest, smartest, and best route to a dog's mind is using a careful observation of how dogs teach and learn from each other, and adjusting that model to a mixed-species pair of teachers and learners.

For the deepest kind of learning in a dog, my feeling is that he should be able to understand everything that's happening. This means he should understand the positive and negative reinforcement, and from where or whom it comes. He sure as hell knew where it came from when his mother gave him a clop with her foreleg when he was a puppy and he stepped out of line and he never ended up hating or fearing his mother. He loved and respected his mother. If you look at puppies and their mothers, they literally worship their mothers. My feeling is, with the natural training method that I prefer, this is what transfers to the owner. The owner ends up with an educated dog who respects and loves and literally worships the owner, and the owner can worship the dog right back. It's perfectly fine.

I'm certainly aware of what other people believe in and the different approaches to training. But I don't believe dogs change. And they are my source for what to believe and how to educate and be educated. The dogs have always been my teachers. After all, they're the ones who have the answers.

JME: *How did you develop the concept of rights for dogs? Did you have a consultant at the U.N.? Seriously, it's a fascinating concept, and the rights are clearly spelled out. I know the U.N. did its charter on human rights and they made it very clear that there were too many people, especially after World War II, that didn't care about rights or had had their own violated or didn't even know that they had any. I think this is happening to dogs, and has been happening to them for years as we dispose of them, utilize them, force inappropriate employment on them, feed them junk, and ultimately kill them when they are too much trouble. What was the whole Pit Bull hoopla about if not another form of ethnic cleansing? Humans always forget the rights of others so quickly. I think charters and lists are important, because they keep us on track. They remind us of the rules. What was the response to that column?*

CLB: The response to this *Gazette* column was very powerful. Apparently a lot of people had these thoughts, these feelings and were excited to see what they also believed in print.

As to where this came from, it has always been my understanding that dogs have a life separate from their roles with humans, as pets or even working companions. Dogs have an existence as dogs which we can observe but never fully comprehend. When you think about this, how could you not say that they have a right to be dogs; to use their noses in preference to their eyes; to greet each other in the special way that they do; to play and mingle with others of their own kind; to have a place and a time to use their voices without being shushed; to contemplate and enjoy the natural environment; and to be seen and appreciated as thinking, feeling beings, not as objects to be experimented on. They have a right to their safety, to have their lives protected, and to be able to give and receive love. I feel these things very strongly. We live in a world where dogs are treated like soda cans: You use them and throw them away. Their lives have an integrity to them and a beauty that is characteristic of their species and different from ours. They are treasures, they are a gift to us, and should be treated as such.

Sadly, we must note for clarity's sake that when we talk about dog's "rights," we are taking a view quite separate from the so-called animal rights groups which do not believe in pet ownership. To them, rights for animals mean freedom from the tyranny of being pets. For the domesticated dog, this would mean the freedom to starve to death or get hit by cars. Dogs, as domesticated animals, need our protection in order to survive. There never were wild Yorkies or Westies or Goldens, so these animals cannot return to the wild. It makes no sense. In addition, the pet dogs I know have wonderful lives. They are cared for, fed, groomed, exercised, and loved. They get to play with each other and with their humans. Their lives are safe and rich, an enviable combination.

JME: *The great food critic M.F.K. Fisher once said in an interview, "When I write about food, I am really writing about love." I was reading* Mother Knows Best *recently and that quote came to mind. You are writing about the mother's love for her puppies and how this translates into the human sphere. It really goes quite deep, which probably explains why the book is such a success. It can be read on many levels. One of the deepest levels is that discipline is love, a truth this ex-monk has no difficulty with. And an even deeper truth is that one does not "own" anything or anyone else. That too is part of the mystery of love. The photograph of Scarlet walking down her road at her own pace at the end of the book makes this very clear. I guess the question is, what is the animating force that spurs love between a dog and an owner?*

CLB: I think I would have to say loving respect, respect for the dog as an intelligent, feeling being and the natural respect the dog transfers from his mother to his owner. True respect breeds proper stewardship and leads to genuine feeling.

One of the things I've observed is that the mother dog doesn't merely *love* her puppies. Her love means educating them. She prepares them to live in the world. She prepares them to live without her.

125

By observing mothers with their puppies, you can see this education going on. When I took the photographs of Chelsea the Boxer and her puppies, for *Mother Knows Best*, during the entire afternoon while I was photographing, Chelsea was educating her puppies. Most interesting is that during the entire time, she only corrected the Alpha puppy, an adorable brat named Lily who was always getting into trouble and leading the other puppies into trouble. By correcting Lily, Chelsea was educating *all* the puppies. Moreover, she was preparing them for their lives as pets, teaching them to accept leadership and to look to their leader for education.

Chelsea could have spent the afternoon lying in the sunshine and letting the puppies do as they would. But she would not have been a good mother to be that permissive, because the puppies would not have learned that there has to be a limit to cheeky behavior and that when someone bigger and smarter gives directions, they ought to be followed. Her education taught the puppies what they needed to know then and also things that would help them as they grew and went out and about in the world.

JME: *So all of this is absolutely natural?*

CLB: Absolutely. And the thing that is so lovely about using the style the mother uses is that you can have near perfect communication. You never see a bitch "repeat" herself when she makes a sound or stops a puppy with her paw. The puppy always understands perfectly what she means. You just never hear the equivalent of the human cry, "If I've told you once, I've told you a thousand times, get your feet off the table!"

I always advise dog trainers to use their powers of observation when they are in the presence of bitches and puppies, dogs playing, or even when they are on the job. Instead of going into someone's home and grabbing the leash and starting to work the dog, I prefer to observe the dog first. You only get one shot to do this. Once you handle the dog, he will view you differently and you won't see it all hang out. And even though the owner hired you to help, he or she won't necessarily tell you all the dog's charming little habits. Patience is the key word. Watch and learn.

Even when you take your dog to play with other dogs, you not only have the pleasure of watching this beautiful activity, you can also be learning. The dogs will be teaching each other, even if it's just something as simple as, "Hey, don't bite my tail so hard." Wherever there are dogs, education is going on. There's communication to interpret and learn from.

JME: *Tell me a little about your cartoons or, if you prefer, illustrations. They're so vivacious and charming. Where did you get your drawing*

126

ability? I have absolutely no artistic talent whatsoever. The last thing I drew was an overdraft from my bank.

CLB: I'm not a trained artist. I just got lucky with the doodling I did when I was on the telephone.

I began to understand the power of cartoons many years ago when I was teaching high school. When I had to give a test, I used to draw a cartoon rabbit onto the mimeograph—there, I'm dating myself once again!—and the rabbit, that was the only thing I could draw, the rabbit would speak for the kids. You know, he'd be lying on the bottom of the test, he'd have an X for an eye as if he'd just keeled over and died, he'd be holding a daisy and he'd be thinking, "Oh, my God, I forgot to study!" I'd give out the test, the kids would look for the rabbit, they'd start to laugh, release a little tension and take the test. One day I came in late, typed up the test in the English office, forgot the rabbit and mimeographed the test. When I handed the test out, my class of eleventh graders went on strike. They refused to take the test without the rabbit. I ended up drawing the rabbit on the blackboard, having him "dis" me, and they laughed and took the test. So I do understand the power of these cute little drawings.

Now my cartoons usually speak the thoughts of dogs as filtered through my own warped imagination. It's a way of teaching a lesson or making an important point without seeming to lecture. People get it, but they don't feel insulted. It helps people to remember things. When I illustrate a book or my *Gazette* column, I often choose the most important things to illustrate. People laugh, but they get it. And they tend to remember it. So it helps their relationship with their dog. That's what I'm always after.

JME: *I think you're the only one who can do that, combine cartoons with writing. For me, it's such a positive, helpful thing because it helps people to relate to their whole background as kids, of seeing comics, of seeing Walt Disney characters...*

CLB: Right. It's friendly...

JME: *Goofy, Snoopy, and so on. It's a way that they can keep going with that cuteness that they want to attach to dogs, and rightly so.*

CLB: There's also another message and that is, if you don't have a sense of humor, you probably shouldn't have a dog. Every dog I've ever had has had a tremendous sense of humor. And sometimes when a dog cracks a joke, he does it by making a fool of the owner. I think it's a great relief to be able to laugh at myself and see myself through dog-colored glasses. Maybe the cartoons remind people to lighten up and enjoy themselves and their dogs a little more.

JME: *Have you ever wanted to be a veterinarian? I've reversed this question, informally, talking with veterinarians, asking if any of them have ever wanted to be dog trainers, at which point most of them scream, "NO!" and rush out to the cocktail bar. But a surprising number of trainers work at veterinary offices and harbor secret desires to get into that field. My secret desire always has been to be a practicing veterinarian. How about you?*

CLB: I was an extremely squeamish child. If I watched my mother pour tomato juice, I'd get sick to my stomach. No, I never thought of becoming a veterinarian.

Many years ago, when I was starting out, I was invited to watch a veterinary surgical procedure, a spay on a cat. I went into the operating room and the technician came in to shave the cat's stomach and as soon as she turned on the clipper, I passed out.

A few years later, I tried again, and I was okay. I watched three surgeries on dogs and found it fascinating. Truly fascinating. But behavior is what really interests me. Actually, the glimpses we get of canine intelligence and humor, those are the things I love most.

JME: *What do you think you bring to dog training that is unique and special?*

CLB: I've always thought that my gift was that of clarity and that's perhaps because I taught for many years. But if you asked the people who read my books and columns what my greatest gift was, I'm pretty sure they'd say humor.

JME: *But isn't part of humor that the joke doesn't come off unless it's clear?*

CLB: Right. I think that's true. In fact, you could say the humor can be a part of the clarity of a seminar or a book. It can be the thing you go away with, that you remember, the funny story or the funny remark, but it was also what made a point clear because it had punch to it. It got your attention.

JME: *It's clear from the interviews I've done with different trainers that all of them come from diverse backgrounds and gain their knowledge in a variety of ways. There's no way that anyone can or should dictate to a budding trainer how to become proficient and respected. I certainly can't ask people to join a monastery for 11 years.*

CLB: I tried. They wouldn't let me in.

JME: *I heard about that. So that makes your background very different from mine. But given your dream scenario, what would be your advice for someone who says, "I want to be Carol Benjamin. I want to train dogs, write books, make a contribution in this field."*

CLB: If someone came up to me and said, "I want to be Carol Benjamin," I'd say, "You can't. The job's taken already." In fact, I have an apprentice right now, and one of the first things I told him was that he was not going to be a Carol Benjamin clone. He's going to be his own person and have his own style. And that's as it should be. He needs to express his own creativity, his own views. The apprenticeship, after all, is not an end. It's just a beginning.

JME: *Do you think everyone should serve an apprenticeship?*

CLB: I don't think everyone can. There are places where there isn't anyone they can serve one with. That's one way. As you said, being in the monastery for 11 years is another. But everybody's not going to do that. I think, from my own background, if you start out as obsessed with dogs as I was as a child, I mean I picked up so much information as a child, reading Albert Payson Terhune and cutting out dog pictures from my mother's magazines, I think I knew all the breeds by the time I was 10 years old, but some people come to this feeling later. I understand you didn't have a background with dogs, you came to it later, and it certainly didn't stop you from becoming a terrific dog trainer and making an enormous contribution to the field. This feels silly to say to you, but I think God works in mysterious ways—you may quote me—and that all the things I did earlier in my life that seemed to have nothing to do with dog train-ing, all feed into it, like learning the value of the cartoons and learning how to be clear when I was a teacher, and learning the breeds on rainy days as a little kid cutting pictures out of magazines. Everything came together, all the games I played with my dogs as a kid were educating me as well as them, and now these are things I teach my clients. I don't think one should ever rue what they did in life before.

JME: *Because it contributes.*

CLB: Yes. It all becomes part of the special view one can bring to the profession. I think when one makes the decision to work with dogs, they should devour every book they can get their hands on. If you come away from a book with one new tip, it's worth the read. You don't have to agree with the person. If you don't, you'll come away believing in what you believe all the more strongly.

JME: *Reading is also very important because that produces a wider vocab-ulary and increases literacy. One thing that makes your books enjoyable is their literacy. I've made jokes in the past that most dog books are like literary Sominex, but that's not the case with your writing.*

CLB: Thank you. Haven't you found that clients sometimes ask about other books? They'll ask what you think of the theories and methods. You have to know what's out there. It's really important to know the field and keep up. It's part of being a professional. In addition to reading, and learning all the proper terminology, I would encourage people to go to dog shows. I used to sit on the grass and watch obedience for hours at a time and figure out why some teams work so well and why others don't. You could see it. It's all there in front of you. New trainers also need to experience as much on-leash handling as possible, even if they have to volunteer at a shelter to walk and train dogs. The more dogs they work with, the better they'll get and the more confident they'll get. The more you work, the more economical your movements become, like the mother dog, the more sure you are, the more clear you become as a teacher of dogs and humans.

JME: *So all of that produces clarity and confidence.*

CLB: And the dog reads that confidence as Alpha.

JME: *And then you add that touch of humor?*

CLB: It can be a great help. It makes it easier for your clients to hear what you're saying. I don't know if it's essential, but most of the dog people I'm close with have great senses of humor. So do most of my shrink friends. Maybe you can't do either job without it.

JME: *Well, to end up, I would just modify one answer that you gave when I asked you what you think that you bring to dog training that is unique and special, and you said clarity and humor. I would say it's not just those two things. It's clarity, humor, and compassion.*

CLB: Oh, thank you. That's so nice. And don't forget beauty.

JME: *And beauty.*

Chapter 17

Amy Ammen

Amy Ammen began training her first dog, Tess, in 1975. Four years later, at age 15, she began instructing classes and private training at all levels and eventually trained dogs while boarding them. In 1982, Amy opened Amiable Dog Training. Now Amy and her five instructors teach pet owners and competitors how to reach their goals.

Since 1990 dozens of organizations throughout the United States and Canada have hosted "The Infinite Instructor" and "Training the Average Dog to Win." These well-attended weekend workshops for obedience enthusiasts have received rave reviews from participants and from hosting organizations alike.

Amy is co-author of *Dual Ring Dog: Successful Training for Conformation and Obedience Competition* (Howell Book House). She is currently writing *Training in No Time*, scheduled for publication by Howell in 1995.

Amy's success with breeds rarely seen in the winner's circle speaks for itself. Consider these examples:

Australian Cattle Dog, Huzzi Bear, Am., Can. UD–#2 Australian Cattle Dog 1978-81

Briard, CH Weaselle, UD–Dog World Award winner, #1 Briard 1982

Flat-Coated Retriever, OTCH Digger–Dog World Award winner, multiple All Breed High in Trial (HIT) winner, #1 Flat-Coated Retriever 1985-87

American Staffordsire Terrier, CH and OTCH Shaker– Specialty and multiple All Breed HIT winner, #2 Terrier 1987 all systems, first CH and OTCH American Staffordshire Terrier

Cocker Spaniel, Jack, CDX–#3 Cocker Spaniel 1985

Amy Ammen and canine buddy. (Courtesy Amiable Dog Training)

Japanese Chin, CH and OTCH Kiwi, UD–First UD Japanese
Chin, multiple All Breed HIT winner, Dog World Award
winner, #1 Japanese Chin 1988, #2 Toy 1989.
Whippet, Orbit, CDX–Dog World Award winner, #1 Whippet,
#3 Hound 1989

THE INTERVIEW

The first thing about Ms. Ammen I noticed, besides her stunning
good looks, was her personal physical carriage. She is tall but not
intimidating. Her voice is modulated and her arms move with an
economy that is the sure mark of a top trainer. While all this might
sound rather strange, good looks, height, and economy in motion
never hurt a trainer. These attributes, in fact, increase self-
confidence and make dogs watch us more carefully, not with suspicion, but with respect and joy. It's uncanny how a trained trainer
detects this in another trainer almost immediately.

We met at Cafe Bianco, behind the restaurant near a bubbling
fountain, the delightful sound of which would have filled any gaps in
the conversation. But I hardly heard the fountain, as there weren't
any lulls in our very good talk.

Young women have a tough time in this field. There is sexism, and there is occasionally the possibility of a really threatening situation—not from the dogs, from the human clients. Culturally, American women (with few exceptions) tend to flail about with their arms, over-gesticulating, trying to please. Wary dogs that are about to be trained (a process they suspect they will hate) do not like this overexuberance. So when a tall trainer presents herself with terrific dignity, it's almost a relief for the dog. We started in on a good interview.

Job Michael Evans: *Most professionals have a way of presenting themselves to a dog, gaining its respect. It's called "presence." What can you say about presence, specifically your presence?*

Amy Ammen: Presence wasn't something I was born with, but developed as I gained confidence in my handling abilities. So what coauthor Jackie Frasier says in the beginning of *Dual Ring Dog* (Howell Book House) about my coordination and naturalness, was a result of six years of very hard work to make it look easy. With dogs, I learned a few things and was eager to go in and *dazzle* them. I was totally focused on *that* dog and studying him or her to determine my next move and bring out the dog's best.

I guess I've learned to do the same with people, but not ever in a cruel or manipulative fashion. Rather, I'm fascinated by people and know I can learn a tremendous amount. I enjoy myself most when I get immersed in the moment, regardless of what I'm doing, and have the best time when I'm engaging with others.

I like to go into a situation with a dog or a person thinking we are both going to feel better after the interaction. With a dog who is going to try to bite me, I tell myself I'll likely be able to diffuse that response. In the worst case scenario, a bite is no big deal and I could live through that. I downplay the risks involved and focus on benefits, and am rarely disappointed.

JME: *As you say, "never in a cruel or manipulative fashion." So many trainers are so brusque—I guess they want to get home in time to watch "Roseanne." If there is anything my mentors have taught me, it is to give of my time, and thus of myself, but also to set boundaries. Did you have a mentor? What would you suggest for beginning trainers?*

AA: I started training my Siberian Husky because after living with her for four months I found her incorrigible and wanted to get rid of her and get another dog. My father said okay, but I could never have another dog. One of my neighbors was taking her dog to training class, so I decided to enroll too. After three months my dog was still biting, jumping, pooping, and running away so I decided to sign up *again*.

133

In 1976 I met Jan Plagenz, who was perhaps my greatest mentor, and to this day my oldest, greatest, and dearest friend. Jan was the groomer at a local kennel and took me under her wing to teach me how to groom, which I did for 12 years. Jan took me to training class, seminars, conventions, and shows. We trained together and she let me show one of her German Wirehaired Pointer pups in conformation. She convinced me to buy Huzzi, my second dog (an Australian Cattle Dog), and took training pictures for *Dual Ring Dog*.

Another person who inspired me to compete and awed me with her common sense and ingenuity was Linda Schaal from Milwaukee. Linda shows Belgian Tervurens in conformation, tracking, and obedience and now has one of the first dogs in history to earn a conformation championship, an obedience trial championship, and a TDX.

My parents weren't involved in dogs, thank God! All they cared about was that I wasn't neglecting them. I proved that would never be a problem. But they rarely took me to events. I was continually scamming rides off every friend and acquaintance I could. Consequently I met, traveled with, and soaked up some knowledge from many great people like Nancy Russell, professional handler and Alaskan Malamute breeder; Dee Rummel, Puli breeder; and Marti Mazanets, Jr., another professional handler. These people and other handlers also taught me the importance of a *good first impression* and the role of "presence" in conformation and Junior Showmanship.

In addition to mentors, I also had gurus. Art Kearns owned a training school in Milwaukee called Arko. In the beginning, my training was very haphazard and influenced by many different and often mediocre instructors. After experiencing difficulty in Open, I knew I had to follow a better plan if I ever wanted to get a UD. So I enrolled in Art's first Utility class and did *everything* he said. Art had only one Utility Dog himself and used the Koehler Method. Unlike most trainers, though, Art understood the method and took nothing out of context, as is so frequently the case when using someone else's method.

Then I started attending Bill Koehler's seminars. He even invited me to visit him and his wife, Lillian, and watch his classes in California in 1983. Bill was a wonderful, caring man and trainer and it angers me to see individuals misinterpreting his techniques that have helped so many dogs when properly used.

New trainers should find someone they respect and trust and whose achievements and status they admire. Then they should believe in and follow their instruction. You see so many "two-week trainers." They initially believe some new trainer is the greatest thing since sliced bread, and the *new* way is the only way to train, and will work like a wave of a magic wand. If something doesn't work immediately, if they don't understand it completely, or a new faddish technique comes into town, they bail ship. This guarantees failure because such trainers have no focus, loyalty, or commitment to direction.

We expect these attributes from a good dog and we have to give it to our instructor. Once we understand a training philosophy after applying it, we are ready to start reading the dog and altering it, if necessary, when we see tendencies in different breeds.

JME: *And there is a certain approach necessary toward certain breeds, a certain technical approach, if you will. Are you a technical trainer and did you start out that way? Do you feel mastery of basic techniques is essential?*

AA: I'm assuming "technical trainer" means a very specific approach to teaching—step by step. Yes, I was and am a technical trainer, since that first Utility class. But for years I followed, carefully, someone else's steps before I adapted my own. Since many methods of training can and do work, when I'm instructing I don't tell anyone what he can and cannot do. I make suggestions. I might suggest things I might not do personally, but there may be a style that student might be more comfortable with, a particular method.

Here is where I believe "presence" comes into play. If the trainer has an objective and a game plan and believes it will work, it almost always will, regardless of how strange it may appear to an observer. To get a "feel" and develop a conviction, new trainers really do need to master the basics following a recipe (usually out of someone else's cookbook) and train dog after dog before varying the method, a method truly their own.

Like you, for many years I had the benefit of training dogs while boarding. That taught me to categorize dogs and develop the most efficient method of training (because I had to produce results quickly) while experimenting with dogs of all ages, sizes, breeds, and backgrounds. There appears to be no substitute for hands-on learning.

JME: *In-board training, as such, which because of my cloistered status I was forced to do for 11 years, does have some benefits, although it is often derided. As you say, there is always a variety of types and breeds of dogs. There is room for humane experimentation without the embarrassment of owners seeing you make a faux pas. I can't agree more that the economical pressure is on. I was expected to work certain set hours and no fooling around. The abbot expected the board/kennel to be kept*

135

booming, and I kept it booming. While I wasn't making any money for myself—I had a vow of poverty—I learned to enjoy work. I wonder, do many trainers really enjoy their work? Not just love it, enjoy it. What would you change about the obedience regulations?

AA: Not much. I hope judges don't try to second-guess how a dog was trained by watching him for five minutes. What I am speaking about is deducting points if the dog doesn't demonstrate "utmost willingness and enjoyment." The point is to prevent handlers from using abusive methods, which is a very noble correction and praise-worthy mission. But saying a "happy" dog has been trained and a timid-looking or lackadaisical one has been roughed up is *nonsense*. Any trainer knows some dogs "come back" after a correction while others require pumping up and lots of precaution to build up any enthusiasm even though they've never been mishandled. After all, the purpose of obedience is not to have a wired dog but rather to have a responsive companion who is a joy to be around. I'd also like AKC competition to be open to mixed breeds.

JME: *I thought* Dual Ring Dog *(Howell Book House) was a break-through. It shattered once and for all the myth that conformation training must precede obedience training lest the dog's spirit be "squelched." The specter of this fills many exhibitors with fear. What has the reaction been to* Dual Ring Dog *and what are your feelings regarding obedience-training conformation dogs?*

AA: The reaction to the book and the seminar "Enhancing Show-manship Through Obedience Training" has been very positive. People want to do more with their dogs (agility, field, herding). Not only do the dogs love it, but it can be used to improve their work in other areas. For example, when a person obedience trains, they personally gain confidence (about their control) and they learn what motivates the dog much quicker and with better, deeper under-standing, than they would be simply conformation training. I believe there are no conformation problems. If the dog exhibits shyness, wiggles, sits, weaves, or is distracted by other dogs, I simulate and resolve it in an obedience setting. That learning carries over to conformation. Then I am able to help the dog do his job—*I facilitate his beauty, through training.*

I think people who look at a dog who isn't showing his best, and say it's because he is obedience trained, should consider there is no problem unique to obedience dogs. Any dog can attempt to sidewind or sit or lunge at bait, but an obedience-trained dog is always easier to work with in conformation.

JME: *You are young, as young as I was when I entered, or more appropri-ately, was forced into the field. Youth can be a hang-up. There are* always the old-timers (who have simply been repeating the same mistakes for years) ready to correct and even condemn. We've a lot of mentors, but they diffuse this insecurity so well; could you talk a little more about them? Who were your role models and who inspired you?

AA: I answered this question partially but I'll gladly continue. After completing the first course with my miserable Husky, I was watching a novice class after training one evening. A teenage girl was heeling her German Shorthaired Pointer off leash and I got very inspired. For the next two weeks I trained diligently for the first time. When I returned to class there was a big difference, I was promoted to the next level, and I was hooked.

As I became involved in competition I read about top trainers around the country. I got so enthused when I saw them at shows and tournaments. Some of the first "hot shots" I met were Bud Burge, Pauline Czarnecki, Barb Goodman, Dick Guetzloff and Kay Thompson (Guetzloff), Bob Self, Ted and Anna Aranda, Bob Adams, and lots of lesser-knowns who showed breeds I was interested in.

When I wanted to broaden my horizons beyond showing, you were my role model. I'd never been to a seminar that was so structured, concise, and organized as yours, and wanted to produce a working, competition seminar version of that. I was impressed by your style, dress, focus, and your accomplishments as a trainer, writer, and speaker. I quietly wondered how you did so much and you were only in your thirties.

Eight months ago I met Judie Howard, a trainer and speaker from Moraga, California. Judy owns one of the largest schools in the country and has at least nine OTCH titleists. Judy and her husband, Gary, invited me to stay in their lovely home and I watched Judie's classes for several days. The Howards are gracious and fun, respectful and kind to one another and everyone else, articulate, and will give their knowledge freely. I respect their character and work ethic and the drive it takes to build an empire. There are many other inspirational individuals whom I've worked with—Jean Taylor, John and Kathryn Haydon, Marilyn Jaqua, Maureen Parolini, and so many others. If I were to answer this question next week I'd probably give a dozen different names because I've been inspired by so many!

JME: *Tell me about your personal dogs. How did you resolve problems and what feelings did that initiate?*

AA: My first two dogs had the typical problems resulting from being trained by a haphazard, beginning trainer—poor attention and sloppiness. Once I improved as a trainer, some of the most outstanding difficulties occurred with the Chin and the Briard; both were very resistant to heeling. After completing the laborious (and atypically difficult) task of lead breaking, we struggled to overcome balking and then lagging and wideness on lead, then back to square one when off-leash work began. They were very slow learners. But by the time they got in Utility they progressed at a quick rate and regularly heeled to perfect and near-perfect patterns.

Frustrations have made me develop a better attitude and new way of thinking. A situation is good or bad only because of the way we perceive it. The process of solving problems always brings me a better understanding of a given dog and much deeper bonding and appreciation. My favorite dogs have *not* been the easy ones. In fact, my two "natural heelers," the Flat-Coat and Whippet, I'm sorry to say, I never really bonded with. That's why I think it is so absurd for someone to tell another that they don't have an obedience dog when we all want something different. Every dog goes through states and as a result of the incredible changes I've seen, *I really believe there is more that a dog can accomplish than that he can't.*

JME: *Yes, we underestimate dogs so easily and then get angry with them when they don't "produce." Meanwhile, I have to ask, produce what? Titles? Ribbons? Dog-food commercial starring roles? Is this really about dogs or dogs as extensions of human ego? I think that is why we need the balance people like yourself bring to the field. What unique thing do you bring to training and what could you work on?*

AA: There is nothing unique about what I do, but I feel strongly about interacting with people. I feel fortunate to have this opportunity and my respect for individuals' choices hopefully allows them to be their best if they want to be.

When I receive criticism, I always end up taking it personally and feeling badly a lot longer than I should. My rational side says I should view criticism as positive because it allows me to see and improve on things I would otherwise be oblivious to. Unfortunately, my emotion (oh no, not everybody likes me) often wins.

JME: *Well, everyone involved in training has had to process such feelings, and just by mentioning your difficulty with criticism, which, by the way, is refreshing because it is honest, means that you are well on your way to conquering any fear of it. I think you are already a fantastic trainer and poised to make a major contribution to our beloved profession.*

Chapter 18

Dr. Ian Dunbar

Dr. Ian Dunbar is a British-trained veterinarian with a special interest in canine behavior. He has published several books and many pamphlets, plus a videotape—in fact, a growing series of videos. He is extremely popular on the seminar circuit and his charm, English accent, and overall presentation make him a joy to listen to. He writes a monthly column on behavior for the *American Kennel Gazette*.

I first met Dr. Dunbar over dinner in New York City, and later in San Francisco near his home. Finally, after much happy socializing, we were able to meet in Toronto to anchor ourselves for this interview. Dr. Dunbar had just taught a five-day, extremely intensive seminar for professionals in dogs. He showed few signs of the strain, perhaps because I was the final speaker, and he had a chance to rest. While we have methodological preferences and differences, I have always felt at home with Ian. He has made a major impact on our field, and what he has to say here will fascinate and help you in your quest to be the trainer and explainer you want to be. The first topic we tackled, of course, was differences between trainers.

THE INTERVIEW

JME: *First I really want to thank you for granting this interview. I think it will really help the thrust of the book, which has some similarity to the type of things we were talking about today. It will be a rich discussion. That is the question of methodology. I know that you and I have differences in that area. It would be easy for anyone who has read our books or pamphlets to figure that out. This has never bothered me because I have always been comfortable with the fact that you're proficient in what you do and I am, in my own way, with my techniques. What I want to*

Dr. Ian Dunbar and Fan. (Courtesy Dr. Ian Dunbar)

ask is, do you find any conflict in any of this? How do you handle poten-
tial problems that might arise because of differences between trainers or
between clients?

ID: I think when you have differences there is a conflict of views. I
don't necessarily see it as a negative thing. I'm usually excited by
someone who does something differently from me. I feel confident
of what I do. When somebody says "No, no, I don't like that, I do
this," and they are excited about that, I think they feel they have
something to teach me, so I really want to listen. By nature, I think
dog training is a profession of just a few philosophers, if you like,
but many thousands, millions of methods. All trainers, really any
two, are going to have different methodologies. I like to promote
that plan A will work well with most dogs and most people. But
when it doesn't you've got to very, very quickly change to plan B. If
that doesn't work then to plan C, and plan D, and plan E. There
will eventually be uses for all the things you have heard from other
trainers. If someone has been doing something for years, and it
works, then there has to be something good to say for it.

JME: *This harks back to what you said during the seminar today. You have*
to memorize in your head what you are going to do. The "what-if" syn-
drome can't be hanging on a thread. When a question comes up you have
to be prepared to answer.

ID: I think another underlying point, since we have different methodology, is, do I have a conflict dealing with you in terms of, let's say, dog behavior training? I mean, obviously, I like you very much as a person. You know I thought it was quite a hoot when we got together in San Francisco. I really enjoyed that. I mean you are just incredibly funny. Today I meant it when I said my biggest fear was I was going to fall asleep, I was so tired. I did not want to offend you. Instead I haven't laughed so much at a doggy thing for so long.

JME: *I had a good time. Laughter is so healing.*

ID: In terms of the differences of opinion, I would not have invited you to be the keynote speaker at the first conference I've ever put on if I thought you were going to say something I didn't agree with. This morning you spoke for the entire morning and there was not anything I took issue with. You were talking about what I think is important and it has actually very little to do with the dog training aspect, it has to do with the *people* training aspect: You were talking about getting people to evaluate their lives and what they are doing, to motivate them to come to class, and to train them to stay in class. There is a much bigger pie here. The dog is the tip of the iceberg, if you like, and getting families involved …

JME: *That is why I warned the audience against this cheap comparison game. Not just between yourself and myself. Thank God it's done on a minor-league level. Trainers will make false comparisons, judgments just about silly things. This is the point I made in the seminar—that you have to train the way that you are comfortable training.*

For instance, I know that I am able to teach with humor and teach balance and discipline. I teach physical discipline techniques that can be used in any emergencies, to solve a crisis or for the troubled dog's behavior. I know there is always somebody who will say that it's overboard or that they prefer to use food, or another methodology. I'll tell you a little secret, I don't teach food well. I've tried. I think there is a point in really looking at yourself, as a trainer and asking "What do I teach well?" Can I "get away" with getting people to discipline? With some there is always the temptation that they will go overboard, but I don't think so, not with the reports I have gotten back. I do not know how to teach food training. I know the principles, the underlying ethos, but I have not had the success I wanted to have. I don't have the necessary temperament I need to do that.

ID: I think that a really good teacher is the best pupil. Someone who is teaching, and really is a good teacher, they are actually learning more than the pupil, but realizing the things you are good at and are bad at. I have found that one silly puppy or one aggressive dog or one owner could teach you so much in a session about the limitations of your methods. I also say to people that I'm just not good at this. If you want to learn real professional heeling, I'm not the person.

If you want to learn to teach a dog not to be stressed around other dogs, I'm really good at that. I think that is really important. We think to be a really good dog trainer you have to be good at all these things. You have to work with every dog without failures. Many trainers set themselves up for tremendous pain and failure because they have to drop out. They beat themselves to death with it. You know, we are not perfect, we try to be as good as we can and then to expand our horizons.

JME: *Can you tell me about when you were a little boy? Did you have dogs and were they your dogs or your parents' dogs? For instance, I think that if someone is raised with dogs, they approach training differently, very warmly in other words but perhaps giving the dog control at heart-rending moments. I have a deprived background in terms of owning dogs—my first dogs were the monastery dogs—only now I do have a Dalmatian pal. I had a very poor attitude toward dogs early on. I remember once when I was seven I took my mother's fox stole (women still wore such things back then) and wrapped it around a roller skate. Then I shoved the skate out onto the street and yelled "Look out for my dog!" I now know I was playing loss out in a childish manner—we had just euthanized a dog. Did you have any similar experiences?*

ID: I guess I had a very animal-rich childhood. I grew up with animals, surrounded by animals. I grew up on a farm. We had farm dogs and we had pet dogs. They were my father's dogs and there was no suggestion that these were the childrens' dogs. I made a promise to myself that I would not get a dog until I got a house.

JME: *Were these dogs for work on the farm?*

ID: Mainly they were either ratter-like terriers or retrievers for hunting and that sort of thing. Both my father and grandfather were very good with rifles and very good with shotguns. I was a terrible embarrassment to both of them since I never could hit anything if it was moving. If it was staying still like a target, I was very good at that. When they had wings and legs and moved I wasn't any good at hitting them. Which annoyed the dogs as well. My first introduction to dog behavior was that they were annoyed at me. They wanted to retrieve and there was never anything to retrieve. I did have the luxury, as well as being surrounded by cows and dogs and cats, of my father and grandfather. My father and grandfather were exceptional in terms of their animal training skills, their son and grandson training skills. I rank them so highly in terms of influences in my life.

Probably the two of them pushed me more in the direction I went as a vet than as a dog trainer. It was, I think, a very privileged upbringing. I don't see many kids having that these days. It was so normal it was ridiculous. I lived on a farm. I spent most of my days out in the fields, always with the dogs, digging holes in the mud and looking at critters and things like that. I spent most of my days out in the fields, quite safely, and then I would come back home. It was just so normal.

JME: *Were they happy when you decided to become a veterinarian?*

ID: I think my mother decided I would become a vet. I don't think I actually made the decision. She decided when I was four that it would be nice, since we were farmers, that one of us would become a vet. Since I was the animal child, she decided I would be the vet. It wasn't until I was at vet college that I actually realized, what am I doing here?

JME: *I think I was at the monastery, I decided that I would be a monk. It used to be, in large Catholic families that you offered up one or two to God. We had 11 kids, a big litter, so we could afford to give back to God!*

ID: So you were the sacrificial offering?!

You know, I never got a dog until I was in my thirties, myself. Although I did spend a lot of time with my father's dogs and my grandfather's dogs, there was no question that these were their dogs and I was looking after them. One of the hardest things for me, and the landmark in my life, occurred when my parents were on holiday and a dog got very sick. I had to make the decision to euthanize it. That was a very hard decision to make. I was about 15 at the time. I have an elder brother and an elder sister, but the decision was left to me, the 15-year-old, to make. That wised me up and made me realize what owning a dog was. There is this very special relationship between dog and human that we can't describe until it happens to us. There I was, making the decision to euthanize my father's dog but it was just so sad because the decision was made by me.

JME: *It is a vulnerable age, 15. It is really very difficult in itself, and then to have to make such a decision—whew! But I think this forces us to grow up, really. You see the vulnerability of the bond between dogs and men. They just don't live as long as we do and you got hit by that at an age earlier than most people.*

ID: I can remember the day my parents came back from Sweden. I rushed out to say hello; they had been away for two weeks. Of course, the first thing I told my dad was that we had to euthanize the dog. He began to weep. Seeing him cry, realizing that I had

143

made him cry—it was a complete role reversal. Like a son was taking responsibility for the father. It was a very dramatic point in my life. But he was very good about it; he said she was a good dog and she lived a good life. She was very old.

JME: *In Anglicized cultures, like America is to a degree, men withhold feelings and don't show feelings. I'm sad that he cried. I'm sad about the dog but it is still refreshing to hear that.*

ID: When I was still a veterinary student I was working and I can remember this day like it was yesterday. I was a student. You have to see a practice before they allow you to really practice your expertise or lack of it, on animals. I was in the clinic and this 60-year-old man came in with this English Shepherd and he was carrying him in a blanket. With him was his 90-year-old father. As for the dog, everything was going. The liver didn't work, the heart wasn't going, the lungs had filled up with fluids. The dog was on the way out. The vet said, "Well, we are just going to have to euthanize him." The owner came up and his father came up and they hugged the dog and they said goodbye to the dog. I held the dog and we euthanized it. It was strange, the heaviness as it dropped. I was holding the dog and I noticed that the grandfather started crying, this 90-year-old man. The son went over to comfort him, and then *he* starts crying. I was quite young then, about 19. I had not seen two men crying together. I started to sniffle and then the vet, he was a big strong man, he started crying. It was a small room, with a dead dog, and four men crying. That was very touching. I remember it like it was yesterday.

JME: *It shows the power of the bond. It shows compassion, sorrow, and dignity. The dignity of death.*

Do you think it matters that you have an English accent?

ID: No, I don't think that is important at all, but it is a tremendous asset. I do actually tone it down so people will understand what I am saying.

JME: *Well, I think you have to, for Americans. It's like when I see Margaret Thatcher on TV; she has such a thick accent, I have a problem.*

ID: I know. You wonder where the plum pits are going to go and where the trees will grow. I was just good at speaking, since I was a kid. I could not act, if I had lines. If I had lines to say I would get nervous. It was difficult. But if I was put onstage I could just do my thing. The first thing I ever did as an entertainer was magic. That is really what giving a seminar is all about, you are relaying information but in a better way than books or videos. So you try to add more in-depth understanding to motivate people. My mother said my first appearance on a stage was the most embarrassing day of her life. Every trick that I did, flopped—such as the egg in the handkerchief. You hit the egg with a hammer and it is meant to be okay when you undo the handkerchief. My egg was broken on the stage. She put her head into her lap and her hand over her head and I just carried on. I said, "That one didn't work, so let's do the next one."

Therefore lecturing without a script has always been easy for me. Even so, I have always done an awful lot of work in terms of looking at people—listening to people that are good and that can catch an audience. For instance, I was listening to you this morning. I was enraptured and giggling away and I saw a couple of skills you have that I don't. But now I have them because I have seen you do them. One is you have a very dramatic pause and it is a very good attention-getter. You start a sentence and three words into the sentence you pause and just take a pause, at which point every head in the audience looks up at you. It is a very subtle and sophisticated way to get attention. I am going to try that out in my next lecture. I look for a lot of skills in all the TV programs we have chatted about. These infomercials—I look at the people there because we are really trying to sell a product. It's a new way to train.

JME: *We do have to "sell" this. For the benefit of all the dogs that are being killed every day. Also to prevent ourselves from being regulated by inappropriate means. But not everyone can lecture effectively.*

ID: I think for a beginning trainer the first thing I would say is, let's differentiate between our dog training skills and our lecturing skills. They are completely unrelated. You may be really good at one and not the other. You may be good at neither. You can also take another, conciliatory approach: "Can we, out of this discord, get together some kind of unity that is better than what you knew as an individual?" By interacting with other people who agree with you, but especially with those who disagree with you, it makes your thinking a lot more sound.

JME: *About writing: You have a monthly column in* Pure-Bred Dogs— American Kennel Gazette. *You are producing books and pamphlets. How do you write? What would you suggest to others who want to get involved in dog writing? You must realize, of course, that as President of the Dog Writers' Association of America, I am honor-bound to promote good dog writing. I know you want to encourage it also—any advice?*

ID: I have much to share here. For years and years it was the hardest thing. I am a terrible writer. I mean awful. It took so much effort. I think of the inscription in my puppy training manual: My English master told me point blank, "Dunbar, you could never write, you can't write now, and you will *never* be able to write." In many ways he hit the nail on the head. I worked at it and worked at it, but my style was very stilted.

Then came along computers. I really like computers better than typewriters. I have a random stream of consciousness, which is good. I have a logical thought process, which is awful. Basically, I take a computer and I take a couple of lines from my own mind—the hardest organism to train, harder than a dog, harder than a dog's owner. One teacher says to pick the best thing you do in life or your worst vice or whatever it is, and if you have a task to do, just do it for 10 minutes and reward yourself. So I decided to write. I will make a cup of coffee and go down to my computer and I will not sip my coffee or light a cigar until I have written one page.

JME: *This is interesting. I have a slightly different method but I also do a reward method. Or I just figure God will punish me if I don't write!*

ID: Basically, I remember when I first did this I wrote something like: "Now is the time for all good men to come to the aid of their party, the party, the dog, the puppy, *the puppy party...*" This was the very first thing I wrote. I then wrote nine pages nonstop; my coffee was cold, and I had not lit my cigar. That was it; from then on writing came easily. I just took the stream of consciousness and then went to a good editor. They are ruthless in pulling it together.

JME: *Would you like to tell us what kind of computer you use? It may sound stupid, but sometimes it makes a difference.*

ID: Yes, I will tell. It is kind of a funny story. I had two computers, both English: an Osborne, which was the first portable, and an Abstract. In one day they both went down, which means all my records, all my writing, all my mailing labels of doggy contacts were hidden on CPM, which nobody even knows what it means anymore. I had to convert it to MS-DOS, then I had to convert the MS-DOS to Mac, to even access the past workings of my brain. When I return from my next trip I am buying an IBM clone—a 486, now extremely cheap, incredible memory as well as incredibly fast.

JME: *What do you think is your special gift?—do not beg off on this question, because in the answer could be help for others—what do you think you bring to dog training that is special to you, and that you share well with others?*

ID: I think probably as a cheerleader. I just look on myself as a cheerleader—a motivator—whether it is in the class scenario or teaching a seminar. I think the information of the instruction is better presented in other media, like the written word, or video is very effective for dog training. I think that the owners really know what you want them to do. The question is, can you get them to do it? I guess I like to rally people around, motivating them, like creating a myth; I guess that is what it is.

Creating almost a situation where people want to belong: They want to do this. It is kind of like in dog training, when you teach the dog what 'sit' means, and the next step is to teach the dog *why* it should do it. That solves a lot of problems. Right there the dog knows, "Hey, I sit and get to be on the couch, or if I sit, you will feed me dinner." I apply that to people: Why should they be here? Why should they be training their dog? Why should they come to a seminar? A lot of information is given out at the dog training class. A lot of information is given at a seminar; no one can take that all in unless they have it in a book with an index to reference. To me a seminar is like a rallying group, like these pyramid sales groups where they get together and say, "Salesman of the month is," and everybody cheers.

JME: *When I came in on the fifth day, I caught the electricity that was still in the air with the participants from the four days of the seminar. One of them said it was like a shot in the arm. People need so much encouragement, and they deserve it.*

ID: I want them to realize that training is like a drug, and if I can get you hooked on it, my problems are solved. I do not have to motivate you anymore. You will *beg* me to tell you how to do it.

JME: *I also noticed that when you did rally them, even if individuals, for whatever reason, had a lack of immediate response, you did not stop. There was a whole atmosphere of "Come on, we can do this, this is not that hard, we can do it, you can do it," which I thought was terrific. Not everyone has that gift. Some people are more in the didactic realm of teaching hard-core, A-B-C type of information.*

ID: I think there is room for A-B-C methodological types of trainers, but there are other types of trainers also. We have the motivators— the direct opposite. I guess in terms of special gifts with animals, I think the best skill I have is taking a nervous dog or a really active or rambunctious dog and calming it down, or an aggressive dog and gently taking the aggression away. People may look at you and say you have a "way with dogs," how do you do that? The dog is growling and lunging at the other dog and you take him and he stops. These are God-given skills. One of the dog owners asked me if I watched myself handling the dogs in my dog training video. I said of course I had. He said, well, when you handle a Malamute you handle it differently than any other breed. You hug it and your hands are constantly, rhythmically moving. I looked at the video and I thought, isn't that interesting. This is a God-given gift. But

147

nicely, it's a skill you can teach to other people when you know what it is yourself.

I think many trainers have a gift but they don't know how to teach to others because they don't know what they are doing. When I realized that, I would teach them—gentle hands on the dog, calm it down, calm it down.

A wonderful illustration of that is: A famous dog trainer, Barbara Woodhouse, had this technique in which you place the dog in a down-stay by taking the second finger and scratching the dog on the brisket really gently. On one of her TV shows, this owner had a Golden Retriever and the owner was scratching the dog using the index finger. Woodhouse slapped his finger and said, "No, not *this* finger," showing the index finger, "but this finger," showing the second finger." It was very funny on American TV. What she didn't convey were two essential points: that to keep a dog in the down-stay you should pet it low and it will sink into the petting; to keep it in a sit-stay, pet it on the top of its head and it will rise up. The other missed aspect: When praising a dog in a stay, you do not give a yell—"Yoooohooo *good* stay." You *gently* pet the dog as praise.

It was very confusing for the owner to remember which finger to use. She taught method instead of teaching the underlying reason. Many trainers are so incredible in training dogs. I will give them that. They are better than I ever will be. But the question is, do they know what they are doing to get the results? Because if they do not know what they are doing, they cannot teach it to others. Sometimes I get irritated because students can't follow directions, but it is usually my fault. If we can't teach someone, shouldn't we change the way we give instructions? It can be humiliating but it teaches you so much. You realize that you are meant to be the teacher and if the pupil doesn't learn you are responsible. Learn how to teach. You should judge yourself by the same standards you are using to judge your pupils.

JME: *So it will be the tough clients, the tough class participants, who will really teach you.*

ID: The failures are successes, because if you want to look at failures and mistakes you will learn so much. But when you are teaching someone who is going to listen to you, it is dynamic. It is explosive. You teach something and they learn so quickly—that is the reward.

We have to acknowledge that we will always have a bunch of people who will not be too good at dog training and a bunch of people who are really good at it. What we will really need to do is spend more time with those who do not grasp it quickly. One success equals one failure. So you fail with a person. Learn from it.

Don't fail with that type of person again. So what if you fail once; you have these successes over here. Let's judge ourselves representatively and not get into this routine of taking the good for granted and bitching at the bad.

This is what people do with dogs. The dog does a straight front in obedience and they say "finish" but if he does a crooked front they say "SIT STRAIGHT!" They take the good front for granted, but for the crooked one they are going to get all over the dog's case. We do this with our pupils and we do this with ourselves. That to me is the most important thing here, I think. You made the point here today—unless you are motivating and training yourself and assessing yourself and you have good confidence and point of view about your own abilities, you ain't no good to anyone if I may speak American for a moment! You will not be a good dog trainer if you are not secure in what you do and how you feel about *yourself*. It will reflect on your work and you will do a bad job. To make this relevant to people, you will kill off dogs. You will kill dogs if you do not look after yourself first. You have to praise yourself, pat yourself on the back, evaluate yourself representatively. Then I think you can be a good dog trainer. And then you will be in the field 25 years instead of burning out at seven.

Chapter 19

Dr. Myrna Milani

Myrna Milani received her Bachelor of Science degree from Capital University in Columbus, Ohio in 1968. In addition to the tutoring duties inherent in her membership in German and Dean's List honorary societies, she routinely did volunteer work with physically, emotionally, and mentally disadvantaged children in the Columbus area. Following her graduation from the Ohio State University College of Veterinary Medicine in 1972, she remained at the University as a full-time academic advisor to the freshman and sophomore students in the pre-veterinary curriculum.

In 1973, Dr. Milani was nominated for an *Outstanding Young Woman in America* award. It was also in that year that she moved to New Hampshire and entered private veterinary practice at the Cheshire Animal Hospital in Keene, New Hampshire. Initially her work included both small animal medicine and larger animals; however, she ultimately focused on the relationship between humans and animals as it affects the behavior and health of both. Because of this interest and the emergence of the human/animal bond as a valid and measurable adjunct to human and veterinary health, Dr. Milani wrote four books for the general public: *The Weekend Dog* (Rawson and Scribners, 1984), *The Invisible Leash* (New American Library, 1985), *The Body Language and Emotion of Dogs* (Wm. Morrow, 1986), and *The Body Language and Emotion of Cats* (Wm. Morrow, 1987).

The Invisible Leash and *The Body Language and Emotion of Dogs* were voted the best in the category of Dog Behavior and Psychology, and *The Body Language and Emotion of Cats* best in the category Cat Psychology, Behavior and Training, by the editors of *The Readers Catalogue*, which lists the 40,000 best books in print. *The Body Language and Emotion of Dogs* has also been used as a textbook for college courses in the human/canine bond and pet-facilitated therapy. *The Week-*

Dr. Myrna Milani and household pals.

end *Dog* and *The Invisible Leash* are still available in Signet paperback editions, and both the *The Body Language and Emotion of Dogs* and *The Body Language and Emotion of Cats* are being released in Quill trade paperback editions this fall. Dr. Milani is currently writing a text on the art of veterinary practice for the University of Pennsylvania Press.

I can't remember exactly why Myrna Milani came to the monastery. She wasn't of my faith, and not particularly religious either. It was, however, immediately apparent that she was deeply spiritual and had embarked on an ongoing quest to learn how, or if, dogs could be integrated into her spiritual quest.

Since I was the guestmaster, it was my responsibility to greet guests, make them comfortable, and then basically leave them alone. Most guests appreciated this, because they often came to the monastery with lots on their mind, and needing to think. They certainly didn't need Brother Job poking in on their personal concerns, and in general, Brother Job didn't, which is probably why the abbot kept me on the job as guestmaster for 10 years.

Something about Dr. Milani, though, attracted me. First, her intelligence; second, her lack of pomposity because she was a veterinarian. Later I learned that she was President of the New Hampshire Veterinary Association, and still later she wrote several sterling books. These were outside the mainstream training trivia efforts; not how-to-train books, but how-to-love books. The most famous has become *The Weekend Dog*.

Because, like the other monks, I was severely restricted in my use of the phone, Dr. Milani and I developed a rich correspondence that has spanned over 20 years. Later after I left the monastery, we were able to enjoy dinners at seminars and veterinary conferences. At my seminars, Myrna would be busy writing notes or listening with what seemed to me to be a look of intense interest. Since she is so knowledgeable in behavioral psychology, ethology, and canine and feline behavior, plus having practiced as a veterinarian for many years, I couldn't (and still can't) imagine what she gets out of my presentations.

Once I asked her. She replied without hesitancy, "Well, the material is extremely interesting, even if I am acquainted with some of it. Also, there's the jokes. You tell great jokes. Also I like to watch the way other women stare at you." We both laughed and then I was rushed to the local hospital for treatment of severe blushing.

Some of this interview is taken from our correspondence—but not all. You will find here a blunt, wise, honest voice, painstakingly critical of her own beloved profession, able to look deeply into the dog owner's psyche, and very much aware of the unity of all life.

THE INTERVIEW

JME: *I suppose we should get the "heavy" stuff out of the way first. For you, that means commenting on your own profession—which I know you love deeply. You're certainly not out there criticizing it, except in very select circles, and I know that right now you are writing a book on* The Art of Practice *specifically for practitioners. I think that's terrific. You're always expanding your horizons. I mean,* The Weekend Dog *would have been enough to secure you a neat niche in the Dog Writing Kennel of Fame. While that book was aimed at guilty owners who just couldn't get over feeling ashamed that they procured a dog they would see basically during evenings or weekends, I also suspect that it was written for those few who, frankly, don't really care that much for their dogs.*

After teaching many veterinary conferences, I find this can be true in that profession as well. I shouldn't be shocked, I guess.

MM: Is there anything worse than a veterinarian who doesn't like animals? My ultimate goal is to teach in the vet schools based on my latest book. I know the toothpaste mentality that permeated the pet food industry since the buy-outs and takeovers would mean fighting a constant battle about product mention in the context of my work.

One of my most favorite professors died recently and that death hit me like what I suspect it must feel like if one were to be subjected to a total vacuum for an instant. There was an overwhelming sense of loss so profound and then all the normal world-air rushed in and it was just a memory. This individual gave me much of my medical philosophy. He was interested in preventive medicine when everyone else was enthralled with wonder drugs and the marvels of emerging technology. He was the source of the 10-80-10 rule that has come up time and time again in virtually all areas of my life. His version says we make things 10 percent better, 10 percent worse with our efforts and 80 percent get better regardless of what we do because the system naturally wants to be healthy. His second major point was that all endeavors have two components: the art and science of technology. Even back in the early 1970s he predicted that medicine was becoming overrun with technicians who had nary a trace of artist within them. How very true that has turned out to be. I think that's what you see in those vacant stares—technicians concerned about picking up some continuing education credits or being seen at a particular meeting. It hurts me so because I feel very strongly about my profession and I see so many I respect getting out of it because of what they see as its following the same dreadful impersonalization as human medicine.

JME: *The crisis within the profession, although it will resolve itself—especially with veterinarians like yourself adding necessary balance—inevitably leads to the deeper question of "Just what are we doing, to cure, to care?" What's up anyway?*

MM: I have come to the conclusion that virtually all treatments are placebos, totally dependent on not only the patients' belief in them, but also that of the person, or system, that prescribes them. I have seen so much evidence of this in medical practice, I gladly champion any treatment my clients believe best for them and their pets. Granted, maybe chiropractic, acupuncture, herbology, homeopathy, voodoo, faith healing, and dancing naked around the tree stump didn't really cure the patient, but then we know 80 percent of them would have gotten better on their own anyhow. The point

153

is that by supporting them, I enable them to come to me for help if their alternative *doesn't* work. Had I criticized their approach and condemned those who espoused it as charlatans, I would have *cut them off* from that support. I am a purpose- rather than process-oriented person. I want to see my patients healthy and happy and that means they pursue a course that seems right and makes sense to them, not me. However, to do this requires a great deal of self-confidence and trust, respect, and love for that other person, enough to allow them to make choices I don't agree with, without undermining that love and respect. That's a tall order and one I couldn't fill until I had the confidence of age and experience.

JME: *Ten years ago, I would have said anything "New Agey" was just bunk and any veterinarian who used or allowed clients to use such treatments—and there are plenty, as you know, present in the behavioral sciences—was just nutzola, Californian, or worse. (It's just a joke, California readers.) Now, I've done a 180-degree turn. I could never understand the point that clients will not come back for standard treatment unless they are "allowed" to have the "control" inherent in trying other treatments.*

MM: Right now, and thanks to you, I'm happy as a little pig putting together my lectures for the Illinois VMA meeting in two weeks. Although my focus is feline behavior, I'm going to try to sneak in a few suggestions regarding the need for some basic philosophical changes among my colleagues. After talking to more than a few pet owners and vets during the past five years, I'm totally convinced that all medical and surgical problems possess a behavioral component as well as a bond component. By focusing all our attention on the diagnosis and treatment of the physiology only, we clinicians make a big deal about "presenting signs and symptoms." Most animals are presented because of what the owner perceives as a change in *behavior*. To them, puking, peeing, coughing, and looking sad are behavioral, not physiological changes. Moreover, these *are* the problems, not the signs or symptoms of it as the medical process maintains. This explains why many clients do not wax nearly as ecstatic as the practitioner when the practitioner spends two days and $350 of the client's money to run tests while doing nothing to stop the behavioral manifestations of illness so as not to louse up those results. If the clinician is so arrogant, he or she can't or won't explain why these tests are being run, or doesn't even ask for permission to run them, we see some very unhappy pet owners. Then there's the paradox summed up by an old New England farmer: "Seems to me the folks in medicine must be getting dumber 'cause it sure takes them a hell of a lot more tests to figure out what's wrong."

JME: *We've talked in the past about human and canine crisis—illness, disease, death in both species. You've always had an interesting take on these topics. You seem to have almost a simultaneous Instamatic camera—a photographic memory of many of your patients. You really get involved. I know some behaviorists and veterinarians just can't. They have to maintain a distance. But is that good? Pure emotionalism won't help one to do one's work either. What's the solution, if any?*

MM: Remember when you wanted to call one of your books something like *Love Is Not Enough?* Lately, I am haunted by the memory of an ancient Poodle brought in to the clinic after midnight by an equally ancient couple. The old dog had been hit by a car, the final assault on a body ravaged by degenerative heart and kidney disease. The owners begged me not to let the dog die, and I promised to do my best. Eventually one inevitably gets to that point when everything that can be done has been done and nothing but waiting remains. As I sat stroking the black curly head I became overwhelmed with the thought, the only time I ever had this thought in all my years of medical practice, that I was the only thing keeping that dog alive. It was my will that kept its heart beating and its lungs inflating. Nothing more or less than me. I became convinced that if I broke the connection with that dog, it would die. Hours later the animal had barely existed on that same subsistence level without change, its fate was decided by nothing more noble than the limits of a bladder stretched to its limits by endless cups of coffee. I went into the restroom and when I returned, the dog was dead.

The second image that haunts me is one from qualitative analysis in which we routinely titrated solutions in the lab. I don't know how familiar you are with the apparatus, but you have a narrow column of clear fluid which you add by drop to the fluid in the beaker beneath it. At some point the fluid added makes the solution in the beaker sufficiently acidic or basic, and it suddenly changes color. If you weren't aware of what was going on, the change would seem most dramatic, miraculous, or senselessly horrible depending on what sort of emotional charge you placed on the change. But if you were aware of the process from the beginning, you knew the change would happen, you didn't know when.

It seems to me a lot of crises in life are like that. When you really take the time to look at them objectively, you discover something so dependent on outside reinforcement it couldn't survive on its own, or a series of insignificant little choices and crises that got lost in the shuffle of daily life. When that's the case, love isn't enough.

JME: *It was terrific to have you at the seminar today, although I can't imagine it's anything but verbal Sominex for someone like yourself.*

MM: (faking snoring) I'll be the judge of that.

JME: *You have said in* The Body Language and Emotions of Dogs *and in other sources that dogs are becoming symbols for humans. Not that they haven't always been, but in an increasingly loveless world, the people/dog attachment can reach neurotic levels. Is this what you mean? It seems to come out in over-permissiveness or rude dominance—give me love, or else!*

MM: Time and time again throughout your presentation yesterday, the phrase from the communion service, "the word made flesh," came to mind. I meant it when I said people are replacing the church with dogs and cats, working through the meaning of self and God via animals. (Have you noticed how very few Christian theologians—actually Western theologians—they don't have to be Christian—say very little about animals save as the human species dominates them?) As a society matures or an individual matures, I think they want to resolve this … dominance versus dominion. Biblically humans were granted dominion, stewardship, over animals, which is quite different from dominance; the problem, however, is that in our egocentric society the concept of stewardship is also distorted to fit the dominance/submission mold—I give, you take; one stronger, healthier, more powerful, intelligent, component taking care of the weaker, intellectually inferior component, rather than a mutual sharing, a communion, the somehow real manifestation of spirit in the flesh.

JME: *Some of this is what the West Africans call "Deep Talk" about animals and it's certainly more refreshing, and, I think, ultimately more helpful for experienced trainers or budding ones to hear it. Yet, training is a business, not just a vocation, and all sorts of cheap ploys happen in certain arenas. It's all become big business.*

MM: What makes it particularly sad is that animals are big business. Organizations are falling all over themselves to fund various programs and the academics are turning out a lot of rubbish. Some of the studies are so pathetic; at one seminar it was disgusting. One vet told us that we should never look a dog in the eye because we were asking to have our thoughts ripped out. Moreover, it constituted malpractice, negligence, basic bad human behavior to allow owners to do so. All around me people were furiously taking notes on this, people I know own dogs they look at *all the time*. They wouldn't own a dog they *couldn't* look at. But this was an expert talking and she had the real scoop—right from the wolves. So all these trainers, vets, humane workers and others are going to tell people not to look at their dogs because their dogs harbor this secret desire to attack them. However, they will undoubtedly continue interacting with their own dogs this way, telling themselves they can get away with it because they're so much more experienced. What they naively don't realize is that their clients will do exactly the same thing because it's such a natural, integral part of pet ownership. Moreover, having received information from the "expert" they choose to ignore, said expert then becomes diminished in their eyes and everything he or she says becomes suspect. However, because the governing criteria are the statistically valid data and not any applicability, the researchers get their advanced degrees or grant money—which is what it's all about.

JME: *God, you can hear such bunkola at some academic conferences! Suggestions to use clickers, quackers, don't use clickers, don't use quackers, train only as one would train a dolphin, don't train at all, meditate, contemplate on the dog's behavior, cook the dog a steak dinner—you name it, it's out there. If these seminars were free, perhaps I wouldn't feel so bad. But you can rack up quite a bill trying to "broaden" yourself—this is a particular problem for the cash-strapped newcomer who is bewildered by the array of seminar and conference choices.*

MM: I attended a seminar on behavioral problems in dogs and cats given by someone from Tufts whose name escapes me, as does much of what was discussed during the seminar. It seemed every other sentence began "My professor says ..." I began to get the feeling I was attending a division of Our Lady of the Pound. If she didn't have data supporting an answer, she refused to offer an opinion and evidently had had no experience outside the university setting. What amazed me was how she was able to supposedly diagnose and treat behavioral problems with almost no interaction with the owner whatsoever. It was as if she believed all owners and pets were exactly the same except for their specific deviant behavior, which resulted from a predictable set of identical circumstances, much as *E. coli* causes diarrhea or *Pseudomonas* chronic ear infections. Then she applied her rigid, canned behavioral modifications just as one would dispense ampicillin or Tresaderm. Between the inflexibility of her approach and her dependency on a data base generated from animals living under laboratory conditions, I was more than pleased I was sitting next to a good friend who was recording this session for someone else. In such a way I was able to amuse myself by whispering obscenities into the tape.

As if that weren't enough, the real challenge to my education, religion, belief in a Higher Power and miracles came toward the end of the afternoon. Evidently even the speaker was getting a bit tired of non-answering question after question with "I haven't any data on that," because she began to whine. She told us we couldn't expect answers on how to treat this or that problem until there was sufficient data and, golly, *there are only five trained veterinary behaviorists in the country.* At that point I had to be physically restrained.

JME: *Then, there is the problem at such academic conferences of exhibitors hawking their wares. While this rarely impacts on my presentations, I'm sure the drug companies try to gain entry into yours. Recently, I had an experience when I was asked about a certain type of collar. I said that I hadn't had much experience with it, but that to fellow New Yorkers, it appeared to look like a muzzle.*

Since it is often "prescribed" for lunging, wild, or shy, retreating dogs, I failed to see how the perception that the dog was wearing a muzzle would help encourage people to initiate social interaction, precisely in order to "train out" the aggression or shyness. I also added that I found the contraption aesthetically ugly. I thought my comments were balanced and on target, but the sellers of the product didn't. They stormed into the conference hall, abandoning their sacred concessionaire venue, and questioned me severely. Eventually, the moderator stopped it all, but I think really I was dealing with salespersons, don't you think?

MM: Whatever happened to professionalism? It seems to have gone the way of caring and ethics and everything else. What really bothers me is when these detail people perceive their behavior as positive—just doing my job—rather than what it really is: aggressive in the worst sense of the word and obnoxious. I got into a minor situation once and suggested the person arrange for his own room where he could expound the virtues of his product for anyone who cared to hear about it. That way he could have all the time he wanted and I could share all the information I'd been asked to share. I totally agree with you that you have to lay it out to these people in no uncertain terms that you won't have them disrupting your presentation. They see your captive audience as a golden opportunity to hawk their product(s) and will do anything to cash in on it. It is, alas, the new and despicable core of PR.

JME: *The Weekend Dog was such a breakthrough book, so helpful to so many, a twist, an innovation on a social phenomenon that no dog writer had yet tackled. Any new thoughts on the theme?*

MM: We now have that new phenomenon known as the latch-key child or children, those kids whose parent or parents work, who come home from school to the dog. Where I've encountered the destructive chewing are situations when the kids develop attitudes toward the pet as a function of their age. I discovered that quite often the kids and the dog had been very close until adolescence turned the child's attention to homework, MTV, the opposite sex, phone calls. Instead of coming home and spending most of their time with the dog, now there is little beyond that all-too-familiar, tension-generating cheerful homecoming. Then the kids go off to do their thing and poor Fido is left in a state of excitement *interruptus*. To relieve the tension, he zeros in on a heavily scented object—a favorite stuffed toy, a baseball mitt, even a hockey mouthpiece—and chews it to bits. This will have to be addressed, and soon.

JME: *I am so sick of reading headlines like PIT BULL GOES ON RAM-PAGE, or BITING FIEND TERRORIZES NEIGHBORHOOD—RESIDENTS HELPLESS AND FLEE IN TERROR! Of course it is a problem, and what we need are not breed-specific laws but strictly enforced dangerous dog laws. After all, a small Yorkie can inflict just as much damage to a kid's face, not to mention a grown man's anatomy, if he just aims or jumps high enough. This will remain a growing problem. Any light at the end of the tunnel?*

MM: Biting dogs are, for the most part, a human problem. Have you ever noticed how many of the homes that sport "Beware of the Dog" signs are places you wouldn't want to visit anyhow? Consequently, reducing the vicious dog population requires a change in human thinking. Although accomplishing such would appear to be impossible, I do see one light in this darkness, one that comes from a rather unlikely source: We are now a population of cat owners, i.e., there are now more cats than dogs in this country. True, we can attribute this to change in lifestyle, but cats are sufficiently different from dogs that those who can't have a dog are not apt to get a cat unless they are willing to accept the cat's differences. One dodges cleaning out a litter box and enduring certain obscure behaviors unless one feels one has something to gain. The way I see it—perhaps idealistically so—is that all the current Pit Bull flap is merely the last hurrah of those who see man as a superior force in the interaction with animals. The idea that one can exert "good" forces to shape or eliminate the "bad" forces now strikes more and more of us as too simplistic. After spending two years dealing with the New Hampshire legislature, I came to appreciate the full implication of animal-related legislation. When I first got involved, I was seeing certain, what I considered valid, laws passed as all there was to it. However, as I traveled through the hallowed halls of politics, I discovered that animal legislation is in and of itself most symbolic; i.e., animal legislation lends itself very nicely to other purposes, such as the advancement of certain people and/or their political goals. These may have absolutely nothing whatsoever to do with the animal legislation. You would be amazed at the totally unrelated legislation that wound up as "footnotes" to some animal-related legislation.

What has all this to do with cats? Owning cats demands that we be at least willing to recognize that some things that are different aren't necessarily wrong. That type of thinking immediately makes us more liberal; we find ourselves questioning those who say all Pit Bulls are vicious, or that all of anything fits a given mold. Anyone who owns a cat knows that such glittering generalities simply do not exist outside the artificial environment of the lab—most certainly not in the real world.

JME: *I like cats too, but it's hard for me to get excited about this as a chance to save the non-biting dogs out there. But in terms of the biting ones, the sociological rise in cat ownership might really reflect a frustration and a desire for safety that dog nuts just don't get. One solution to the problem has been the institution of the Canine Good Citizen Test (CGC), which was pooh-poohed earlier on and then gained this tremendous acceptance. Now the idea has been expanded to include certification by different groups for active trainers.*

I have been heavily involved in one such entity, but there are ups and downs. I recently quit, in fact. What are your thoughts, coming from a profession that is highly regulated and professionally ethical? Enclosed are some brochures from various organizations. The main one I am involved with is consumed with in-fighting. Much of the squabbling concerns who should certify whom. It has all been very disturbing and I am essentially now out of the process. This is not just happening to me, but all over the country. Some of the objectors seem more interested in eating than training.

MM: I found the certification concept sound and the brochure very professional, so it would seem that the troublemakers find this bothersome. It surprises me, nonetheless. I would have expected these people to come out of the woodwork during the Reagan/Bush years, but then maybe they did. Maybe the reason they're being so obnoxious now is because they see the handwriting on the wall.

Should you fight it/them or not? If you enjoy it, then I'd say go ahead. But if you don't, forget it. We have a brave new world in which animals have become exceedingly potent symbols, often of power and Messiahdom, which are merely different ways of saying love. Consequently, you can't reason with these people and fighting them takes on all the characteristics of a holy war. As I'm sure I needn't tell you, such confrontations are often more brutal and bloody than your standard military operation. Frankly, I have no stomach for it. You've got 35 certified people out there. It seems to me that if they feel the program is valid as it exists independent of the board, then they should be willing to speak up for it. Let's face it, you're up against a woman with a major chip on her shoulder, and all those who embrace food training and electronics are making a very powerful statement about self-image and love. *They can't imagine that even a dog would want to do something for them unless they bribed it or shocked/forced it.* When you and your committee come along and say dogs will learn to do things because they want to please others, that flies right into the face of these people's beliefs. Because they lack the self-confidence to trust their love for others or others for them, it rankles when someone suggests—and perpetuates the idea—that such could be true. It seems to me that the lesson that love simply is simply a gift one can neither earn nor lose is what's at stake here. For those who want to believe they can force or bribe another to love them, such a statement is most threatening. Thus the position of your committee violates the foundation of the lady's personal philosophy. You may see yourself fighting for the perpetuation of a sound and logical system, but she might see its continued existence as a proof that her most intimate beliefs about herself, which she projects on dogs, are wrong.

JME: *That reply went deeper, and was more helpful than expected. So let's move to our last topic which is even more difficult. It's death. Most veterinarians have secret thoughts on this topic, and only those with accompanying behavioral insights seem to have something really sensitive to say. In each of my books, even dating back to the monks' book* How to Be Your Dog's Best Friend, *I wrote about it. And we've talked about lost friends, many, many times. Of course there are Elisabeth Kübler-Ross, John Bradshaw, all those people who teach us to accept and move on (sometimes I think they really want us to "move on" to their next book ...).*

MM: In terms of Kübler-Ross, I do think her five steps are most valid, but I expect that Elisabeth would now add a sixth—joy. It is not enough that one accepts what is occurring in one's life. One of the problems I have with the Alcoholics Anonymous credo is the belief in the "sleeping demon" within one, just waiting for one to botch up, to overwork, to wander into a bar, to yield to temptation. I simply can't buy that, perhaps because I'm such a coward. If there's going be something living in me, buster, it sure as hell ain't gonna be no demon. It's going to be, and is, God Him/Herself because my body is, first and above all, a temple where love dwells and from which love radiates. And if there are, or at some time will be, cancerous or other unsound inhabitants, they will not be demons, but merely that God/love in a different form. It will be my choice to remodel my temple to meet my needs because I know I am loved and I love totally and without reservation. There are and will be no demons within me because I don't want them there. I don't need them and I don't feel their presence necessary to fulfill my purpose here.

JME: *But people feel so sad, so cheated by their dog's death. They can't make the human connections with the grief "process." Nobody listens. They get into real pain. I guess it has to be dealt with, ultimately alone, the loss of any dear friend, human or canine. You are alone in the night with it, and baby, that's it. Maybe you have a friend who understands. I know I do.*

MM: I know there's a lot of New Age as well as religious garbage out there relative to love, and yet to me the most powerful aspect of it was noted by no one more unlikely than Machiavelli in *The Prince.* What he said, and what is backed up by both physiology and religion, as I believe your own perusal of the Bible during your last days at the monks' proved, is that fear and love cannot coexist. It's like trying to blow out air and defecate at the same time, a less than elegant analogy but a technique that is routinely used to keep women in delivery from trying to expel the infant too soon. *So whenever the fear sneaks up on you, do what I do. Find that little corner of yourself that for some strange and beautiful reason we share, and go there just as I have so many times lately. And there you will find love. Now and forever. I promise.*

Part Four

—

ON DOG WRITING,
AND AN ANNOTATED
BIBLIOGRAPHY

Chapter 20

—

How to Avoid Dog Writing

Here are some tips on how to avoid writing about dogs, or for that matter, about anything. The first mistake is to believe the maxim of Thomas Alva Edison, who said that genius is one percent inspiration and 99 percent perspiration. Any writer who has written one word knows that this is patently false. Writing is one percent inspiration and 99 percent *procrastination*. With the exception of wordsmiths like Mordecai Siegal (the Joyce Carol Oates of dog and cat writing—and a damn good writer, I might add), most of us like to hedge our bets with our dog writing. Maybe we'll write, but maybe we won't.

Like a dog burying the proverbial bone in the backyard, we bury ideas hoping that they will still be fresh when we decide to write the dog book to end all dog books. We engage in various evasions, subterfuges, and even outright self-defeating ploys to get out of writing. We then look to other writers to tell us how to write.

At the symposium on dog writing given by the Dog Writers' Association of America a few years ago, I had the appalling nerve to offer to present a talk entitled, "How I Write." Participants listened in rapture as I described how I triple-space and edit. It was a rather disgusting exercise in self-revelation. Thank God nobody was paying for my speech. When we have a real lag of material in the newsletter, or when I want to be officially censured by DWAA, I will reproduce that speech.

For now, let's talk about how not to become a dog writer or get any dog writing done whatsoever, because strangely enough, reverse psychology often inspires as well as motivates. Here are my tips:

1) *Exhibit* Get that RV and slap on the obligatory decals pertaining to your breed/group/self/political beliefs/food preferences. Sure, you want to be a dog writer, but this way you can do both. Hubby or wife will drive the RV from show cluster to show cluster while you will be cheerfully and creatively typing away on the PC in the rear. Sure!

Instead, here's what will happen. You will power up the PC, or worse, try to balance a typewriter on a rickety "table," your driver will hit a sharp curve—everything, including you and your machine, will shift. Not one word will get typed because dog Exhibit A is now whining full throttle and Exhibit B has puked within and without his cage. It's not a normal puke. This will require a stop—a paper towel and spray stop. Does this have anything to do with your dog writing? Well, yes, everything and nothing—precisely, nothing, because not one word has been typed. The show went well. You even won. Not one word of yours has been published.

2) Volunteer.   Preferably everywhere for every doggie cause. After all, you're collecting vital information, even though when you see those "Increase your Vocabulary!" ads on television you really think maybe, just maybe, you should apply. Your animal shelter experience will certainly provide you with new verbs, but any adjectives you may become acquainted with will quickly become inadequate due to the carnage you've seen. Yet, you feel you have to write as fast as you possibly can in order to stop that very carnage. Hurry! Write! You're not writing fast enough! Animals are dying—and you're their only hope. You are their Messiah. You'll break, probably over a typewriter, and write *zilch*.

Don't get me wrong; there is everything laudable about volunteering to help in dog-related organizations. It's just that very few individuals can balance the demands of voluntarism in too many organizations with the demands and concentration needed to write. Balance is the key. It's everything.

3) Teach seminars.   This is a nifty ploy to pull on oneself. This will be your reasoning: "Well, perhaps I'm not that great of a writer, but I know how to run a class and do a little public speaking. People seem interested in what I have to say about dogs. So, I'll simply tape my talks and transcribe them into articles or chapters." Unfortunately, it doesn't work that way. First, the transcription will read untrue in print. You will try to clean it up. But every noun is off, every verb is somewhat inaccurate, and every adjective rotten. This is not writing. It is transcription. The only possible hope is to employ a secondary source (essentially, a ghostwriter) who can make sense of it all. But then you are not the writer, are you? Someone else is. And you probably had to pay that person to prop you up as a fake writer! Get real!

4) Teach your dog to retrieve, or get a retriever (any breed) or a Dalmatian. Now you're really doomed not to write a word, unless you enjoy typing with one hand and throwing a ball with the other. Even the output of a genetically proficient writer is cut in half once one hand is out of commission. Remember, as much as we love our dogs, they will not write one word for us. Not even at gunpoint. Dog writer's rule: Do not play with your dog while you are writing about him! You will only teach him to sabotage your writing since he secretly thinks you are penning something critical about him or his behavior anyway.

5) Write one book or article and convince yourself you've told it all. This is the ultimate self-subterfuge. Since the piece you just published was so excellent, how could anyone expect anything more of you? You are now excused from writing another word. Besides cheating your own intelligence, since you have much more to say (and you know it), don't expect any article payments or royalty checks to continue to roll in. Nevertheless, you won't have to write another word. You're on top. You've said it all. Dog writers who employ this ploy usually try novels next. The trouble will then be that in their evasion of dog writing they are well acquainted with ploys, not plots. Novels thrive on the latter. Another dog writer bites the dust. Is a novelist born? Better to alternate the two genres, if you can.

6) Get sick. This is a foolproof mechanism for avoiding typing one word. Claim neuropathy of the fingers. Get a good walker; the aluminum models are the lightweight choice these days, I understand. While I jest, getting sick is a routine maneuver writers use to avoid their job of communicating. Drink is another: Consider Hemingway, Proust, F. Scott Fitzgerald, Lillian Hellman, or just do a secret stakeout at your local liquor store and see how many writers show up— specifically non-writing writers. As my Slavic grandmother used to say, "Avoid the drink—it leads noplace."

WRITE OR FACE YOUR PLIGHT

So there you have six of the top ways to escape dog writing. Are you "guilty" of any of these excuses? If yes, why? Throw out excuses, that's my advice. Adopt a production rule for yourself—say, five to ten pages of writing a day. Now, get to it. Make everything and everybody else take a back seat. Remember, sometimes writing requires fighting—fighting down psychological side-step routines, descaling one's love of myriad activities that are evasions from writing, and finally keeping your focus on the written word flowing out of your mind and experience onto paper and into the minds of others who read your work. You want to write, otherwise you wouldn't be reading this chapter. Don't deprive yourself of something you want to do.

Ask yourself: What's the reason you want to write? You know you have something to say. You feel you have the talent to say it publicly. Of course you love dogs. But do you love to write? The one love can lead to the other. It is a permissibly adulterous relationship, in a sense. For the truly called, everything else is an evasion. Write!

Chapter 21

—

My Own Book Sale, or Last Bra Sale at Bloomie's

Recently, I decided to move from my Upper East Side condo to a simpler rental in the Village, or somewhere where writers and other weird types outnumber investment bankers, old-money widows, or mayoral employees. (I live near Gracie Mansion, the only real "house" in Manhattan—yard, swing set, the whole deal). Besides, I consider the neighborhood boring.

To simplify such a move, many a Manhattanite will mount a household sale. In my case, this included warehousing or selling a literal wall of dog books. Most of these I had purchased over the years, but I had accumulated some by serving as book reviewer for *Dog Fancy* for five years, and after leaving that job, review copies continued to flow in. In fact, while I did review briefly for *Horse Illustrated* and *Cat Fancy*, suddenly titles about gerbils, snakes, and monkeys started to arrive. For one moment, I thought I must be Michael Jackson; otherwise why would I be receiving such stuff?

Of course I didn't return any of it, although I did call the snake book editor and tell her that I really wasn't interested, but the rest accumulated. I yanked out the dog books I was interested in, lined up everything else according to species and title and did some on-phone advertising about a "private sale" of well-titled animal books. I invited five people for a sedate cocktail-look-and-see party; no pressure to buy. The group arrived punctually, seemingly thrilled to be given access to my library. Cocktails were consumed, and serious searching began. The silence was almost monastic.

Because these were serious book collectors, and in some cases, serious writers, the selection process was slow. This was immediately noticeable. Here's what I consider the experts do at a book sale—and please remember any Waldenbooks, Barnes & Noble, or B. Dalton is, essentially, an ongoing book sale:

- They looked at the cover carefully, very carefully.
- They immediately turned the book to its *spine*; here is where co-authors often make their appearance—co-authors who are not listed "up front."
- They turned to the editorial blurb information on the front and back inside covers, but if it sounded false or fakey or there was just too much of it, they immediately turned to...
- The table of contents or the index.
- Then and only then did this savvy group flip through the entire book. Usually, at that point, content clarified or condemned, they would make a decision—and often the quality of the photos or the layout of the book sealed their idea as to whether they wanted the book or not. What's the point here?

Well, "judge what you buy before you buy it" sounds simple enough, but more deeply, as a writer, if you had any training in expository writing in college or high school, remember what you were taught about evaluating a book—basically it's the above procedure, with your individual flourishes, needs, and desires.

For instance, one lover of books on rare breeds was simply "forced" (her term, not mine) to snap up every title in that genre. But others grabbed randomly, as if they were rehearsing for the second, much larger, invited group.

The second "private sale" included invitations to 25 individuals. I had asked participants to bring their own duffel bags, shopping carts, or moving vans to transport whatever they claimed at the sale. While the first group obeyed, and paid, with a minimum of effort, the second tier of trainers definitely showed why they were just that. Instead of examining a book, they would approach me with questions like "What's in this book?" or "Is this book well-written?" Three seconds of educated perusal gave the answer to the first set of buyers, but not to these folks. They wanted *reassurance*, which is so important to the insecure, especially the insecure dog trainer. They would also bend bindings inappropriately, handling the books roughly, as if any writer wouldn't know about "brittle book syndrome" or books over 20 years old. These young writers are out to lunch!!

That's disturbing. If what they wanted, instead, was top quality, time-saving, tight, useful literature or nonfiction on dogs, I would have been thrilled. Instead, I felt like Oprah Winfrey moderating a talk show on which authors are best "guests" and which to invite into your home. Since I do not review on the spot, I told them to make their own decisions. Meanwhile, I hasten to add, the "sale" books were either free or topped out (for deluxe books at $10.00), so money was a minor factor. Lack of critical judgment, especially among younger dog writers, was much more of a revealing factor. Frankly, it was sadly revealing.

The mania, the acquisitory attitude, the obsession to get that one particular title in one's library seemed understandable but somehow frivolous. What are writers if they cannot find their *own* voice, their *own* way, their *own* methodology, their *own* special "tilt" in writings or in seminars? Of course research is essential, but so is creative, individual thinking. Otherwise one is not a dog writer but a copycat.

I am glad I had my book sale. I sold a lot of books. I watched some crazed behavior—most of it indicating that the less mature trainers hoped they would somehow, finally, once and for all find the "secret" to dog training that had been hidden for years in some obscure book. All of this taught me mounds about what it is to be a dog writer—it is a profession in which one is idolized, then possibly ignored, and then re-revered.

Chapter 22

City Dog Bashing

There are many ways of owning a dog, and many ways of writing about the experience. Writers often get into a jam because they feel there are words and phrases that they just can't utter on paper—lest the entire fancy rise up in arms. Most often, this problem arises concerning where dogs should live and who should own what dog.

After World War II, it was standard dog writing practice to decry the ownership of dogs in cities. Check the literature; it's all there in black and white. At about this time also, of course, the great exodus from the cities to the suburbs began, and it was decreed that your dog should have an enclosed, grassy yard, hardly any neighborhood friends, and live the so-called easy suburban lifestyle. Dog writers followed the trend, some of them moving to the suburbs themselves. Ironically, many suburban owners now keep their dogs inside half the year because they are terrified of Lyme disease. Meanwhile, city dogs are taken out on leashes and can easily be steered away from likely Lyme-generating patches.

Yet city dogs continue to get bashed in the dog press. Not with the same regularity or moralistic zeal, but often a column comes across my desk chanting the same old chant, "You know, dogs are really much happier in the country." Says who?

First, what does the term "country" mean? I think it means suburbia. I think it means anywhere but midtown Manhattan or the Chicago Loop. I think it means many dog writers have never, and probably will never, have the experience of raising a dog in the city and that they should just shut up and write about what they know—which sure ain't city life.

There is a 14,000-year-old skeleton in storage in Israel. It is a man or a woman (the pelvis was crushed, making it impossible to determine the sex), a member of the Natuftian culture—hunter-gatherers

Enough city dog bashing! Dogs have lived and intermingled in cities for centuries, like this entangled group. Not everyone wants (or can have) the proverbial "country home." (Charles Hornek)

who were probably the first to adopt dogs. The person is embracing a four- or five-month-old puppy. The two skeletons, locked in this embrace, were found under a limestone slab, which was part of a large city in Israel—in fact, one of the largest cities at the time. In short, the concept of dog ownership probably was part of the city genius, an integral part of the urban ethos, as it remains today.

So with the scientific artifacts codified, with the scholarly study complete and filed as to the great benefits city dogs offer their owners, plus the anecdotal reports of trainers like myself (*Evans Guide for Civilized City Canines*), can the remaining writers who down dogs for living in cities please lay off? If you don't like cities, which usually translates into "I don't like filth, noise, different ethnic groups, scrawny trees, etc.," just stay away from any metropolis. Just don't write about what you think life is like for a dog in a city in a negative vein. Believe me, the return of the dog to the cities will continue to happen, and if you proclaim in print that no dog can survive there, you will look rather foolish. They can and do live, happily, I'd add.

I own a rooftop garden in a brownstone. I'm out now, having finished this diatribe, to toss a ball for my rooftop Dalmatian. A 44-story high-rise juts over on the next block. On weekend days we have been known to tease high-risers out onto their balconies to applaud and cheer difficult retrieves. I have one hell of a happy spotted friend. Breeders: Learn which dogs do well in town. Writers: Stop bashing city dogs—they were there first! You wouldn't have a job unless they had infiltrated cities first. Don't ever forget that.

—

Chapter 23

Red Ribbons at Westminster

I had seen the red ribbons on the Oscar awards telecast on many occasions. Then they started to crop up at the Emmys, the Grammys, and other awards shows or special events. I learned later that an actors concern group, Broadway Cares, had begun the tradition of the red lapel ribbon over eight years ago, and that wearing it meant that one was concerned about the world-wide epidemic of AIDS. I suppose most of you know this by now.

So it was with a certain strange sense of relief, gratitude, and acceptance that I viewed so many active dog enthusiasts sporting red ribbons at Westminster. Near the entrance site to the main runway, a table was set up distributing leaflets with attached ribbons that said:

By the end of 1993 there will be millions of men, women, and children infected with a disease that strikes as much terror and pain, paranoia and misinformation in the hearts and minds of mankind as the infamous plague of the Middle Ages. The disease is AIDS. Tragically, within the dog fancy, our own family has been profoundly affected by this disease. In recognition of this crisis we all are facing, the June edition of *Kennel Review* will include our first annual AIDS Awareness Feature. A portion of all advertising proceeds will be donated to a charity to assist in the fight against the AIDS epidemic. The charity will be a fund established for dog people, by dog people. Further details will appear in the April issue of *Kennel Review*. On the outside of this card you will find a red ribbon which has become the symbol of your support for those whose lives have been touched by AIDS. *Kennel Review magazine.*

Well, this was a breakthrough. After 13 years of the AIDS epidemic, and after many closeted and not-so-closeted AIDS deaths within

The Red Ribbons on the handlers (and even on some dogs) at the 1993 Westminster show weren't just for show—but instead expressed a deep sense of loss within the fancy. Hopefully, the several groups dedicated to keeping those with AIDS with their pets until the last possible moment will be able to function vigorously as long as they are needed. (photo A. Kaplan, used courtesy POWARS, NYC)

the fancy itself, the fancy was finally "getting it." Great thanks are due to *Kennel Review*, which sponsored the ribbon action. Millions saw top handlers wearing the ribbons on national television.

Since this is a book about dog training and writing and not about disease, I'd like to offer some writer's tips on how to proceed if you wish to write about AIDS and its impact on the dog world. I have collected this information from the *New York Times* style book, from the press advice given at Gay Men's Health Crisis (GMHC) in New York City, the Alliance for the Arts, and other sources.

First, people with AIDS prefer to be called PWAs—not victims or survivors—just people with AIDS. Calling PWAs "patients" is also inappropriate (although many of them have been more than patient since the PWA is a patient only occasionally, but lives with the disease constantly). Remember, the words writers use shape the thoughts that our readers think, so proper terminology is important.

Secondly, an extraordinary number of PWAs own dogs. While no definitive study has been done, it is significant that several organizations have sprung up coast to coast to keep PWAs together with their pets as long as possible. They are listed as resource services to aid your writing. They will be found at the end of this chapter. The point to realize is that the ratio between PWAs who keep pets is radically higher than the national owner/pet ratio—thus the need for these groups, and for our concern. You can write to the listed organizations for press kits for full information on these groups, the services they perform, how they started, and how they have grown. Perhaps you noticed the short piece in *Pure-Bred Dogs*—about Pet Owners With AIDS Related Service (POWARS), its incredible growth in volunteers, and how they strive to keep PWAs and their pets together until the last possible moment. It was a good piece—another "wake-up" call to the fancy.

Since photographs enhance any article, you should know that POWARS (the group servicing New York City) has a series of stunning, award-winning photographs that are available for reproduction. Most have been done in poster form and contain an incisive message about the AIDS/pet connection. If your editor will not let you use the poster reproduction itself, you may be able to clip off the glossy and simply convert the poster text to a caption.

WE MIGHT AS WELL WAKE UP, FOLKS

Please remember that "denial" is not a river in Egypt—it is a disease in itself that affects others, slows research, and stifles progress. Don't add your voice to the denial of AIDS within the dog fancy by your silence. While I fully realize that many of you do not have an appropriate forum for addressing this issue in print, I also know that many of you certainly do. Just as we've bombarded the media with warnings about parvovirus, Lyme disease, brucellosis, and other maladies that affect our dogs, now we must sound the alert against AIDS—and signify our concern about this disease within the fancy. We have waited far too long. We have lost too much. There are some writers and fanciers who have run out of fingers to count the number of friends they have lost to this dreadful disease. The least we can do to show we care, and that we have hope, is to promote the organizations that keep best friends together.

RESOURCE SERVICES FUTURE SAFE

Estate Planning for Artists in a Time of AIDS is a 35-page free booklet available from The Alliance for the Arts (212 947-6340) or write The Alliance for the Arts, 330 West 42nd Street, New York, NY 10036. This is an invaluable resource book, especially for any writer with AIDS who must secure his work, or any writer in research.

Some organizations that provide press materials to writers and may have pre-cleared photographs available are: POWARS (212 744-0842), or write Steve Kohn, Executive Director, Pet Owners with AIDS Related Services (POWARS), P.O. Box 1116, Madison Square Garden Station, New York, NY 10159.

In Washington, D.C., there is Pets Washington DC (202 234-PETS) or write Pets—Washington D.C., 1747 Connecticut Avenue, N.W., Washington, DC 20009.

In San Francisco you can contact PAWS (Pets are Wonderful Support—for People with AIDS), 539 Castro Street, San Francisco, CA 94114 (415 241-1460).

Chapter 24

Friends

I am sitting on my roof deck on a bright, scintillatingly beautiful day—yes, we have such days in New York City—and thinking about friendship. I am with my best friend, at least in the canine world, my Dalmatian, Sport. He is exhausted after a hard half-hour of rooftop ball chasing, and has fallen at my feet, ball still in mouth, content that his play quota had been met for today. This leaves me free to call a human friend, a fellow dog writer. Luckily, her dog is exhausted also. So we talked—and talked and talked.

Then, another close dog writer friend called and we talked, and talked and talked. In both cases, we talked about what we had read recently in *The New Yorker*, or in *The New York Times*, and I also recall discussing what had appeared in *The Atlantic*, *Partisan Review*, *The New Republic*, and even *The National Review*. Well, I did train William F. Buckley's dogs.

TALK ISN'T ALWAYS CHEAP

The point is, we talked about the art of writing: who wrote what, what we liked, didn't like, style points, layout, thrust, researching of a piece, and all that "stuff" that makes for good writing. In discussing such matters over so many years with these and other writer friends, I like to think that I have become a better writer. Since I have won a few accolades along the writing way, I like to think this is true, but I continue to have serious doubts—thus the ulterior motive in discussing writing with writers is often to bolster self-confidence. I figure, well, so what if that is a motivation? It's probably a good one.

So what is the point of all this? Briefly, I think it's extremely important, if you want to be a good writer, to talk with and hopefully be friends with other good writers. There is a magical exchange that can transpire between writer friends. It has nothing to do with becoming a "clone" of that writer, or plagiarizing, or competing—as long, of course, as you do not participate in any such activities. If you can find a writer/friend, I would advise you to be extremely careful about any copycat activities. I would also advise you to cultivate such friendship at every opportunity.

I can tell you that such friendships are often extremely productive. The comfort and caring expressed between the two friends very often flows out to others—humans and dogs. A good writer is a happy writer, and happy dog writers are not just happy about their dogs, they are happy in their friendships and love relationships. Remember, *we* make our lives happy.

THE SECRET TO SUCCESS

Twenty years "into dogs" and dog writing, I am so often asked, "How do I become a dog writer?" While research, study, literacy, vocabulary extension, and style are important, perhaps they are not of central importance. A friend who appreciates and understands what you are trying to do could be. Dog writers, who certainly outplay many "regular" writers in the loneliness department (and sometimes in self-pity, which some writers think is better than none at all) need to realize the importance of reaching out.

You might not need an agent, and if you do, perhaps you sought one out because you needed an ally in your writing. As long as you understand the psychology behind what you may have done in seeking one out (and possibly paying big bucks to secure one), I think that's fine. On the other hand, if your only writing fan or friend is your agent, editor, publisher, spouse, or dog, you need to expand your writing horizons.

Look around. If you check out the local scene, there are probably a few groups for writers, and they need not be dog writers. Most probably they won't be. Especially in any university town, writing groups will exist. It might mean a drive once a month, but it will give you a chance to share and read your material aloud to an interested audience.

Believe me, the other writer/participants will be fascinated in what you have to share because almost everyone is fascinated with dogs. Give it a try, and in the meantime, look for that special friend who loves dogs and dog writing as much as you. This is, in fact, the core purpose of DWAA, and if we can't see each other as a group as often as we may prefer, we can encourage each other in friendship and in love for each other and our chosen compatriots, our dear dogs.

An Annotated Bibliography

How do you do a bibliography for an eclectic book like this? It's about training, but no one I know wants to read *Pumping Iron*. It's about explaining, and here we could turn to Julia Child or M.F.K. Fisher on food, or practically anybody who explains how to do anything. This will lead us nowhere.

The smartest course is to chart one's own course and sail confidently into your reading career. I've already made my basic contributions. You will find full and specific bibliographies in *How to Be Your Dog's Best Friend* (Little, Brown), in *The Evans Guide for Counseling Dog Owners*, and in the more recent *People, Pooches and Problems* (all Howell Book House). Each has a specialized bibliography.

A CHANGE-OF-PACE BIBLIOGRAPHY

So, as a change of pace, I've included books that train a little and explain a lot, since that's the point of the book. I didn't find too many, which is probably why I got into writing this book. Even the trainers who *do* know how to train, often can't explain it!

The wise writer then snoops out other research sources—like increasingly rare book stores with full pet sections. Of course the AKC Library and its gracious staff can be your outposts. The AKC Library is an invaluable source when you draw a blank elsewhere. The phone number is 212/696-8245.

A word on actually getting dog books—it's often easier just to call the publisher's 800 number and order the titles you want. Many dog people who are not regular visitors to book stores are often shocked that the "Pets" section now resides (25 books in all) under "Nature."

It's all marketing—but store frustration is one of the reasons you have a phone!

Since I've covered my preferences in counseling, training, and problem-dog texts elsewhere, let me caution you about the "other" types of dog books around. Precisely, I mean the type of books that talk "around" dogs, "about" dogs, but never tell you what to do if a dog does anything bad.

Authors of these books do not like to address this topic. Behavior is an abstract concept for them and usually the college dorms they reside in don't allow dogs anyway. The text will sound good, read terribly, and ultimately, you'll realize you're with a research lab author. Get out of it whatever you can. I hope you borrowed it from the library.

Finally, remember as you search for books that are not mundane, please understand that some boring texts *must* be read in the early portion of any dog-related career. Don't fall for texts that look ever-so-unmundane, but are really college Ph.D. theses in book form. Here, you'll get diagnosis without any real help as a trainer.

PUBLISH OR PERISH—STILL THE RULE

"Publish or Perish," the perennial dictum of all the high arts and certainly of all the high sciences, still rules supreme. It facilitates peer review and forces research (usually lab style), but doesn't help one to a career in training and explaining as presented in this book. So, while I can't dictate which books you should read, I can hint at which to avoid. I've done that in the reviews, and believe me, I haven't reviewed all the books I'd liked to have reviewed.

Most of all, keep reading. As my previously quoted grandmother who read for one hour in bed each night before she went to sleep used to say, "My darling, with a book, you are never alone." She was always reading one of those involved Russian novels—too many names for me—but the point was clear.

READ AND YOU ARE NEVER ALONE

The books mentioned here are listed in no particular order, and I would advise perusal at the largest mall or city book store you can find. You don't have to buy a book if it doesn't ring true. Buy smart.

Here's a tried and trusted test used by book reviewers: Read the front and back covers, then the inside jacket flaps. Now read the copyright page (rich with information—tells the year of publication, how many printings, and more). Next read the introduction—by the author, not his background (this usually means the first chapter). Next open up randomly and read ten pages, even out of context. Now, finally, read the last ten pages. Do not impulse-buy anything but an ice cream cone—especially not a dog book. Quality, quality, that's your goal—ask yourself, "Will I refer to this book again?"

Here are some of my current favorites. Needless to say, by the time this book is published, you will have your own. The main point: Take *joy* in your dog reading, *revel* in it, and don't think for one second that we dog writers don't appreciate you. We do, and very deeply so.

Start with *What the Dogs Have Taught Me*, by Merrill Markoe (Viking Penguin, 375 Hudson Street, New York, NY 10014; 1993). I thoroughly enjoyed this book. While only half of the chapters deal with dogs, they are brilliantly, scintillatingly written. Most deal with what dogs think about *us*. Since as a professional trainer I always like to see the tables turned, this was fine with me. The dogs converse with the humans—an excerpt:

> It is late afternoon. Seated at my desk I call for my dogs to join me in my office. They do.
> *Me:* The reason I've summoned you here today is I really think we should talk about something.
> *Bob:* What's that?
> *Me:* Well, please don't take this the wrong way, but I get the feeling you guys think you *have* to follow me *everywhere* and I just want you both to know that you don't.
> *Stan:* Where would you get a feeling like that?
> *Me:* I get it from the fact that the both of you follow me *everywhere* all day long. Like for instance, this morning. We were all together in the bedroom? Why do you both look blank? Doesn't this ring a bell at all? I was on the bed reading the paper ...
> *Bob:* Where was I?
> *Me:* On the floor sleeping.
> *Bob:* On the floor sleepi ...? Oh, yes. Right. I remember that. Go on.
> *Me:* So, there came a point where I had to get up and go into the next room to get a Kleenex. And you *both* woke up out of a deep sleep to go with me.
> *Stan:* Yes. So? What's the problem?
> *Bob:* We *like* to watch you get Kleenex. We happen to think it's something you do very well.
> *Me:* The point I'm trying to make is why do you both have to get up out of a deep sleep to go *with* me. You sit there staring at me, all excited, like you think something really good is going to happen. I feel a lot of pressure to be more entertaining.

183

Bob: Would it help if we stood?

Stan: I think what the lady is saying is that where Kleenex retrieval is concerned, she'd just as soon we not make the trip.

Markoe is co-creator of the "Stupid Pet Tricks" on the David Letterman show, a wildly successful section of the show. This might lead you to think that Markoe is the last person who could train a dog to do anything or explain anything to a human. In fact, she's brilliant at both, and with humor. The book is a smash-out belly-laugh for dog lovers. It will help you train and explain with humor.

Some trainers, in fact, use the "anthropomorphic" techniques Markoe uses to such great comic effect here. I'm not saying, as they say in her own trade, go ahead and steal her lines, but probably you can think up your own. If you're a trainer with humor deficiencies (we've already alluded to how deadly that can be), the book will help. While so many academics are writing endless tomes on how the canine mind works and the subsequent product is literary Sominex or worse, a Merrill Markoe is sudden sun on a rainy day. One more excerpt:

> I *pick dogs that remind me of myself*—scrappy, mutt-faced, with a hint of mange. People look for a reflection of their own personalities or the person they dream of being in the eyes of an animal companion. That is the reason I sometimes look into the face of my dog Stan and see wistful sadness and existential angst, when all he is actually doing is slowly scanning the ceiling for flies.
>
> We pet owners demand a great deal from our pets. When we give them the job, it's a career position. Pets are required to listen to us blithely, even if we talk to them in infantile and goofy tones of voice that we'd never dare use around another human being for fear of being forced into psychiatric observation. On top of that, we make them wear little sweaters or jackets, and not just the cool kind with the push-up sleeves, either, but weird little felt ones that say, *It's raining cats and dogs.*

Then there is a more recent effort called *The Hidden Life of Dogs* (Houghton, Mifflin, Boston) which from my point of view was a pleasure and an absolute hoot. I consider this a first class, well-written book. It got top billing in the *Times* and I found it fascinating.

Author Elizabeth Marshall Thomas claims she doesn't even train her horde of dogs, since they follow the alpha dog's example. Would that such an arrangement worked in every multi-dog household, but then again, one never knows what "training" means to one person or another. But the writing is good and that's such a concern to me, so an excerpt:

> On the other hand, dogs are dependent on people, and it is not always to their advantage. Every day the humane societies execute thousands of dogs who tried all their lives to do their very best by their owners. These dogs are killed not because they are bad but because they are inconvenient. So as we need God more than he need us, dogs need us more than we need them, and they know it.

Watching Out

How much do you watch your dog? A lot, you might say, but the truth is, your dog probably watches you more than you watch it. After all, what else does your dog have to do but watch you? It's not as if it has to go out and earn a living to bring home the dog food. Dogs are great watchers of humans—they know our every move.

There are two books that will help you learn to watch your dog and understand what you see. If you can watch *and* understand, you may not only be well on your way to solving any behavior problems your dog may have, you will also enjoy your dog to the hilt. This is because your eyes will be opened to the infinite variety of a dog's actions and their meaning. That alone is reason enough to own both these books.

Desmond Morris's name might ring a bell with you. He wrote *The Naked Ape*, a controversial book published in the 1960s. This time, in *Dogwatching* (Crown Publishers, 225 Park Avenue, New York, NY 10003; 1987, 192 pages) the renowned zoologist, animal expert, and author of two other books that encourage readers to watch (*Catwatching* and *Bodywatching*) is set on explaining why your dog does what it does.

In fact, nearly every chapter heading begins with "why." Why do dogs bark? Why do dogs howl? Why do dogs invite play? Why does a dog bury a bone? Why does a pointer point? And, the question countless dog owners have been asking for the last 15,000 years: Why do dogs sometimes roll in filth? The answer to the last query is that dogs like to "put on" scents the way we like to put on fancy clothes. Rolling in some putrid substance, like a dead fish, gives the dog a distinct odor that is readily appreciated by other canines, says Morris. I would add only that it also gets the dog a lot of attention from humans who try to wash the offending scent away using baths with fine shampoos and even tomato juice (most dogs love the taste). Sounds like a good deal to me.

Many of Dr. Morris's answers home in on what's in it for the dog—a train of thought that often provides ready answers to complex canine riddles. For instance, you may wonder why your dog is dragging its rump on the ground. According to Morris, it may be trying to release impacted anal glands. Why do dogs pant so much? Well, once you understand that that's how dogs perspire, you can see that there's a lot in it for the dog to pant, pant, pant—and no anti-perspirant made for humans will make a dent!

Dogwatching is a handsome book, tightly written, informative, sometimes wry, but never condescending. Even a small matter like why a dog wags its tail receives a full and insightful treatment. By the way, tail-wagging does *not* necessarily mean that your dog is happy. There are astounding layers of meaning even in tail-wagging. That's what I like about this book: the author's respect for level of meaning, for nuances and subtleties. Get this book, then watch your dog. You'll be amazed at your new understanding of its actions.

If you want to give yourself a double treat, you should also invest in a book by Myrna Milani, a veterinarian whose writing style and economy I have lauded and whose interview appears in the previous section of this book. Her *Weekend Dog* is a favorite for guilt-ridden owners who must work but still want a well-adjusted canine pal. Her *Invisible Leash* helped owners who want their dogs to enjoy off-leash freedom to obtain that goal. Now, with *The Body Language and Emotion of Dogs* (William Morrow and Co., 105 Madison Avenue, New York, NY 10003: 1986, 285 pages), she has penned a book on understanding your dog's body language and thus, your dog's emotions.

Milani discusses the "St. Francis Syndrome," which can mean intervening in all matters to the pet's detriment. Milani says that what we need over our pets is not "dominion." Dominion means *wanting* to care for your dog, *wanting* to educate it, wanting to *dominate* it if necessary. Other authors have called this "stewardship," but I like the contrast between "dominance" and "dominion." Milani is a first-class writer—direct, cogent, and easily read.

MONGREL MIRTH

About once a month, editors at *Dog Fancy* send me a large envelope stuffed with letters that readers have written to me in care of the magazine. Most are notes of thanks from people who purchased (or in some cases, avoided) books that I have reviewed. Others ask for help to locate certain books (I am happy to help if I can), and a few are critical of what I have said about a given book. Some complain that I am ignoring a certain breed, behavior, or health problem, or, in one recent instance, a whole "race" of dogs.

A reader wrote that in the five years that I was the *Dog Fancy* reviewer, I had never once reviewed a book on mixed breeds. The writer went on to say that I was just another "purebred chauvinist" who was "anti-mix."

Nothing could be further from the truth. To me, a dog is a dog is a dog, and I love mixes and purebreds equally. The fact is, in my tenure as reviewer, I've never seen a book written exclusively about mixed breeds—and believe me, there are very few doggie book titles that fail to cross my desk.

So, as I was wondering how to redeem myself from a sin I hadn't even committed, another large envelope arrived from *Dog Fancy*. In it was the answer to my prayers: a book about mixed breeds or, as they are still known in England, where author Angela Patmore lives, mongrels.

I read the book, *The Mongrel* (Popular Dogs, distributed by David and Charles Inc., North Pomfret, VT 05053; 1988, 205 pages), in one sitting—amazing, considering that most dog books are not page-turners. The writing is excellent; the topic has been ignored for too long. Mongrels of the world will be full of mirth: They now have a book of their own, a champion of their rights in Angela Patmore, and a dog-book reviewer with a happy reaction.

Patmore says there are more than 150 million mongrels on the face of the earth, and in her opinion they have purebred dogs beaten hands down. In fact, she says it is purebred dogs that are genetically corrupt. She calls them "freaks," concocted by breeders who make up wild histories trying to convince the public that a given breed has ancient roots.

"Even 50 years ago, modern 'purebred dogs' generally looked very different from what they do now, as you can see from early photographs," Patmore says. "Their breeders would have been hard pressed to show you a family tree without mongrels in it, and some went to extraordinary lengths to cover their tracks, inventing 'myths of origin' to account for their 'ancient' breeds. Pride and no little money was at stake."

Breeders of purebreds come in for even more criticism in the areas of health and temperament. Patmore lists health problems purebreds are prone to in a litany that takes up a full page. What she doesn't mention is that some mongrels also get the same diseases. The book's main fault is an anti-purebred stance stated early on and repeated to the bitter end. The argument wears thin after a while and even becomes tedious. It's like preaching to the converted, because most readers will already be enamored of mongrels and probably own one or more.

Well, is the author right? Are mongrel dogs of greater integrity structurally and mentally? The answer is probably a quiet, qualified yes: Mongrels do have fewer congenital defects and structural faults, and they are as easy to train as most purebreds. But the argument always comes back to aesthetics and the question of beauty, which as we all know is in the eye of the beholder, or, in this case, the owner.

Patmore revels in the unpredictability and quirkiness of the looks of mixes. Indeed, the dog selected for the cover of her book is a pop-eyed, white-muzzled charmer, and I would defy any professional dog person to trace its lineage.

Even the Queen of England, purebred fan that she is, breeder of handsome Corgis and working Labradors, is a member of the mongrel fan club. She concocted her own mix, a "drogi," by allowing her Dachshund and Pembroke Corgi to mate. The purebred clubs in England had a fit. They informed Her Majesty that even she could not randomly create a new breed. For purebred fanciers in England, "never mix, never worry," is the maxim to obey, and the battle lines between mongrels and purebreds are drawn more fiercely than they are in the United States. This vehemence might surprise American readers, and in this respect, the book will mystify. Further, the listing of British service organizations will not be of any use to American readers.

Otherwise, this is a long-awaited treasure trove for mixed-breed owners, featuring (besides the justification and defense chapters) solid essays on exercise, health and care, mongrel behavior, superstar mongrels (Benji, take a bow), and mongrels that have served mankind. There is a short but accurate section on training and a hilarious description of the top dog show in England for mongrels: Scruffts, a take-off on the name of the top purebred exhibition in Britain, Crufts. Show categories include happiest dog, dog most like its owner, best trick, best bone-finder, and even best lamppost-user. Yes, an actual lamppost is installed so that the dogs can compete for the prize.

All of this should have mongrel owners celebrating and no few purebred owners sniffing in disdain. The nicest point is that the dogs couldn't care less.

DOGS THROUGH HISTORY

Maxwell Riddle is a giant in the dog fancy: a writer, judge, and exhibitor. He is truly the grand old man of the dog world, and only he could write a historical overview like *Dogs Through History* (Denlinger's, Fairfax, Va.).

This book does not claim to be an exhaustive study of dogs through the ages—rather, it is a grouping of nicely-written essays surveying dogs in different areas of the world. This geographic approach is refreshing and will allow you to read selectively. Although I read the book cover to cover, I will tell you that each chapter stands quite well on its own. So if you are interested in dogs in the Arctic, you can "break the ice" with this book on page 133, and if Egyptian dogs are your concern, go ahead and start with that chapter. I like books like this one—they give me freedom as a reviewer and as a reader to pick and choose my areas of special interest, and yet not lose anything along the way.

That said, I do want to encourage you to read the first four chapters, especially if you are interested in wolf-pack theory and if you are puzzled about the immediate ancestors of domestic dogs. Current theory, with only a few dissenters, holds that wolves are the direct ancestors of dogs. Riddle questions this, and his discussion is *very* persuasive. "Darwin's theory of evolution," says Riddle, "postulates that occasional mutations toward a superior being occurred over immense periods of time, even over epochs. But today many scientists, anatomists, evolutionary geneticists and paleontologists suggest *another* form of evolution. A *random leap* or *jump* may come all at once to make a vastly superior organism"—that is, your dog.

In other words, Riddle seems to apply the punctuated equilibrium theory, so popular now in examining human evolution, to dogs as well. Your dog might not be just an evolved wolf, but a mutation of that or another species, in many ways light-years ahead of its wild relations. The author does provide myriad justifications and evidence for this view, but they are too complex to repeat in a review and really should be examined in context. Suffice it to say that I find this absolutely fascinating, as you will. If Riddle is right and the domestic dog *is* a superior mutation, we might have to re-evaluate some of our veterinary and behavioral research on our best friends.

Several chapters stand out. The essay on dogs in Palestine is exceptionally well written, and it comments on the Bible's view of dogs. "Here one runs into a puzzle: every mention of the dog is in some way with contempt," Riddle writes. As both a former monk and dog lover, I've always been embarrassed by the biblical condemnation of dogs. Riddle's essay helped me see the situation in perspective, and my face has since become a little less red.

TO BENEFIT BREEDERS

Whether you are a professional breeder or have helped whelp only one or two litters of puppies, you know that breeding dogs is an art and a science that can be a study in organization and *disorganization* at the same time.

While most breeders give long, hard thought to their breeding plans and carefully arrange their chosen matches, when the actual whelping day arrives, matters can get hectic. But after reading Muriel Lee's books, no breeder will have any excuses anymore—and even newcomers will be able to enjoy what is really a miraculous event.

Let me hasten to add that I am in no way encouraging more people to begin breeding dogs. The pet population situation in our country is way out of control and has been for many years. We hardly need more unwanted pups. But if you are a serious full- or part-time professional breeder, or know one, you might as well have these two excellent guides on hand.

One gem: "Talk to other breeders in your breed, read up on your breed, and acquire some knowledge about breeding, whelping and puppy problems. All whelpings are different. If you are raising Pomeranians, you will have more problems than you would with the Coonhound that produced 12 pups—all of which lived—in a box in a garage. If you are raising a litter of Westies, you will probably have more problems than the breeder of Old English Sheepdogs. And if you raise a litter of Bulldogs, you will probably have more problems than anyone else!"

"DEAR VET" BOOKS

The Animal Doctor's Answer Book.
Dr. Michael Fox
New Market Press
3 East St.
New York, NY 10017
1984, 300 pages

Small Animal Health Care, A Primer for Veterinary Clients
Amy Ward, DVM
Veterinary Medical Company
690 South Forth St.
Edwardsville, KS 66111
1983, 152 pages

Veterinarians spend about half of their professional time answering questions from clients. Happily, their patients aren't as cantankerous as the human versions—and, if they could talk, their questions would probably make more sense than those of their owners. But regardless of how silly the questions may be or how difficult they may be to answer, two veterinarians have published what are essentially answer books.

Dr. Michael Fox has been writing a syndicated column about pets for what seems like eons, and most of the questions that he answers are from troubled dog owners. New Market Press has brought out this compilation in an extremely attractive format, with small (but reliable) type, neat illustrations, and good organization.

Fox's book is on responsible ownership and stewardship of pets. His philosophy is one of reverence for all life and has philosophical and religious roots. He manages to slip in quotes from Albert Schweitzer, Pierre Teilhard de Chardin, and Jesus Christ, within the scope of answering questions for a syndicated column! He continually directs the readers' attention to broader horizons, often referring them to other books and sources. If the format limits him in what he can say, he uses the question as a reference source and pulpit.

A lesser known but no less brilliant veterinarian has put together *Small Animal Health Care*, which is almost totally free of any publisher's hoopla but no less valuable than Dr. Fox's book. Dr. Ward has written a primer for veterinary clients that will answer most of their questions in a reassuring and intelligent manner. This book is an excellent addition to any veterinary clinic's waiting room.

Beginning with health concerns like vaccinations and parasites, Dr. Ward explains complex medical problems like pancreatitis, hip dysplasia, and surgical procedures. All of this is done in a clear, no-nonsense style—ideal for stressed clients waiting with stressed animal patients. "My clients ask tough questions," says Dr. Ward. "They deserve thorough answers."

Dr. Ward has also provided sections on training your dog and on psychological stress in dogs and cats. This latter feature should be a normal part of such handbooks, and probably will be in the future. I must admit that it has not normally been included in past efforts. Some veterinary practitioners seem to be unaware that their patients have minds, emotions, and feelings in addition to hearts, livers, and lungs. No such myopia plagues Dr. Ward; she is admirably concerned with the whole dog—body, mind, and, yes, soul.

TRAINING THE PROFESSIONALS

Teaching Dog Obedience Classes: The Manual for Instructors
Joachim Volhard and Gail Tamases Fisher
Howell Book House
15 Columbus Circle
New York, NY 10023
1986, 384 pages

Ten years ago, general care books were the stock-in-trade in the dog publishing business, with training books as a steady sideline. Breed books have always been popular. But there were few places for the professional to turn for help with his or her special concerns. Business advice was gleaned from professional associates or through the school of hard knocks—and hard knocks could sometimes mean losing considerable income.

But the industry is changing. Today we have books on dog owner counseling, veterinary/client relationships, constructing a boarding kennel, managing an animal shelter—and now an entry on running an obedience class.

With professionals setting higher standards for their fields of experience through such books, it can only mean better care and training for our canine friends. What more can we ask from a "dog book"?

Jack Volhard and Gail Fisher have given obedience instructors little excuse for running a poor class. They lay out high standards of performance in *Teaching Dog Obedience Classes*. As anyone who has ever been in an obedience class, let alone taught one, knows, training people to train their dogs is a complex task that calls for a full measure of humor, patience, tact, and skill. This book should prove a trusted guide for the obedience class instructor.

The first part of the book talks about the student's dog, with sections on understanding canine behavior. It discusses how a dog learns and some of the influences on learning behavior, including temperament, sensitivity, touch, health, and eating habits.

The second part deals with educational psychology: how people learn, their retention rates, and tips on how to develop your ability to teach and truly observe the progress of students in your class. Unless the bond between student and instructor is strong, and the student feels the instructor really cares about his or her progress, the dropout rate in any class is bound to skyrocket. Teaching an obedience class is serious business, but it should be approached both methodically and joyfully.

Volhard and Fisher also cover administrative details such as advertising, liability, and renting a training site. This book concludes with a section on dealing with problem students and problem dogs.

What are problem students? There is the "Belligerent Personality," who "complains about the method or the equipment or the facility or something else that isn't to his liking … usually loud enough for the instructor to hear." There is the "Demanding Student," who is "an exhibitionist … he or she wants to be watched … always asking the instructor, 'Would you watch me? I don't think I'm doing this quite right.'" And there is the "Helpless Student" who "stands there waiting for his neighbor to comply with an instruction and then watches to see what he should do … the one who calls you over saying, 'I can't do this, you do it.'"

The author's advice? Excuse the belligerent student from class if he or she becomes too much of a problem and help the demanding student or helpless student. Then ignore him.

Don't let the length of the book frighten you; you'll enjoy the fine writing and economy of words. This book will send you into your classes with a renewed sense of dedication.

COUNSELING FOR YOU AND YOUR DOG

Better Behavior in Dogs and Cats
William E. Campbell
American Veterinary Publications, Inc.
5782 Thornwood Dr.
Goleta, CA 93117
1986, 287 pages

William Campbell's first book, *Behavior Problems in Dogs*, caused a sensation among dog people. It was the first book that discussed at length the concept of counseling dog owners, helping them identify problems in their relationships with their dogs and then rebuild those relationships.

He has now written that book for the layperson. He says his first book "is still popular and useful but too technical as a 'how-to' guide for the average pet owner." Campbell's new offering speaks directly to you, the distressed dog owner, in language that is humorous, insightful, warm, and personal. In fact, as you read *Better Behavior in Dogs and Cats*, you will feel as though you are having a private consultation with the author.

Campbell calls his treatment of problem behavior "the causative approach," focusing on the source of frustration that causes the dog's problem behavior. "When you uncover the answer to the question," he writes, "and then do something about it, many problems can stop in a very short time—a couple of days in some cases, as long as six weeks in others." He kicks off the book with a look at various solutions to a common and obnoxious problem: excessive barking.

I can hear you saying now, "Okay! okay! Tell me what he suggests, Evans. I have a problem with my dog." Well, although I'd like to help you, I can't put Campbell's suggestions into two sentences, nor would I want to. In fact, Campbell never hands out quick-fix solutions to problems. Instead, he prescribes a holistic program that changes the overall relationship between dog and owner, resulting in a lasting "cure." The stopgap measures dished out in some other dog training manuals are just that—emergency actions that bring about temporary peace. Campbell doesn't deal with owners and dogs that way. Here are some hints about the techniques he uses for problem behavior, but I urge you not to employ them without reading the book.

First, he advises owners of problem dogs to stop all praise and petting. Make them earn praise and petting by performing a command (such as "sit") before being rewarded, he says. Second, he suggests that owners feed their dog twice a day, not once, to alleviate any tension from hunger.

Campbell's methods can produce speedy results in many cases, but this often depends upon the honesty of the owner in confronting the problem. In the chapter "The Dog's Problem: People," you will be asked to evaluate your own personality. Here you'll find descriptions of owners like "the name droppers" who sit around and talk about the dog all the time, using its name and then complaining when the dog doesn't respond to its overused name; or "the whirling dervishes," who are always late for work and whirl around upsetting the dog, who then chews out of frustration when the owner leaves. Perhaps you are a "domineering owner" or an "ambivalent owner"—whatever shoe fits, don't just wear it; with Campbell's help you can change your method of handling your dog. You must know yourself and how your personality affects your dog if you truly want to help your pet.

The best writing on canine behavior problems always drives home one central point to the reader: You must be your dog's leader. Some writers call this role "Alpha," but Campbell calls it "having IT." "IT is a sense of having control over your dog's feelings, as well as its behavior. You will have IT when you see your pet's emotional energy and attention directed to what you want, rather than what it wants," Campbell writes. Either you have IT or you don't. If you do, your dog might have an occasional problem, but it won't be a problem. There's a difference. If you don't have IT—if you're not your dog's leader—get ready for headaches and heartaches. Campbell's concept of IT is where it's at. I urge you to read his book.

Quantity Versus Quality

The Weekend Dog
Myrna M. Milani
Rawson Associates
597 Fifth Ave.
New York, NY 10017
1984, 207 pages

Some readers may look at the subtitle of *The Weekend Dog*—"How to Choose, Raise, Housebreak, Train, Exercise, Feed, Breed and Otherwise Care For a Dog You See Only Nights and Weekends"—and comment that anyone who sees a dog only nights and weekends shouldn't have one. The fact is, however, millions of such souls do have dogs—and in this book they have an excellent manual that addresses the special problems of the weekend dog and its owner.

In fact, Dr. Milani's book is so refreshingly honest and helpful that it is a good guide even if your dog is underfoot 24 hours a day, so please don't deem this a book only for busy career persons or "uncaring" owners. Although it is certainly inclined toward the weekend owner, it will be of help to all.

If you have been following my reviews in this chapter, you know how strongly I feel about poorly written dog books. Unfortunately, the market is teeming with them. Even if a book is factually correct and overflowing with helpful knowledge, I hesitate to suggest it to readers if it is a form of literary Muzak. Dr. Milani's text is crisp, clear, funny, concise, and absolutely positive on dogs and what they are and can be for us. It is doggone good writing.

The biggest problem for the weekend dog is being left alone all week and then being the center of attention all weekend. Sometimes the contrast is just too much for the dog, and he or she breaks down behaviorally. Milani suggests de-emphasizing hello and good-bye scenes, and emphasizing structured exercise and proper nutrition. She devotes whole sections to the last two topics.

On exercise, for example, Milani asks the dog owner to evaluate the situation as it is: "If the dog is a real sluggard but its owner is gung ho about rigorous daily workouts, or if the dog craves constant activity while the owner prefers to sit in front of the television set, relationships will suffer unless something changes." She then asks the owner to remember some options concerning what we can do with our dogs—options she hammers home at every opportunity in this book:

- Accept the situation as it exists, including how we feel about it.
- Change the way we feel about it.
- Change the dog to align its behavior with our beliefs.
- Get rid of the dog.

This is a wonderfully honest approach to exercise or any other aspect of the dog/owner relationship. Dr. Milani continually asks the reader to examine the quality of his relationship with the dog. Throughout, she stresses that there is a difference between the quantity of the time we spend and the quality of what happens within that time. For example, it is not all that uncommon for a dog that is held and cuddled to feel lonely and frustrated because it never gets to see its own species or explore the world from floor level. Its cuddling owner might dismiss this book if he saw it in a bookstore, though: "Thank God I don't have a lonely weekend dog, and don't need that book," might be the inner thought. Meanwhile, even though Fifi is held and fondled continually, she still soils the house, chews destructively, goofs off, barks, whimpers, and generally acts like a hooligan. There is, indeed, a difference between quantity time and quality time.

Other chapters include "When the Weekend Dog Gets Sick"; "Old Age, Death, and Euthanasia"; and "Sex and the Weekend Dog." Recently I watched a book-browser in a New York bookstore read the inner flap of this book, the back cover, and the table of contents, and then watched him turn immediately to the sex chapter. He may have been disappointed to find no illustrations.

I suspect Dr. Milani, however, would find the vignette amusing, and that is the last aspect of this fine book I'd like to highlight—its wonderful sense of humor. She relates an incident when her own dog stole a layer cake off the kitchen counter and ate it, getting a stomachache in the process and leaving a sticky mess of icing and crumbs everywhere: "I considered my alternatives:

- Scream at the dog
- Ignore the dog and angrily clean up the mess
- Feel guilty because my own negligence had caused my dog great discomfort
- Laugh"

This is the first training and care book I've read that instructs owners to laugh. I'm a strong advocate of discipline and training dogs, but Milani is absolutely right in including a section entitled "It Doesn't Hurt to Laugh." Sometimes it's the only sane thing to do.

FIRST-RATE READING

Second-Hand Dog
Carol Lea Benjamin
Howell Book House
15 Columbus Circle
New York, NY 10023
1988, 96 pages

Back in 1985, when I received Carol Benjamin's book *Mother Knows Best: The Natural Way To Train Your Dog*, I said that she was the finest dog writer of the day. Others apparently agreed, and that year Benjamin received not one, but both of the top awards that dog writers can earn: The Dog Writers' Association of America's Writer of the Year Award and the FIDO writer's award. With the publication of *Second-Hand Dog*, I'm happy to report I have no reason to change my mind.

Here's a little book with a mighty mission—to save second-hand dogs from being "disposed of" once again. In a nation that currently euthanizes more than 15 million dogs and cats each year, the enormousness of the educational task is obvious, and could be overwhelming for a less experienced and knowledgeable writer.

Benjamin's breezy, funny, incisive, and even curt style moves *Second-Hand Dog* along at a fast clip, facilitating the educational process and turning a situation that might be viewed as a problem into a pleasure. What second-hand *dogs* really need, she says, is not love, love, love, but a solid training program that will help them present themselves as such angels that they will never be bounced out of home and hearth again.

> In order to become a terrific pet, your second-hand dog will need more of everything at first: an extra dose of R and R (Rules and Regulations), more good food, more grooming, more contact, more company, more bonding activities, more long solitary walks with you, more exposure to your particular environment, more exercise, more rides in your car, more games, more patient training, more room to himself.

While many owners of second-hand dogs truly believe that love will be enough to shape their pets—and love is often the motivating reason that they rescued the animals from the street, shelter, or other source—Benjamin reminds them that love necessarily includes discipline, education, and realistic expectations.

> You've got your work cut out for you. But there'll be rewards too—unqualified love, loyalty, companionship, someone to greet you when you come home, someone to make you laugh, to keep you feeling young, someone to get you out or keep you happy to stay in, someone who will place you above all others for as long as he shall live.

We are then taken on a tour of how a dog learns (by repetition, example, reward, or punishment, and even by accident) and what to do to become a leader in the dog's eyes. Far and away the best chapter, in my opinion as a trainer, is "An Alpha Primer (Because You Must Be in Charge)." Here is a list, eight solid points in all, of things to do and steps to take to make your saucy second-hander regard you as The Boss instead of a bimbo. Some excerpts:

> Always praise your dog as if you own it. Put your hands firmly on your dog. Hug the dog. Pat him so that your hand gets warm from the contact. Do not praise in an offhand or timid way.

This is great advice, for second-hand owners often fall into two extremes in terms of praise and petting. Either they are too timid, unsure of the mysterious creatures they've adopted because they do not know the animal's background, likes, or dislikes; or they are overly affectionate and stroke, stroke, stroke all day long, thinking this version of "love" will make everything all right.

> Do a sit-stay. My own very laid-back way of becoming alpha in five to ten minutes is to put the dog in a sit-stay. If he's a wild animal and doesn't know the meaning of the word *Obedient*, all the better. When he breaks, and he will, I put him back. If he breaks 14 times, I put him back 14 times ...

Take it from another trainer: Any static exercise, forcing a dog to stay in one place in a sit-stay or a down position, will establish you as Head Honcho, pronto.

You'll also get a short course on dog training, tips on second-hand dogs and kids, and some hints on problem solving. While the focus is not on specific solutions to specific problems, these sections can help you establish dominance, train, analyze a problem, and often stop bad behavior in its tracks. Remember, as a second-hand owner, you've got a challenge ahead of you but also an advantage: The dog doesn't know you either, or how loose or firm you will be. If you show firmness quickly, the dog might not even try (or will stop trying) some of the tricks it pulled on its last owner.

I'd like to see this book at the front desk of every shelter in the country. Add to those locations veterinary offices, grooming salons, and, of course, bookstores. I suspect that the author felt that if she saved even *one* dog from oblivion with this book, writing it was worth it. My estimate would be more likely in the thousands. A great book—it is simply sterling.

APPENDIX

I am adding this excellently written appendix because it will help those who want to understand more fully the mystery and complexity of what it means to be a dog trainer. As you will see, Ms. Weinberg, in this previously unpublished paper, weaves together the work of the famed family therapist Virginia Satir, my own work, and the work of some other trainers. It is an excellent synthesis, complementing nicely what I have said in this book and what many of those interviewed discussed. It brings this book full circle—and I just couldn't resist sharing it with you.

The Human–Canine Relationship: Lessons in Communication

Dani Weinberg

"The dogs really love you," said my student Jenny at the end of our dog obedience training class. "My Patrick never likes anyone, but he loves you. You're really good with dogs."

That evening's session had been a difficult one, as Week Three of my course usually is. Most of my 10 students had accepted the challenge of learning to train their dogs and were now in utter chaos—struggling to coordinate hands, feet, bodies, and brains as they moved about the room with their suddenly unfamiliar canine companions at the other end of the leash. Watching 20 living creatures, empathizing with their hard work, straining to be heard over the din of dominant barkers—all this had left me exhausted.

So when I heard Jenny's words, I started a rapid descent down my own personal Rabbit Hole of Interaction. Here's how it felt on the inside, as the interaction proceeded. (See Figure 1.)

The process began with
>*Sensory Input*, or what I heard and saw:
>>"The dogs love you.... You're really good with dogs," says Jenny, smiling, making eye contact, and leaning towards me.

I immediately gave a meaning to what I saw and heard in the form of an
>*Interpretation*: She admires me and is praising me.

How I chose to interpret the sensory input led me to a
>*Feeling*: Pleasure!

That might have been just fine and the process might have stopped right there. Or, I might have become aware of a
>*Feeling about the Feeling*: Embarrassment.

Having reached this point in the process, I was probably feeling threatened, and some old tapes from childhood were triggered in the form of a

Survival Rule: "Don't shine." (Who did I think I was anyway, to be noticed and appreciated for my gifts and competencies? Besides, you have to earn love, and I wasn't sure I had earned this offering.)

Now that I was down to a survival issue, I needed some form of

Defense: Dissolve into the woodwork. If that's not possible,
a. Try Placating. If that's not appropriate,
b. Become SuperReasonable.

After the split second it took to go through this entire process, I might have given the following

Response:
a. "Aw, heck, anyone can do it." (Placating), or
b. "Knowledge of canine behavior dictates that we resist the temptation to anthropomorphize the dog, especially if it's a juvenile or in the second Fear-Imprint Period." (SuperReasonable)

In this specific case, I managed to collect myself just before the Defense step in the process. I paused, swallowed, and said, "Thank you for telling me that. I appreciate it."

To be perfectly honest, none of this analysis came to my awareness until the next day. I realized only then what a brilliant, if unconscious, recovery I had made the night before. The incident tapped deeply into my lifelong struggle with issues of competence, perfection, and conditional love.

As an anthropological consultant to organizations, I work with the human-human bond, teaching my clients how to raise their awareness and enhance their effectiveness as communicators. I have found that the same principles apply to the human-animal bond, in particular to the relationships between people and their dogs. In this essay, I will draw on another part of my experience—as a dog trainer, behavior consultant, and obedience class instructor. I will use the human-canine relationship as a metaphor to explore how people communicate with each other.

Studying how people interact with their dogs, we have some distance and objectivity that is not always easy to achieve with human students or clients. We can permit ourselves certain illuminating liberties of reasoning because in our culture, dogs, as pets, belong in the unserious domain of home, family, and leisure activities. As we study the canine-human communication process, we can be irreverent,

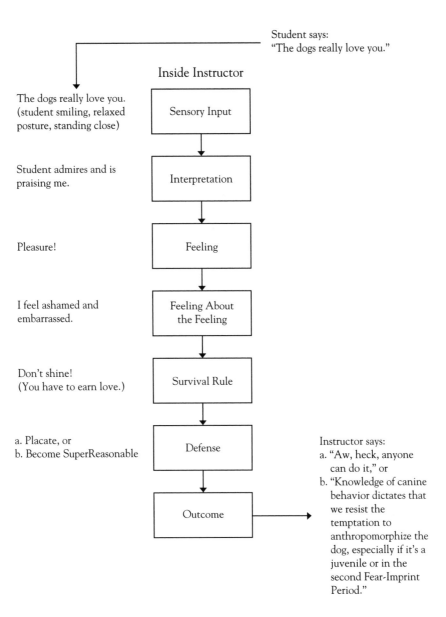

Student says:
"The dogs really love you."

Inside Instructor

The dogs really love you.
(student smiling, relaxed
posture, standing close)

Sensory Input

Student admires and is
praising me.

Interpretation

Pleasure!

Feeling

I feel ashamed and
embarrassed.

Feeling About
the Feeling

Don't shine!
(You have to earn love.)

Survival Rule

a. Placate, or
b. Become SuperReasonable

Defense

Instructor says:
a. "Aw, heck, anyone
can do it," or
b. "Knowledge of canine
behavior dictates that
we resist the
temptation to
anthropomorphize the
dog, especially if it's a
juvenile or in the
second Fear-Imprint
Period."

Outcome

Figure 1. The Inside View of an Interaction

outrageous, wildly imaginative, and even totally absurd—all necessary conditions for creative thinking and understanding. The intellectual freedom we gain from the study of dogs enables us to understand our own species better.

LIVING WITH DOGS

My life with dogs began only in full adulthood and out of conscious choice. As a child, adolescent, and young adult, I was actually terrified of dogs (and cats). This makes sense, knowing some of my family history.

From earliest childhood, I had been taught that the world was a terrible place, filled with danger and loss. For my parents, these were understandable beliefs. We had fled from Nazi-occupied Czechoslovakia in 1939 in a way that would have delighted filmmakers of that era. We Jews were advised by a non-Jewish friend to leave the country immediately. I was barely three years old and, according to family legend, almost responsible for our three lives. Because I had a cold, my parents hesitated to make the trip. Fortunately, they decided to go anyway, and, the story continues, we were in the last car of the last train that was allowed to cross the border out of Czechoslovakia. After spending some time in France where we endured air raids, where my mother badgered the Gestapo for exit permits, and where we finally found passage on a ship, we arrived in New York.

The high energy of heroism soon dissipated as we faced the realities of our losses—home, family, friends, social standing in the community, material possessions, familiar language and culture, and even my father's profession. My father was not an adaptable man and never fully recovered. He passed on to me his perception of the world as a dangerous place. My mother continued to live a quietly heroic life, enjoying the rich unfolding of new experience. She gave me my sense of adventure and joy. She was never able, though, to keep a pet. Holding the pain of loss at arm's length would be too difficult for her with such an obviously mortal and short-lived creature as a dog, a cat, or even a bird.

I accepted my legacy and learned to live in this perilous world. I learned to be a keen observer and to make sense of my observations. I learned to be with people and to understand their behavior. In short, I became an anthropologist. But when it came to other animals, I reached the limits of my willingness to risk uncertainty, danger, and loss of control. Looking back now, I realize that I lacked a template for understanding dogs and cats. Because I had no models for or experience with their behavior, I found it unpatterned and unpredictable. Given this combination of history, beliefs, and experience, it made sense for me to fear animals.

Only when I realized that there was pattern and meaning in the behavior of dogs and cats was I able to get past my fear and learn to communicate with them. In these terms, "communication" meant recognizing and accepting the animal's behavior pattern and under-standing how our different behavior patterns engaged with each other—sometimes colliding and sometimes in fine harmony. I soon learned that congruent communication greatly reduced the probabil-ity of danger in my interaction with animals. I have since learned that this is equally true in my interaction with people.

At the age of 34, I met Heidi, a golden German Shepherd, and began my love affair with dogs. Now, more than 20 years later, I am a reasonably competent dog trainer and an excellent teacher of people who want to train their dogs. I'm active in the sport of obedience, showing my own dog in obedience trials and working my way up through the hierarchy of skill and polish. With dogs, as in many other aspects of life, I have recreated myself in my own image, rather than playing out the script my parents wrote for me. For this reason, Jenny's praise in my obedience class moved me deeply and reached down into the very core of my life. It gave me yet another opportu-nity to measure my growth and to discover joyously how tall I can stand now.

The incident also gave me insight into another one of my issues: what to do with the enormous gift of being loved, whether by canine or human. When I do not love myself, when my self-worth is low, I cannot receive the gift of love from others, no matter how desper-ately I want it at that moment. Instead, I concentrate all my energy on protecting my vulnerable self from perceived threat. The behavior that results from this process is incongruent in that what I express outwardly does not correspond to what I feel. In fact, my behavior is designed to mask my inner state, from myself and others, in a mis-guided effort at protection.

As a teacher, and a lifelong student of the learning process, I have seen how people with their dogs (and other pets) replicate this cycle of low self-esteem, the sensation of imbalance, the perception of dan-ger, and the incongruent coping strategy. Our life with dogs offers us a stage on which we can reenact old issues, replaying old family stories and beliefs.

DOGS AS QUASI-PERSONS

In addition, our culture's definition of dogs as quasi-persons offers yet another justification for using dogs to learn more about human com-munication. Through years of scientific breeding, we have literally created this domesticate to our own specifications, selecting for the behaviors and physical conformations that fit our definition. Although dogs were originally bred and kept as mundane working animals, today we speak of "companion" dogs and value them for such anthropomorphic qualities as "intelligence," "courage," and "loyalty."

The official breed standard for the German Shepherd, for example, describes the dog as:

> strong, agile, alert and full of life … quality and nobility. The breed has a distinct personality marked by direct and fearless, but not hostile, expression, self-confidence and a certain aloofness that does not lend itself to immediate and indiscriminate friendships…. It is poised but when the occasion demands, eager and alert. (*The Complete Dog Book*, 17th Ed, 1985: pps 617-618)

The Maltese, a Toy breed weighing from four to six pounds and usually bedecked with a bow in its topknot, is described as:

> gentle-mannered and affectionate, eager and sprightly in action, and, despite its size, possessed of the vigor needed for the satisfactory companion…. the Maltese seems to be without fear. His trust and affectionate responsiveness are very appealing. (*The Complete Dog Book*, 17th Ed, 1985: pps 461-462)

The Great Dane, one of the largest breeds, is described as exhibiting

> in its distinguished appearance dignity, strength and elegance…. the Apollo of dogs. He must be spirited and courageous, never timid. He is friendly and dependable … (with a) majesty possessed by no other breed. (*The Complete Dog Book*, 17th Ed, 1985: pg 293)

We attribute "masculinity" and "femininity" to dogs, far beyond the physical characteristics of sexual dimorphism. We take advantage of their instincts to assign them quasi-human occupations such as guarding, hunting, and herding. We name them and take full advantage of their neoteny—the lifelong retention of juvenile features—by feeding them, clothing them, providing quasi-human shelter (dog "houses"), seeing to their needs for recreation, caring for their health, parenting them through their reproductive functions, and finally mourning their death.

We talk to our dogs and thrive on their "unconditional positive regard." Some people abuse their dogs as they abuse their children, both physically and emotionally. Most of us at least attempt to discipline our dogs, to teach them to "behave."

CONGRUENCE

In my role as obedience instructor, I have to deal with this anthropomorphic view of dogs. Dogs also serve as a psychological projection screen. People recreate with their dogs their own unresolved issues and relationship patterns. This is evident in the behavior of first-time dog owners coming to a beginners' obedience class. Human "moms" and "dads" dotingly escort their canine "kids" into the training building, exhibiting a mixture of concern, apprehension, and love. As they begin learning how to train their dogs, they reenact their own practiced reactions to stress. Like any other learning experience, this one usually begins with a challenge to the owner's self-esteem, perhaps accompanied by a vague sense of danger and a felt need for protection. At that moment, an automatic coping strategy takes over, and the person is in the grip of mindless and unproductive behavior that we call "incongruent."

The idea of congruence was central in the thinking of Virginia Satir (1888–1976), a therapist who focused all her work on teaching people to be congruent, even in the face of severe stress. Satir developed the "systems model" of family therapy to its finest realization and revolutionized family therapy in two major ways. First, she demonstrated that the "identified patient"—that is, the family member who actually came to therapy—could not be successfully treated outside the context of his or her family. Second, she brought to all her work a belief in the essential goodness and potential for health of all human beings. I have found her ideas useful in helping work groups and organizations. I have also used her models successfully in my work with people and their dogs.

SELF-WORTH

In my obedience class, I witness the entire range of canine-human interaction. I see the class as a portrait, slightly distorted and comical, of Virginia Satir's models of the human-human interaction process. In Satir's view, good communication depends on respecting and balancing the needs of the Self, the Other, and the Context. When my self-worth is high, I behave congruently and achieve this balance. When my self-worth is low, I defend myself by mobilizing an incongruent coping strategy—and in the process, upset the balance and disturb the communication.

Satir's model of self-worth may be likened to a thermometer that registers how the core of my being reacts to an event. (See Figure 2.) It is not the event itself but rather my self-worth "temperature" that

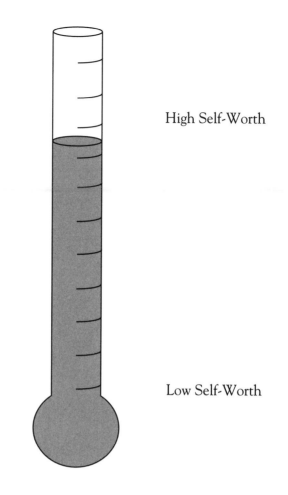

High Self-Worth

Low Self-Worth

Figure 2. Self-Worth Thermometer

determines this reaction. The identical event may trigger entirely different responses in you and me because of the condition of our self-worth at that moment.

In the early weeks of my obedience class, I see students being dragged around the room by their canine partners. To the untrained eye, the dogs all seem to be enjoying themselves hilariously—pulling, leaping, lunging, spinning, barking, and sniffing. In fact, however, their behavior reveals their stress and uncertainty in these early stages of learning.

Their owners, too, exhibit a variety of emotional reactions including embarrassment, defensiveness, fear, and hopelessness. For example, a novice dog trainer reports some of the feelings she experienced in her first obedience class:

Clumsiness, vulnerability, frustration at my own inadequacies, guilt that I can't help my generous and willing dog more, and a serious lack of self-esteem ... (Capra, 1993)

A big part of my job as instructor is to help people shore up their failing self-worth in the face of this very natural—and stressful—part of the learning curve.

Teaching a dog to walk pleasantly at your left side and adapt its pace to yours is no trivial matter. Most of my students, though, are accustomed to a comfortable level of competence in most things they do. They are college professors, parents, store clerks, managers, lawyers, office workers, sales professionals, psychologists, and writers. The rude shock of learning something completely new and being clumsy in the process may be enough to squash down their self-worth. I help them by acknowledging their feelings ("This is tricky!"), by reinforcing their positive efforts ("You've been practicing this week!"), and by empowering them to take charge ("Look how well you've taught Bear to sit!").

Some of my most moving experiences as an obedience instructor have come not from watching the dog's progress but from seeing the growing self-worth of the owner. This is especially evident in some of my women students whose culturally prescribed role of caretaker includes responsibility for the family dog.

Betty, for example, came to class with Samantha, a six-month-old mixed breed. Samantha was destined for destruction if Betty couldn't stop her from nipping her four-year-old daughter, "leaking" on the rug, and running away when turned loose outdoors. Betty reported that her husband liked "spirited" dogs like Samantha. He would bring them home as puppies, rough-house with them and his three children, and leave them in Betty's charge—over-stimulated and out of control—when he went off to work.

Neither he nor Betty knew anything about training dogs, yet he reprimanded her for not being able to control Samantha. His previous "gift" to his wife, a bouncy Golden Retriever pup, soon became a physical threat to their then-two-year-old daughter and was euthanized. Betty turned her face away from me as she told the story. "This time, I want to do it right," she said.

The day after our first class meeting, Betty called and told me how discouraged she was. Wouldn't it be better, she asked, if her husband trained Samantha, since the dog always obeyed him? I pointed out that this was exactly why she, Betty, should do the training. She was still dubious. Only when I told her that it would confuse Samantha to change trainers in midstream did Betty agree to stay in class. Here was a clear case of low self-worth, reinforced by a domineering and thoughtless husband, and supported by our cultural stereotype of the helpless wife. Betty's self-worth "temperature" was so low that her strongest motivation to act was for the benefit of others, in this case to spare Samantha's confusion.

After three weeks of class, Betty began to appreciate Samantha's progress and to enjoy their daily training sessions. As the weeks went by, Samantha gradually became my star pupil, and Betty's pride and joy grew commensurately. When I asked Betty to come to the first meeting of my new obedience class and demonstrate the basic exercises with Samantha, she agreed with pleasure. "This is the first time I've been able to do something well," she told me.

THE COMMUNICATION WHEEL

Self-worth is basic to any kind of performance and accomplishment. As an obedience instructor, I must also keep in mind the balance required for good communication. Imagine the wheel of an old-fashioned, horse-drawn cart. The wheel is composed of three pie-shaped sections—Self, Other, and Context—and turns on a hub of Self-Worth. (See Figure 3.) When my self-worth is high, the wheel turns smoothly and easily as I honor the needs of each of the three components.

When the cartload of stress becomes too heavy, however, my self-worth may drop. Then I channel much of my energy into protecting myself from perceived threat and my own painful feelings. Instead of maintaining the nice, easy balance of the wheel, I unconsciously withdraw my attention from one or more parts of it. Instead of congruently feeling and expressing my vulnerability, I go into a mindless state and behave in ways that are out of my control and awareness. Satir described four of these unbalanced states as the major Coping Strategies: Blaming, Placating, SuperReasonable, and Irrelevant.

The following examples of these incongruent coping styles are drawn from a workshop on Communication that I taught for instructors of obedience classes. Most of them were skilled dog trainers and experienced obedience instructors. I had asked them to describe their biggest problem as an obedience instructor. Their own words reveal clearly which of the coping strategies are their "favorites" for dealing with stress.

Donald: "I am unable to keep a smiling motivating face if I have one of those extra-stupid, extra-untalented classes."

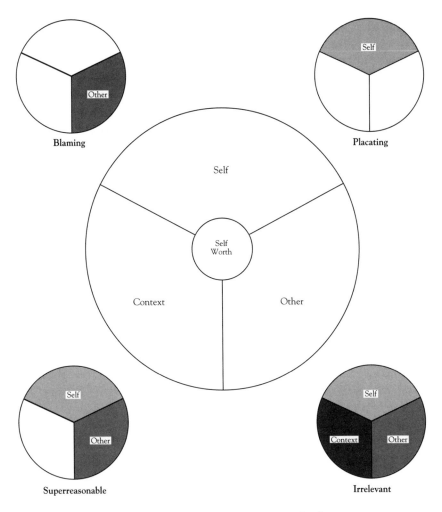

Blaming

Placating

Self

Self
Worth

Context

Other

Superreasonable

Irrelevant

Figure 3. The Communication Wheel

Donald deals with his stress by discounting Other on the communication wheel. He points a *Blaming* finger at his students. It's their fault. Of course, he doesn't make this statement directly to them but conveys his feelings in subtle, and not-so-subtle, ways by his words and tone of voice. He begins sentences with "You ..." He uses a lot of "shoulds" in his instructions. He talks in absolutes about his students' efforts: "You *always*...," "You *never*..." He asks questions beginning with "Why (do/don't you) ..." that can be answered only by an admission of guilt or ineptness. Not surprisingly, Donald reports, "My students are afraid of me."

Noel: "I feel that sometimes my instructions might not be clear enough. I also can be drawn into giving one person too much attention and I may not be firm enough."

Noel discounts *himself* when he's under stress, using the incongruent coping strategy of **Placating**. His words are tentative and his manner uncertain. He finds fault only and always with himself. Satir taught about placating by creating a concrete, exaggerated, physical picture. The placating person is a supplicant, down on his knees with one arm reaching out and the other pressed against his heart. He is wrong, and the Other in the communication wheel is right. The placater discounts his own needs and submits to the Other's wishes and judgments.

Evelyn: "[My biggest problem is] dealing with the under-achiever or low-energy handler. I have a theory that achievers, or their achievements, are so admired by the less active that the goal changes from performing the feat to acquiring the trappings of those who perform the feat. During the initial telephone interview, I stress the amount of work to be done at home with the dog, point out the waste of time and money if the work is not done, and the resultant embarrassment in class."

Evelyn deals with her stress by adopting the **SuperReasonable** coping strategy. She discounts her Self and the Other—that is, the living, breathing human beings in the conversation—and pays attention only to the Context, the class requirements. She speaks in abstractions and uses the passive voice. She spins theories out of her head, anesthetizing all other parts of her that are located below her brainstem. She seeks refuge from her painful feelings by totally denying them and concentrating instead on "the facts."

Robert: "When students ask me difficult questions about behavior, I just don't know where to begin. I shoot a volley of questions at them about the dog's health, living conditions, diet, exercise, place in the family.... Before they have a chance to answer even the first question, I start telling them about hip dysplasia, barrier frustration, orthomolecular medicine, rage syndrome, acupuncture, and separation anxiety. Finally, I get so frustrated, I just want to walk away."

Robert seeks relief from his stress through the incongruent coping strategy of **Irrelevant** behavior. He discounts all three parts of the communication wheel. He protects himself from perceived threat by distracting attention from himself, the student, and the classroom situation. As he himself realizes, his responses are not appropriate and do not address the student's question. These conversations often end with bewilderment on the part of the student and a feeling of helplessness in Robert.

COPING WITH CANINES

I see the same incongruent coping strategies in my obedience class, employed by students with their dogs. The human-canine relationship can be just as stressful as the human-human, especially in the early stages of obedience training when both dog and handler are novices. The resulting incongruent behavior has been described with wit by Job Michael Evans, a professional dog trainer specializing in canine behavior problems. He uses Satir's coping strategies as a framework to help him understand his clients and their dogs (Evans 1986: chap. 9).

Evans met Satir in the 1960s when she was working with his psychologist father. He read her books and was heavily influenced by her ideas. He uses her systems approach to help his clients—typically, families that are "dysfunctional" in relation to their dogs. He realizes that incongruent coping strategies come into play when people are low on the Self-Worth thermometer. Recognizing that the dog may be falsely viewed as the "identified patient," Evans focuses his "counseling" efforts on understanding and reframing the human-canine communication patterns in the family.

For the **Blaming** dog-owner, everything that goes wrong in training is the dog's fault. She or he discounts the Other—in this case, the dog—on the communication wheel. As Evans says:

> The voice is hard, tight, often shrill and loud. This person is also over-verbal with the dog but in a loud, bossy way.... The blamer begins sentences with the dog's name ('Rover chews.... Rover knows he's done wrong.... Rover just does it for spite.... He's a bad dog.... He gets into everything.... He never listens'). Watch for words like 'never,' 'always,' and 'absolutely.' (Evans 1986: pg 52)

The blaming dog owner anthropomorphizes the dog, attributing to it levels of intelligence, consciousness, and morality that we know do not exist in the species.

Contrary to prevailing belief, dogs do not know right from wrong, and they do not feel guilt. When a normal, healthy dog is scolded harshly by its owner, it may react by displaying submissive behavior towards the dominant "pack-member"—avoiding eye contact, making itself small, putting its tail between its legs, rolling onto its back, urinating, and, when those behaviors only elicit more scolding, running away and hiding. This canine behavior often increases the rage, that is, the characteristic emotional state of the blamer. As the owner's anger display increases, so too does the submissive behavior of the dog, until they find themselves in an impossible, hopeless cycle.

The **Placating** dog owner also anthropomorphizes the dog, but from a position of discounting Self on the communication wheel. The dog, in the placater's view, can do—and has done—no wrong. Everything is the owner's fault. The placating dog-owner is essentially passive, backing off at the first difficulty encountered in training, lacking confidence to influence the dog's behavior, and exhibiting fear as the characteristic emotion:

> The placater always talks in an ingratiating way, trying to please, apologizing. They talk too much in long whiny sentences. The placater tries to elicit obedience out of the dog by bribing, often with food, by cajoling ('C'mon, lie down, will ya? Please? C'mon, you know that would make me happy. C'mon, pleeze, pleeeze?').... While this dog owner knows that he or she needs help in handling the dog, he will rarely blame the dog for bad behavior ('He's really *good*, he just gets nervous and bites, that's all.... It's probably my fault.... If I had only completed that obedience course everything would be different; I know it's my fault'). Unless the counselor is skilled, the placater will also try to placate the counselor ('I know I've failed, just tell me what to do, I'll do anything, really, anything'). (Evans 1986: pg 50)

The **SuperReasonable** dog-owner, having discounted Self and Other in the communication wheel, is emotionally anesthetized and disconnected from all the physical aspects of training dogs. He or she is

> very correct, very reasonable, with little feeling ... calm, cool and collected.... The voice is often dry, flat. Often commands are given to the dog in a monotone or using big words ('As I look at you, Rover, I see a recalcitrant dog, one that should be lying down'). Of course most dogs just think this is hilarious.... The client will often have great difficulty mastering obedience techniques. Since they are often very rigid physically, the hand motions and body positions necessary in good training will be difficult as will verbal animation and any display of praise.... Unfortunately, due to a misreading of training books or a

misunderstanding of the tenets of good training, some … will think that this response is the ideal in their relationship with their dog: say the right words, show no feeling, don't react. (Evans 1986: pg 55)

Irrelevant behavior in dog training is manifested as inconsistency and frequent changes in training method and schedule, all dictated by the owner's frequent changes in mood. The person in this state is not paying attention to any part of the communication wheel, and the overall emotional message is what we call craziness:

> Whatever he or she says is always irrelevant to what anyone else is saying or doing, including the dog. You get a dizzy feeling when you are around this type. The dog will often be extremely hyperactive in response to this handling. The voice is very singsong, going up and down ('Ooops there he goes, watch it, cup of coffee, oops, boom, well time to go to the store!'). This type of person often tries to do several things at once and may be physically uncoordinated. The erratic body language is very confusing to the dog and makes training and discipline difficult.… In handling the dog they will praise and discipline at the same time, completely ignore the dog, forget the dog's name, or call the dog by several names. Occasionally they will not have chosen a name for the dog. (Evans 1986: pg 57)

CONGRUENT TRANSFORMATIONS OF COPING STRATEGIES

We can see incongruent human behavior clearly when we observe people interacting with their dogs. We also see how encumbering and disabling it is to the primary purpose of training a dog. Should we then concentrate on getting rid of these incongruent coping strategies? Shouldn't our highest goal as humans be to behave congruently all the time?

Satir believed that this goal was impossible, unrealistic, and maybe even undesirable. Because her entire approach was built on her view of people as marvelous "manifestations of life," she chose instead to work by a positive Principle of Addition, rather than a negative attempt to subtract. One of her great gifts was reframing "undesirable" behaviors into an exalted picture of the wonderfully imperfect human. She made us sharply aware of our subjugation to the prevailing Threat-Reward model of life. People, according to this model, either are too much of something (negative) or not enough of something (positive). Instead, Satir taught that we need to learn how to love and accept ourselves.

But how can we reframe our incongruent behavior so that it becomes a friend to be cherished rather than an enemy to be destroyed? How can we harness all the energy that goes into these incongruent coping strategies and use it in a positive way? We can learn something about this from our canine companions.

Remember the Blamer's dog who became submissive in response to harsh scolding? According to the rules of canine social structure, this dog was reacting correctly and appropriately to the person it perceived to be the dominant "dog" in the pack. The dog's submissive behavior was perfectly congruent with its inner state. Wolves and other canids, in their natural state, are constantly reaffirming or revising the dominance hierarchy in this way. Even in the human household, dogs live together harmoniously by keeping their "coping strategies" in good repair and using them when necessary. These instinctive skills actually become strategies for survival.

The submissive survival strategy—head down, ears back, body lowered, tail tucked between the legs—looks like a canine parody of the human incongruent coping strategy we call Placating. The dominant survival strategy, on the other hand, reminds us comically of Blaming: The dog makes direct eye contact, holds her ears erect and her tail up, growls, and raises her hackles (the fur just behind the shoulder blades).

But what we are actually seeing in dogs are the transformations of these coping strategies into positive, constructive behaviors. The dog sees a present or, at least, potential, danger and mobilizes one of several powerful survival strategies which, in the wild, were usually successful at keeping it alive.

We see congruent transformations of the SuperReasonable and Irrelevant coping/survival strategies in the behavioral repertoire of other animals as well. Some of our mammalian relatives, for example, respond to survival threats by freezing in place and thus becoming invisible to their predators. This is what Robert Burns' mouse did in one of his most famous poems, "To a Mouse"—"Wee, sleekit, cowrin, tim'rous beastie." When the poet startled her by "turning her up in her nest with the plough," she reacted in a parody of SuperReasonable behavior, as if Self (the mouse) and Other (the poet) did not exist and paying attention only to the Context of danger. This strategy works for mice because their main predators, hawks, cannot spot them unless the mice move.

To witness a survival-based transformation of Irrelevance, we need only watch a squirrel, cornered by dogs, go into a frenzy of flight behavior—dancing and leaping in the air, running in quick circles, and thus avoiding its canine predators who cannot change direction as quickly and don't have the visual apparatus to follow such quick movements.

In people, too, each of these strategies is genetically coded and, in situations of real danger, can serve us well. In their congruent transformations, these coping styles become valuable strategies for survival. Knowing how to attack, submit, freeze, and take flight are precious gifts, part of our genetic inheritance, and charged with energy. It is only when we use them incongruently, from a position of low self-worth, and in a situation of *imagined* threat, that we deplete energy and defeat our deepest yearnings. Sadly, this is another marker of the huge difference between human and non-human animals: the capacity to be self-reflective, enabling us to feel high or low self-worth and then to use our behavioral "survival kits" inappropriately.

TRAINING CONGRUENTLY

Satir taught us how to transform these tools into congruent behavior by applying our powers of awareness and choice—by attending to our self-worth and thus moving into a state of consciousness. In this way, we can transform the energy of Blaming into assertiveness, Placating into empathy, SuperReasonable into the decisiveness required in an emergency, and Irrelevant into creativity. In my obedience class, I teach people to use these congruent transformations with their dogs. Assertiveness, empathy, decisiveness, and creativity are all essential qualities of a good dog trainer.

The assertive trainer is clear and firm in giving commands and signals to the dog. Impatience and anger (Blaming) have no place in dog training. They are human emotions that lose a lot in canine translation, as we saw with the Blamer's dog. I tell my students to stop training when they feel frustrated, lest they start blaming the dog for their own ineffective teaching process. Volhard and Fisher put it more forcefully:

> To become successful in your training, banish the notion that your dog is wrong. If he fails to respond to a command, or if he does something you don't want him to do, it is your responsibility to train him to respond or to refrain from the undesired action.... If he makes a mistake it is not because he is spiteful but because he needs more training. (Volhard and Fisher 1983: pps 28-29)

The need for empathy is supported by current thinking among animal behaviorists that training is best accomplished using positive reinforcement (Pryor 1984)—in other words, Satir's Principle of

Addition. The dog learns more quickly and retains the learning for a longer time. Training with empathy also supports the philosophical position that we humans share the planet with other animals. If we abuse them, either physically or emotionally, we only dehumanize ourselves.

As dog trainers and dog owners, we sometimes need our ability to be decisive, to focus entirely on the Context, ignoring Self and Other. When my dog Honey met her first porcupine, I had to get her to the veterinarian as quickly as possible, without delaying to reassure her and to soothe my own frightened feelings.

Finally, creativity is an essential part of dog training. There is no training methodology that will work perfectly for every dog, because each dog is a unique individual—or, as Satir would have said, a singular and marvelous "manifestation of life."

HOW TO BE A GOOD COMMUNICATOR

Dog training is essentially a communication process, and communicating effectively with dogs is not very different from how we deal with people. There are three essential qualities of a good trainer/communicator—appreciating differences, observing accurately, and giving feedback effectively.

The dog trainer, like the human communicator, must be aware and respectful of gross (species/cultural) differences, as well as individual variations in temperament and learning style. This principle echoes Satir's careful attention to both the universals and the differences. She described successful relationships as those in which people "treat each other as unique, are aware of and build on their sameness, and grow and learn from their differences." (Satir, *The New Peoplemaking*, 1988: pg 382)

At the very first meeting of my obedience class, I remind these new dog trainers that their dogs belong to a different species. In order to train them effectively and live with them happily, the owners must know what these *human-canine differences* are and take them into account. For example, we make use of the canine dominance hierarchy to establish ourselves as "alpha dog" (the top dog in the pack). We do this during the first week by teaching the dog the Long Down—having the dog lie down and stay in that position for 30 minutes, until we release it with a specific command. The Long Down puts the dog in a subordinate posture which the owner enforces by quietly repositioning the dog every time it starts to get up. Giving the releasing command further reinforces the owner's alpha standing.

An essential feature of this exercise is the calm, quiet confidence exhibited by the owner. Repositioning the dog is framed as teaching rather than punishing. The owner begins to understand that alpha status does not derive from force but rather from the knowledge that his or her "superiority" is only intellectual. The owner learns that as "alpha dog," she or he must exercise leadership, not raw power. Kevin Behan, in his excellent book, *Natural Dog Training*, supports this respectful and collaborative approach to training:

> A master cannot be arbitrary, so an owner must be governed by two skills: sensitivity and decisiveness. To be a master an owner must be sensitive to the needs, the desires, and the limitations of his dog.... (Behan 1992: pg 87)

As the dog owners begin to appreciate this difference between our two species, I introduce them to another: Dogs are more directly motivated by their fundamental drives than we are. For training purposes, we focus on three of these drives—Pack (the instinct for affiliation), Prey (the instinct to pursue food and anything in motion), and Defense (the instinct to fight or flee a threat).

Wendy Volhard (1991), a professional dog trainer and behaviorist, teaches people how to recognize drive-generated behavior, how to identify the individual variation in strength of drives in their own dog, and how to use this information in training. For example, you can easily and humanely train a dog high in Prey drive to Heel properly (walk at your left side, adapting its pace to yours) by the systematic use of a toy or treat as you move along. The dog will focus on this "object of attraction" and eventually transfer that intensity from the object to the handler, and ultimately to the activity of Heeling itself. The traditional method of teaching Heeling by "correcting" the dog into position with pulls and jerks on the leash will only put the dog into Defense drive. He will either actively and noisily resist you (Defense-Fight) or become a pathetic, cowering dead weight at the end of the leash (Defense-Flight).

Because we cannot persuade our dogs with analytic and symbolic means (as we do with people), we must use the "language" of instinct to influence their behavior. If we fail to honor this important difference between our two species, we wind up in a power struggle with our dogs, competing for control instead of collaborating to enhance the relationship.

Recognizing and respecting differences is essential to good communication. In addition, whether we are working with dogs or people, we need good *observation skills* in order to get accurate and useful feedback on our communication process. Satir expressed this as the first of her Five Freedoms: "The freedom to see and hear what is here instead of what should be, was, or will be." (Satir, 1976) Outstanding dog trainers share this ability with human educators to seek out and take in information through their senses—all six of them.

Dog trainers must learn to "read" their dogs. One of the most common, and costly, mistakes that beginners make, for example, is failing to recognize when the dog is stressed beyond the point of being able to learn. Some dogs (like people) are "negative stressors," shutting down when they are over-stressed. Their eyes narrow, their movements slow almost to a halt, and they become essentially somnolent. Other dogs (like people) are characteristically "positive stressors," becoming agitated when over-stressed. They are in constant and jerky motion, panting excessively. Understanding the universal stress response to learning and recognizing its unique manifestation in our own dog, we stop training when these signs of stress indicate that the dog is past learning.

Finally, both canine and human teachers must know how to *give information and feedback effectively*, through congruent communication. The desired outcome in obedience training is that the dog will respond reliably and quickly to specific verbal commands and hand signals. Beginning trainers, however, often fail to appreciate the subtlety of this process.

Dogs (like people) are always responding to all manner of cues of which we are not even aware. Chief among these are the posture and voice of the trainer. If you turn and lean over your dog as you command "Sit," you may not get the response you desire. Your body posture may put the dog into Defense-Flight, causing it to back away from you. If you then repeat the command "Sit" several times in a high-pitched voice, you will probably have a dog in frantic motion at your feet. Research has demonstrated that short, repeated, high-pitched sounds tend to stimulate motor activity in dogs (McConnell, 1991)—in effect, putting them into Prey drive. In both cases, you have given the dog an incongruent double message. Similarly, if you want to teach your dog to come when called, you will do it most effectively in the early stages of training by crouching, opening both arms wide, and smiling as you call the dog to you in a happy voice—eliciting Pack drive.

These three characteristics of a good communicator—respecting differences, observing, and giving feedback congruently—are woven into the rich fabric we call personhood. They enhance any relationship, whether with a dog, another person, or oneself.

APPLYING THE LESSONS

The German Shepherd Heidi, my first canine friend, gave me an intensive course in communication. She taught me to observe—to see her as she was, rather than as my previous picture of the unpredictable and dangerous dog. She demonstrated ways in which we were different. She showed me, by her own congruent responses, how to let her know what I wanted—to play or to rest, to walk with her or be left alone.

There have been many dogs in my life since Heidi. Living together, training one another, and performing as a team in the obedience ring, we have all learned important lessons. For me, the most important of these was about my own personhood. There is no question in my mind that these were reciprocal relationships. Therefore, I do not hesitate to call this human-canine bond "communication" and to draw broader lessons from it that apply to human-human communication.

Virginia Satir dreamed of "a world in which peace is possible," because "all five billion persons" would understand and practice "the essentials of congruent living":

> To communicate clearly
> To cooperate rather than compete
> To empower rather than subjugate
> To enhance individual uniqueness rather than categorize
> To use authority to guide and accomplish 'what fits' rather than force
>   compliance through the tyranny of power
> To love, value, and respect themselves fully
> To be personally and socially responsible
> To use problems as challenges and opportunities for creative solutions
> (Satir, *The New Peoplemaking* 1988: pps 369-370)

These principles apply equally well to human-canine relationships. Canine obedience training offers us a laboratory in which to examine our human communication processes and to practice new ones when we choose. We can learn by observing our ups and downs of Self-Worth; how we balance (and unbalance) the communication wheel of Self, Other, and Context; which incongruent Coping Strategies we prefer in times of stress; and how to transform these into congruent behaviors.

We can also learn by observing our dogs. One of the great differences between our two species is the fact that dogs seldom lie. They are, almost by definition, incapable of incongruent behavior. What they experience is what they express. Their lives are well regulated by the biological imperatives of food, defense, and reproduction. These basic drives have been shaped and tempered by the centuries-long process of domestication. We have consciously bred dogs for neoteny, to be our pets or our working companions, and they remain perpetually and charmingly childlike and dependent. Even those dogs that perform important and intricate tasks—such as police work, therapy, service for the blind or deaf, and search-and-rescue—never really "grow up." They never go beyond their species-determined world of instinct and the dominance hierarchy that makes their lives stable and predictable.

As culture-bearing animals, we surpass dogs in our capacity to think, to learn, and to communicate by means of the symbols we create and the meanings we make. The price we sometimes pay for all this is the loss of simplicity and directness in our relations with each other—what Satir called congruence. Living with dogs is one way to recover some of that loss and get in touch again with our humanness.

Acknowledgments

I am grateful to Melissa Bartlett, Kevin Behan, Karen Schlipf, Jack and Wendy Volhard, and Pinny Wendell, who made helpful suggestions on the canine side of this paper, and to Mary Pipher and Jerry Weinberg on the human side. Their thoughtful comments have contributed considerably to the quality of the paper. At the same time, I take full responsibility for any remaining errors or misconceptions. My thanks also go to my students and clients, both human and canine, who have taught me so much about communication. In order to protect their privacy, I have changed the names of all dogs and people and altered the details of each story.

References

American Kennel Club. 1989. *The Complete Dog Book.* 17th ed. New York: Howell Book House.

Behan, Kevin. 1992. *Natural Dog Training.* New York: William Morrow.

Capra, Lu. 1993. "Let the Dance Begin, Or: The Relationship Between Learning to Train a Dog and Learning to Teach Writing." *Front and Finish* 22:7, 12.

Evans, Job Michael. 1986. *The Evans Guide for Counseling Dog Owners.* New York: Howell Book House.

McConnell, Patricia B. 1991. "Lessons from Animal Trainers: The Effect of Acoustic Structure on an Animal's Response." In *Perspectives in Ethology,* 165–187, ed. P. Bateson and P. Klopfer. New York: Plenum Press.

Milani, Myrna M., DVM. 1986. *The Body Language and Emotion of Dogs.* New York: William Morrow.

Pryor, Karen. 1984. *Don't Shoot the Dog: How to Improve Yourselves and Others Through Behavioral Training.* New York: Simon & Schuster.

Satir, Virginia. 1976. *Making Contact.* Berkeley, CA: Celestial Arts.

———.1988. *The New Peoplemaking.* Mountain View, CA: Science and Behavior.

Volhard, Joachim, and Gail Tamases Fisher. 1983. *Training Your Dog: The Step-by-Step Manual.* New York: Howell Book House.

Volhard, Wendy. 1991. "Drives: A New Look at an Old Concept." *Off-Lead Magazine,* 26:9, 7–16, 26:10, 10–18.

Epilogue

The following is excerpted from the April 1994 issue of *DWAA Newsletter*, the official publication of the Dog Writers' Association of America. In it Job Evans shares some of his trial, joys, and remembrances with DWAA members. It was Job's wish that this appear in *Training and Explaining*. These are his own words and say better than anything else what this truly remarkable individual was like.

TO THE DWAA MEMBERS ... BY JOB

Today is August 17, 1992, and I've decided to write this to you because today I had a serious scare. A serious scare for a writer, at any rate. I've been experiencing neuropathy in my fingertips, but today it has enveloped my whole hand, and it's difficult to type. Writing longhand is out of the question. What's the numbness from? Probably from toxicity, from the more than seven medications I swill down each day to keep my AIDS in check. As I write this, I realize that neuropathy in my hands might be one of the least bothersome problems I may deal with in the future. But for a writer it's a very serious problem.

So before or if things get worse, I am prompted to write a few words to you, my fellow writers. First, don't give up. Write. You will not become a writer by not writing. Each day sit down at that typewriter and write. Some days it will flow, even in great gushes. Other days, it will be a torturous experience and the typewriter will be the equivalent of an aggressive dog you are trying to train. Just go on. Try setting a limit—and an obligation—on yourself of five pages a day. If you are tooling around with your computer, stupidly rearranging things, tinkering with your own writing, just shuck that computer and go back to a manual typewriter for a while. Yes, a manual (or primitive electric) typewriter. You'll be surprised how it clears your mind and enlivens your prose. Just don't give up.

Well, enough about dog writing, now let's talk about me. That's a joke, a small joke, but a joke. I was diagnosed HIV positive on May 3, 1989. I had become quite sick two weeks earlier. At my side in the doctor's office when the results were announced was my friend Carol Benjamin. The news hit us like acid poured on an already open wound. Still, as I stumbled out of the office, I was happy that I had followed my doctor's orders: "When I tell you your HIV status, I want you to have your closest friend nearby."

Carol Benjamin is a wise woman who knew enough not to comfort me, or even attempt to cheer me up. Not that I was weeping or hysterical. Instead, there was a strange calm, an eerie feeling of relief and even peace. Now, we knew.

Throughout the succeeding months, and luckily, it turned out, years, we made our way through the incredible morass of my having HIV and her being friends with an HIV-infected individual. Because of the stigma of AIDS, because I wanted to continue to work, because I knew that if my health condition was revealed I might lose work, I swore Carol to silence. How difficult it must have been for her not to be able to turn to others in our association, to confess her hurt at seeing her dear friend so ill and troubled. Of course it is easy for everyone to sit back now and say, "It wouldn't have been any problem for me to have known," but Carol and I were well aware of the cold, hard realities of the response of society to this illness. If you are somehow disturbed with me for not having told you personally, you simply must take time to reflect on the pressure we were under. As a writer, you are certainly used to deep reflection: so, think—what would you have done or said, under similar circumstances?

When I was elected President of DWAA I was somewhat apprehensive because of my health and because I didn't know exactly how much work was involved. I was already a board member, but I didn't want to trust what I had heard about how hard officials need to work. So I paid a visit to my dear friends Hal and Mary Sundstrom at their exquisite home in Virginia for a serious talk. Hal has a skill at diplomacy (it was, after all, his former career) and Mary has a skill at charm. I have a skill at accepting orders (this was, after all, my role as a monk for 11 years) and so charm, diplomacy, and lingering monastic obedience all came together. Arriving with every intention of turning down the job, I left thrilled to accept it. I sometimes wonder if it would have made any difference in the offer had I revealed that I was HIV positive at the time. I think not. At any rate, at that time I was essentially asymptomatic, and it was not irresponsible for me to accept the post as your president.

Later, around May of 1993, things worsened. I had a spell in the hospital, a disastrous course of chemotherapy, a subsequent collapse, high fevers, the loss of many friends, many of whom I tended, and generally one hell of an awful time. Throughout, there were dog writers who called—just out of friendship, not because they knew my situation—and a tremendous outpouring of support from DWAA. I tried to write good, non-gossipy columns about what it's like to be a dog writer, and always, always I had the membership in mind. You cannot accomplish much in the time I had, but you can try.

I guess most of all, I wanted to say that DWAA had been one of the happiest, most constructive, non-controversial and sweetest experiences of my life. *We must always keep it that kind of group.* Sweetness adds spice to life and a happy writing life makes for a good-hearted writer. You have all been so kind to me, and I hope we meet again. Meanwhile, if you pray, would you pray for me? I can't tell you how much my family and I would appreciate that.

And get busy on that next piece!

Love
Job Michael Evans